THE MIDDLE CLASSES
IN AMERICAN POLITICS

LONDON : HUMPHREY MILFORD

OXFORD UNIVERSITY PRESS

THE MIDDLE CLASSES
IN AMERICAN POLITICS

BY

ARTHUR N. HOLCOMBE
PROFESSOR OF GOVERNMENT, HARVARD UNIVERSITY

CAMBRIDGE · MASSACHUSETTS

HARVARD UNIVERSITY PRESS

1940

E
183
472

9/2/41. Cosp #1.87

20921

Preface

THE first part of this book can stand by itself, but it serves also as a somewhat extended introduction to the second part. Portions of the material in the second part of the book have been printed elsewhere, and I wish to take this opportunity to acknowledge my obligations to the publishers, who have kindly granted permission for reprinting them here. Chapter i of Part II was originally printed under the title, "Present-day Characteristics of American Political Parties," in *The American Political Scene*, edited by Professor Edward B. Logan of the University of Pennsylvania and published by Harper and Brothers (New York, 1936, revised edition, 1938), pp. 1–52. Chapter ii of Part II is a revised version of the *Bacon Lectures on the Constitution of the United States*, delivered at Boston University in April, 1940, under the title, "Sections, Classes, and the Constitution." The revised version of the first of these three lectures has also been printed in the *Boston University Law Review* (June, 1940). I am indebted to Mr. Gaspar G. Bacon of Boston, Massachusetts, for the opportunity to deliver these lectures, and have his gracious approval for printing them here. Chapter iii of Part II was originally printed under the title, "Thoughts and Afterthoughts on the Future of Democracy in America," in *Bryce's American Commonwealth, Fiftieth Anniversary*, edited by Professor Robert C. Brooks of Swarthmore College and published by the Macmillan Company (New York, 1939), pp. 112–154. Chapter iv of Part II is a presidential address originally delivered before the American Political Science Association in Chicago, Illinois, December, 1936, and published in the *American Political Science Review*, XXXI, No. 1 (February, 1937), pp. 1–11. Though written for different occasions, these chapters have their appropriate places in the development of the subject of this book. I am also deeply indebted to the publishers of *Fortune* magazine for their kind permission to reprint certain statistical information concerning the strength of the middle classes in the United States from their *Fortune* Survey: XXVII (February, 1940), and to my colleague, Professor Walter B. Cannon, for kind permission to quote certain passages from his book, *The Wisdom of the Body*, published by W. W. Norton and Company (1932). The Notes on Books, which complete Part II of this book, contain references to publications which readers who desire to pursue the subject further may find of interest. Finally, for efficient aid in preparing this book for the press, I wish to record my gratitude to Mrs. Mary A. Keenan, Secretary of the Department of Government, Harvard University.

ARTHUR N. HOLCOMBE

Cambridge, Massachusetts,
June, 1940.

CONTENTS

PART I

PART II

PART I

In Defence of the American Way

I

THE American way in politics implies a purpose and a method. The purpose is clear. In the last analysis it is to maintain a kind of state which will serve as well as possible the ends of politics set forth in the Preamble to the Constitution of the United States.[1] The method is more obscure. It must harmonize with the essential traits of the national character as revealed in the whole American way of life. It must also employ instruments suitable for the purpose. What are the essential traits of the American character is a question to be determined by weighing the evidence. The suitability of available instruments is likewise to be determined by logic and experience. This book is mainly an inquiry into the proposition that the most suitable instrument for maintaining the American kind of state is a strong and enlightened middle class within the American people.

The importance of the middle classes has long been recognized in American politics. Recognition of their importance had already begun at the early period when discussion of the fundamental principles of political science was most active, the period of the adoption of the Federal Constitution. In the Federal Convention itself there was little explicit reference to the class-structure of the American

---

[1] I have explained my understanding of these ends in my book, *The Foundations of the Modern Commonwealth* (Harper and Brothers, 1923).

people, though there was much consideration of arguments on behalf of special privileges for the wealthier planters and merchants. In the State ratifying conventions, middle-class consciousness was more openly expressed. One of the most striking expressions of a middle-class political philosophy occurred in the New York Convention of 1788.

The spokesman for the middle class was a merchant and lawyer of New York City, Melancton Smith by name, who had been elected to the Convention as a delegate from Dutchess County. Smith had been born of humble parents and had made his way up from the rustic obscurity of his native county to a prominent position in the life of the metropolis. In New York politics he was a lieutenant of Governor George Clinton and in the Convention he acted as the floor-leader of the Anti-Federalist faction. He was a strong opponent of ratification of the proposed Constitution, until a satisfactory bill of rights should have been adopted, but yielded at last to the eloquence of the Federalist leaders and the logic of events, particularly the news of ratification by the prescribed number of states necessary for putting the new Constitution into effect. In short, he was an exceptionally competent specimen of the typical urban middle-class American of that time.

A debate arose in the Convention over Smith's criticism of the provisions in the Constitution for the election of the federal house of representatives.[2] Smith contended that the proposed ratio of one congressman for every thirty thousand inhabitants would make the representative body too small. "The number of representatives should be so large,"

[2] Jonathan Elliot, *The Debates in the Several State Conventions, on the Adoption of the Federal Constitution, as recommended by the General Convention in Philadelphia in 1787*, 4 vols. (second edition, Washington, 1836). See II, 245.

he argued, "as that, while it embraces the men of the first class, it should admit also those of the middling class of life. I am convinced," he continued, "that the representatives will generally be composed of the first class in the community, which I shall distinguish by the name of the *natural aristocracy* of the country. . . . Every society naturally divides itself into classes. . . ." And Delegate Smith went on to explain what he meant by a natural aristocracy, an upper class resulting from real differences in birth, education, talents, and wealth, which, he urged, "create distinctions among men as visible, and of as much influence, as titles, stars, and garters."

Melancton Smith's theory of the natural classes in a political society deserves closer examination. "In every society," he continued, "men of this [that is, the "first"] class will command a superior degree of respect; and if the government is so constituted as to admit but few to exercise the powers of it, it will, according to the natural course of things, be in their hands. Men in the middling class, who are qualified as representatives, will not be so anxious to be chosen as those of the first. . . . The great easily form associations; the poor and middling class form them with difficulty. . . . The circumstances in which men are placed in a great measure give a cast to human character. Those in middling circumstances have less temptation; they are inclined by habit, and the company with whom they associate, to set bounds to their passions and appetites. . . ." It was therefore desirable, Smith thought, that both classes be duly represented in the house of representatives.

Delegate Smith supported his theory of representative government with a suitable political philosophy. "My idea is, that the Constitution should be so framed as to admit this class [that is, the "first" class], together with a sufficient number of the middling class to control them. You will then combine the abilities and honesty of the community, a proper degree of information, and a disposition to pursue the public good. A representative body, composed principally of respectable yeomanry, is the best possible security to liberty. When the interest of this part of the community is pursued, the public good is pursued, because the body of every nation consists of this class, and because the interest of both the rich and poor are involved in that of the middling class. No burden can be laid on the poor but that will sensibly affect the middling class. Any law rendering property insecure would be injurious to them. When, therefore, this class in society pursue their own interest, they promote that of the public, for it is involved in it."

The leading representatives in the Convention of what Smith called the natural aristocracy hastened to join in combatting both his theory of representative government and his political philosophy. Alexander Hamilton, John Jay, and Chancellor Livingston all agreed in denouncing his conception of classes and his notion of a good system of representation. These big guns of the "aristocratic" party fired such a heavy volley at the spokesman for the "middling" class that Smith was forced into a strategic retreat. He retired to a previously prepared position, and dug in. In other words, he appealed to higher authority. "My idea of aristocracy," he countered, "is not new; it is embraced by many writers on government. I would refer the gentleman for a definition of it to the Hon. John Adams, one of our natural aristocrats. This writer will give him a description the most ample and satisfactory." [3]

[3] Elliot's *Debates*, II, 248 and 281.

John Adams' *Defence of the Constitutions of Government of the United States of America*, to which Melancton Smith referred his opponents with so much confidence, was well known to them. It had been written, while the author was sojourning in London as the first American minister to the Court of St. James, for the purpose of defending the constitutions of the thirteen original states, and particularly the Constitution of the Commonwealth of Massachusetts, which Adams had had a large part in framing, against the strictures of European critics. Of this massive work, the most learned and all things considered the most substantial writing in the field of political philosophy by any American statesman, the first volume had been received in America at the very moment when the members of the Federal Convention were preparing for their task. It contained a vigorous, though discursive, exposition of certain principles of government embodied in the Massachusetts Constitution. These same principles greatly influenced the framers of the Federal Constitution and determined many of the leading features of the proposed government for the new and more perfect Union.

John Adams was a zealous student of politics. "I know not how it is," he once wrote, "but mankind have an aversion to the study of the science of government. To me no romance is more entertaining." [4] He was extremely confident of the correctness of his opinions. They were supported, he declared, "by facts, observations, and experiments," like the doctrines of the natural scientists, and he was "as clearly satisfied of the infallible truth" of his political doctrines as "of any demonstration of Euclid." [5]

[4] *Works of John Adams* (Boston, 1850–56), IX, 567.
[5] *Ibid.*, VI, 479; 252.

The system of government which he recommended was, he declared, "the only scientific government; the only plan which takes into consideration all the principles in nature, and provides for all cases that occur." [6] The views of so eminent a statesman so strongly recommended were bound to attract the attention of his contemporaries.

Adams' political philosophy contained much which the representatives of the "natural aristocracy" found greatly to their liking. "Nature," he declared, "which has established in the universe a chain of being and universal order, has ordained that no two objects shall be perfectly alike, and no two creatures perfectly equal." [7] Men may have been created equal with respect to their rights and duties, but not in other respects. On the contrary, in all societies, even the most democratic, "there are inequalities which God and nature have planted there, and which no human legislator ever can eradicate." [8] The most important inequalities seemed to Adams to be of three kinds, inequalities of wealth, of birth, and of merit. All three are causes of superiority, and the first two are no less creditable to their lucky possessor than the third, Adams argued, since to be born with superior talents is as much a matter of chance as to be born in a rich family or of famous ancestors. [9] Such superior persons would naturally possess influence over others, which in Adams' opinion was the essence of aristocracy. A natural aristocracy, therefore, is an aristocracy of wealth, of birth, or of merit, or of any combination of these qualifications, "the rich, the well-born, and the able," as Adams liked to put it. Such a natural aristocracy, he

[6] *Ibid.*, VI, 44. Cf., C. M. Walsh, *The Political Science of John Adams*, chap. i.
[7] *Works*, VI, 285.   [8] *Ibid.*, IV, 392.   [9] *Ibid.*, VI, 396.

maintained, existed everywhere regardless of artificial distinctions of rank and condition established by law or
custom.

Adams' political philosophy contained also much which
the natural aristocrats greatly disliked. The aristocrats, he
lamented, are prone to carry their good qualities to excess.
They easily become too greedy, too proud, or merely too
smart. Their covetousness, arrogance, and contentiousness
create disorder and confusion. The members of the superior
rank or order — Adams did not like the word class — he
wrote toward the end of his life, "are the most difficult
animals to manage of anything in the whole theory and
practice of government." [10] Despite their small numbers,
they may easily become too strong for the rest of the state,
strengthened as they generally are by "their connections,
dependents, adherents, shoe-lickers, etc." [11] The proper
way to treat them, Adams concluded, is to acknowledge
their superiority and assign them a suitable but necessarily
restricted share in the government, "giving the natural aristocracy in society its rational and just weight," but not
more.[12]

How to limit the power of the natural aristocracy is,
according to Adams' "Defence," one of the first problems
to be solved by a true science of government. The solution,
he believed, follows from the nature of the classes which
form the structure of society. But what are the natural
ranks or orders, as Adams would have said, among the
people of a state? To this question Adams did not give a
clear and consistent answer. Sometimes he spoke of "the
three natural orders in society, the high, the middle, and

[10] *Works*, X, 51.
[11] *Ibid.*, IV, 355.   [12] *Ibid.*, IV, 463.

the low." [13] More frequently he spoke of "the great and perpetual distinction in civilized societies . . . between the rich, who are few, and the poor, who are many." [14] He sometimes put the two-class scheme of social classification very dogmatically: "The people in all nations are naturally divided into two sorts, the gentlemen and the simplemen." [15] In one place he referred to "the middling people" as the most industrious and frugal,[16] and again, this time following Aristotle, he mentioned a division into "the very rich, the very poor, and the middling sort" [17]; but in general whatever may lie between "the rich" and "the poor" escaped his attention.

Adams' theory of government was derived from the scheme of social classification which seems to have been generally uppermost in his mind. Since the greatest danger to the stability of states, he thought, was caused by the mutual jealousies and animosities of the rich and the poor, it was necessary to check each by the other and maintain a balance between them. This could be done, he believed, only by introducing a third power, which would be independent of both and would represent the whole body of people, both rich and poor. This third independent power, he argued, should be the chief executive and should possess an absolute veto over the acts of the representatives of the two conflicting classes. Thus he reached his conclusion that the best form of government was a monarchical republic, as he called it, like that established in Great Britain. A president, eligible for reëlection to an indefinite number of successive terms, seemed to Adams a more natural type

---

[13] *Works*, V, 90, 183.
[14] *Ibid.*, IX, 570.
[15] *Ibid.*, VI, 185.
[16] *Ibid.*, V, 41.
[17] *Ibid.*, V, 458.

of chief executive than a king for the United States, but the function of the president would be the same as that of a king. He should act as a mediator between the natural aristocracy and the common people, keeping the representatives of each in their proper place and maintaining a true balance between them. The middling sort of citizens were left to shift for themselves between the rich and poor. It never occurred to Adams to utilize them as the mediator between the natural aristocracy and the lower ranks or orders. Hence, his dogmatic insistence upon the mediating function of an independent chief executive. To his way of thinking a strong president could make the public interest prevail over any partial interests, whether those of the rich and the poor, or those of the high, the middle, and the low.

Such a theory of government satisfied scarcely anybody in the United States. The natural aristocrats saw no prospect of gaining more power under the Federal Constitution than they thought they deserved and could use to good advantage. Outstanding realists among them, notably Alexander Hamilton, regarded Adams as a pedant, if not a traitor to his class, and never afterwards trusted his political leadership. Eventually that distrust helped to wreck the Federalist party of which Adams unwittingly became the nominal head. Opponents of the natural aristocracy, like the Clintonians in New York, might cite the authority of Adams for their own purposes, as Melancton Smith cited it in the New York Convention of 1788, but they could not wholly trust a statesman who did not trust the common people much more than he trusted the aristocracy. Adams was destined to become a lonely figure in American politics as well as in American political philosophy, and his reputation has never wholly recovered from what he himself called the mountain of unpopularity which fell upon him. His political philosophy has been almost as completely forgotten as that of Anti-Federalists such as Melancton Smith with their peculiar views concerning the function of the middle class in American politics. The special political role of the middle class remained an inarticulate major premise in the subconscious thinking of middle-class Americans.

The political philosophy of the American Revolution was written under the aegis of the Newtonian physics. The laws of motion, the principles of celestial mechanics, the grand conception of the equilibrium of the sidereal universe, cast a spell over the minds of intelligent men. Political philosophers dreamed of a natural harmony between the various political ranks and orders and of the permanent stabilization of the rightly constituted states. But the eighteenth century passed away in the midst of sanguinary revolutions and violent warfare of unprecedented extent and destructiveness. To the widespread belief in the natural perfectibility of men and states succeeded an uneasy feeling that all attempts to improve the lot of mankind would be frustrated by the consequences of its own follies and vices.

II

The conception of a rational world to be quickly perfected by reasonable men, who, having lost their faith in princes, would at last be free to act consistently with their faith in themselves, gave way to that of a more romantic universe in which perfection awaited the end of a long process of gradual improvement through the struggle for existence and the survival of the fittest. The nineteenth-century doctrine of evolution, like the eighteenth-century laws of motion, cast a spell over the minds of intelligent men and inspired new dreams of progress in politics as well as in other branches of human thought and action. The harbinger of the new theories of political evolution was a short but meaningful essay by the German philosopher, Immanuel Kant. Written in the period between the American and the French revolutions, Kant's *Natural Principle of the Political Order* was little known by either Americans or Frenchmen.[18] Nevertheless, it marked the beginning of a new era in the understanding and control of political behavior.

Because Kant's theory of political evolution is still not well enough known by those whose interests it was designed to serve, a summary of its essential features may strengthen the foundations of belief in the principles of modern constitutional government. Kant was convinced that, though the actions of individuals seem incapable of explanation by any rule, yet the affairs of mankind occur in accordance with constant natural laws. The weather, he pointed out, is so inconstant that it can not be accurately predicted in detail for long periods of time, yet temperature and rain-fall do apparently conform to some rational law. They can not be relied upon to behave normally at any particular moment. Nonetheless, they do not fail to maintain the flow of rivers, the growth of plants, and the various processes of animal life in harmony with the traditional character of the region. "Individual men, and even whole nations, little think," he added, "while they are pursuing their own purposes, that they are advancing unconsciously under the guidance of a purpose of nature which is unknown to them,

[18] Immanuel Kant, *Eternal Peace and Other International Essays* (Boston, 1914), pp. 1–25.

and that they are toiling for the realization of an end which, even if it were known to them, might be regarded as of little importance."

Kant was well aware that men, viewed as a whole, are not guided in their efforts purely by instinct, like the lower animals; nor do they proceed in their actions, like the citizens of a purely rational world, according to a preconcerted plan. The fact must be recognized that a rational conscious purpose can not be supposed to determine the whole course of the actions of mankind. But a scientific observer might be able, Kant believed, to discover a universal purpose of nature in the paradoxical movement of individual men. In view of this possible purpose the behavior of more or less civilized men who proceed without a plan of their own may be found to conform to a determinate plan of nature, in the light of which the philosophy of history would acquire new meaning and practical utility. "We will accordingly see," Kant concluded, "whether we can find a clue to such a history; and in the event of doing so, we shall then leave it to nature to bring forth the man who will be fit to compose it. Thus did she bring forth a Kepler, who, in an unexpected way, reduced the eccentric paths of the planets to definite laws; and then she brought forth a Newton, who explained those laws by a universal natural cause."

Assuming the modest role of the investigator who would merely state the problem which political science at its best has to solve, Kant was content to leave to others the more difficult tasks of reducing the eccentric paths of political behavior to definite laws and of explaining these laws by a universal natural cause. The purpose of his *Natural Principle of the Political Order*, consequently, is to enter a plea for faith in the possibility of a progressive political order in the world, the realization of which becomes the ultimate problem of political science. The grounds for this faith are set forth in the form of nine propositions, which constitute the substance of Kant's epochal essay.

The first proposition in Kant's statement of political faith was based upon observation of the development of all forms of animal life. An organ which is not to be used, Kant affirmed, or an arrangement which does not attain its end, is a contradiction in the teleological science of nature. If the idea of purpose animating the phenomena of the natural world be rejected, then natural phenomena are no longer conformable to law, and, as Kant put it, "the cheerless gloom of chance takes the place of the guiding light of reason." Preferring the guiding light of reason, Kant resolutely turned away from the cheerless gloom of chance. He chose to believe that *all the capacities implanted in a creature by nature are destined to unfold themselves, completely and conformably to their end, in the course of time.*

The second proposition follows closely upon the first. *In man, as the only rational creature on earth, those natural capacities which are directed toward the use of his reason can be completely developed only in the species and not in the individual.* Reason is a faculty capable of extending the powers of the individual far beyond the sphere of natural instinct, and knows no limit in its efforts. It depends for its practical operation, however, upon long-continued observation and experience, and its greatest accomplishments must be the result of persistent experimentation and the gradual accumulation of wisdom. The life of a man is far too short for the reason of any particular individual to produce all the fruits of which human reason is capable. Therefore the production of a thoroughly rational world can be the achievement only of an indefinitely long series of generations, each profiting by the accumulated wisdom of its predecessors.

Recognition that the attainment of this goal may properly be regarded as the rational aim of the individual's existence leads to the third of Kant's preliminary propositions for a science of politics. *Nature has willed that man shall produce wholly out of himself all that goes beyond the mechanical structure and arrangement of his animal existence, and that he shall participate in no other happiness or perfection than that which he has procured for himself, apart from instinct, by his own reason.* In fashioning man nature seems to have taken pleasure, Kant noted, in exercising the utmost parsimony, and to have measured man's animal equipment with the greatest economy. Compared with other animals man is a poor creature but for the gift of reason, being incredibly deficient in strength, speed, endurance, and other useful physical qualities. Through the accumulated wisdom of the ages, however, man is able greatly to surpass the lower animals, and each generation strives patiently to prepare a better world for its successors, knowing that it is to be the happy fate of only the latest generations to dwell in the building upon which the long series of their forefathers have labored with no possibility of participating in the happiness which they were preparing.

The fourth proposition introduces a way of thinking which, even more than the first three, must have struck Kant's contemporaries as new and bold. *The means which nature employs to bring about the development of all the capacities implanted in men is their mutual antagonism in society, but only so far as this antagonism becomes at length the cause of an order among them that is regulated by law.*

By this antagonism Kant meant the consequences of the paradoxical disposition of mankind to lead a gregarious life and at the same time to do as they pleased. The struggle for a satisfactory existence develops the talents which are latent in mankind and enables the successive generations to make more of themselves as well as to accumulate wisdom. The most precious fruit of this struggle is the development of a sense of justice and a will to seek liberty under law.

The greatest practical problem for the human race, to the solution of which it is compelled by nature, is the establishment of a civil society, universally administering justice according to law. It is only in a society which possesses the greatest liberty, Kant believed, that the highest purpose of nature, that is, the full development of all the capacities implanted in mankind, can be attained. But if such liberty can not be reconciled with the maintainance of an order which can satisfy the natural sociability of mankind, the full development of man's latent capacities will not be attained. Hence, the formation of a society in which the greatest possible liberty under law may be combined with the greatest possible power to enforce the law and maintain order, that is to say, the formation of a perfect civil constitution, is the supreme problem prescribed by nature to man. "It is with men as with the trees in a forest: for, just because every one strives to deprive the others of air and sun, they compel each other to seek both from above, and thus they grow beautiful and straight; whereas those that in freedom apart from one another shoot out their branches at will grow stunted and crooked and ugly."

The preceding proposition leads directly to the next, which is, that *this problem is likewise the most difficult of its kind, and will be the last to be solved by the human race.*

"The difficulty which the mere idea of this problem brings into view is, that man is an animal, and if he lives among others of his kind he needs a master. For he certainly abuses his freedom in his dealings with his fellow men; and, although as a rational creature he desires a law which may set bounds to the freedom of others, yet his own selfish animal disposition leads him, wherever he can, to put himself above the law." The authority behind the law must be capable of perfect justice, and yet must remain a man. Kant conceded that a perfect solution of so difficult a problem is impossible. "Out of such crooked material as man is made of, nothing can be hammered quite straight. So it is only an approximation of this idea that is imposed upon mankind by nature."

With the seventh proposition Kant emphasized an aspect of the problem of finding the right constitution for mankind which surely seemed in his own time, as in ours, to give a tantalizingly visionary character to his political speculations. *The problem of the establishment of a perfect civil constitution is dependent on the problem of the regulation of the external relations between organized states according to law; and without the solution of this latter problem the main problem can not be solved.* However visionary the idea of a parliament of man and a federation of the world may seem, Kant was convinced that it must be the ultimate goal of all rational effort in the field of human relations. Nature works through wars between nations, as through the antagonism of individuals, to carry out her purpose. "And at last, after unmeasured devastation and destruction, and even the complete exhaustion of their powers, the nations will be driven toward the goal which reason might have easily impressed upon them without so much sad experience."

The eighth of Kant's propositions is the one which has exerted the greatest influence over the political thinking of later years. *The history of the human race, viewed as a whole, may be regarded as the realization of a hidden plan of nature, to bring about a political constitution internally, and for this purpose also externally, perfect, as the only state in which all the capacities implanted by her in mankind can be fully developed.* This proposition is a corollary from the preceding proposition. The organized bodies of people which we call states can not fulfill the highest purpose of their being unless not only the relations between their members but also those between the states themselves are successfully governed by just laws. The happy result may be remote, but the possibility of contemplating it is an indispensable condition of a rational life.

These and similar considerations led Kant to his ninth and final proposition. *A philosophical attempt to work out the universal history of the world according to the plan of nature, aiming at a perfect political union of mankind, must be regarded as possible, and even as capable of helping forward the purpose of nature.* It seems at first sight, Kant conceded, a strange and even an absurd proposal to suggest the composition of a history of the world according to some idea of how its course must proceed, if it is to conform to rational laws. The remoteness of the establishment of a perfect constitution for mankind and the difficulty of discerning in the apparently senseless course of the rulers of the states which Kant knew best the manifestation of any rational purpose seemed to condemn to futility such a study of history as Kant suggested. War, and preparation for war, prevented contemporary rulers from rendering the constructive services to their subjects which more rational rulers would have delighted in undertaking. Nevertheless, if it be assumed that nature does not proceed without a rational plan, the idea of a universal history designed to reveal such a plan may be regarded as practicable. The contrary assumption, namely, that the natural course of human events is devoid of purpose or reason, makes life excessively uninteresting to a reasonable man.

Thus Kant concludes his search for a clue to a philosophy of history and a science of politics. One can not help feeling a certain repugnance, he acknowledged, in looking at the conduct of men as it is exhibited on the great stage of the world. Occasional glimpses of wisdom appearing in individuals did not greatly alter the general character of the political scene. The whole web of human history seemed to be woven out of vanity and folly and destructive frenzy. Yet if nature had produced a Kepler and a Newton to reduce to order and to explain the confused and apparently inexplicable relations of physical bodies, Kant could believe that likewise men would be produced capable of discovering a rational order in the phenomena of human relations.

That nature has not yet produced the Newton or even the Kepler of political science would doubtless be conceded by Kant, if he could return to earth and compare the statesmanship of the present time with that of the world he knew. But the endless adventure, which is the experience of those who practice the art of government, has not been wholly barren. In America the Federal Constitution was framed three years after Kant wrote his essay on *The Natural Principle of the Political Order*, and Americans at least will not hesitate to contend that some progress has been made towards a science of politics. In Europe also the development of the British system of parliamentary government

and its extension to the Continent seem to have added something to man's understanding of the governmental art. It is
still possible to believe, as Kant did, that a Kepler of political
science will be an eventual product of the study of politics.
Meanwhile, ambitious philosophers have essayed the role of
the politico-scientific Newton without awaiting the production of the politico-scientific Kepler. Outstanding
among these ambitious philosophers are Kant's disciple,
Hegel, and Hegel's disciple, Karl Marx, the two leading
apologists for the most dynamic political movements of modern times, nationalism and communism.

Hegel contributed to the philosophy of history a conception of the universe, a method of reasoning, and a theory
of the state. His conception of the universe led him to
believe that history has meaning because it is the manifestation of a supreme and absolute power or spirit. His
method of reasoning led him to find meaning in history in
terms of persistent struggle between conflicting ideas. His
theory of the state sought to explain how order and progress
may be derived from such struggle and conflict. Thus his
philosophy of history is an attempt to rationalize the intelligent citizen's faith in his country and in its government as
the indispensable instruments of order and progress.

Hegel's idea of the nature of the state merits closer examination. Men naturally wish to do as they please, but the
impossibility of all doing as they please without injury to
one another compels them also to desire order. The desire
to do as one pleases gives rise to the idea of liberty and the
desire for order gives rise to the idea of authority. But
authority and liberty seem to be mutually contradictory.
Each idea, carried to its logical conclusion, excludes the
possibility of the other. Either liberty or authority is pos-

sible without a state, but not both. States exist in order that the blessings of both authority and its antithesis, liberty, may be enjoyed at the same time. How is this possible? Because the state is a synthesis of the two conflicting ideas. It transmutes authority into justice and enables the man who obeys those exercising just powers to do what he really pleases and therefore to remain as free as before. He does what he really pleases, when he obeys those who speak in the name of the state, because, in a rightly constituted state, they command him to do what it is reasonable that he should wish to do. As Hegel liked to put it, what is rational is real.

In the march of history progress is revealed through the succession of states in which authority and liberty are synthesized on ever higher planes. In the oriental empires of antiquity, according to Hegel, liberty and authority were synthesized in the person of a single despotic ruler. He possessed supreme authority and he was also free, but he alone was free. In classical Greece and Rome larger parts of the population were admitted to a share in freedom without the impairment of authority. The establishment of the Greek city-state, based on a broadening sense of community, and of the Roman Empire, exemplifying a generous effort to maintain a reign of law for all citizens, though not for other subjects, represented great achievements in the development of more advanced types of states. But man's greatest political achievement, according to Hegel, was the establishment of the Germanic monarchies. There at last, he argued, supreme and efficient power was skillfully united with universal liberty under law.

It is easy to see now that Hegel's enthusiasm for the early nineteenth-century Prussian monarchy was ill-founded.

The decisive test of the degree of advancement of a particular state is the character of its government. A government which is to command even the qualified approval of
the political philosopher must be so constituted as to establish a harmony between the processes of law which it main-
tains and the principles of justice in which the people of the
state believe. If a people's notions of justice are crude, a
very imperfect kind of government may be regarded as
suitable under the circumstances. If a people's conception
of justice is more refined, the processes of government must
be more skillfully fabricated and more trustworthy. A
rightly constituted government in a very advanced state
will secure the citizen against any political restraint upon
his personal liberty except by authority of just laws and
will establish a kind of justice which can command the
citizen's ungrudging consent. No doubt the early nineteenth-century Prussian monarchy still left a good deal to
be desired by the intelligent citizen. There is much to be
said in principle for Hegel's effort to vindicate the claims
of the well-ordered state to the allegiance of the intelligent
citizen. In practice his attempted vindication of the Prussian state as theoretically perfect was discredited by the im-
perfection of his theory of government. Kant had suggested
that nature must produce a Kepler of political science before
it could produce a politico-scientific Newton. Hegel pre-
sumed to play the role of a Newton in political science without waiting for its Kepler and succeeded in showing, not
that Kant's proposal for a science of politics was necessarily
sound, but merely that, if sound, it had better be carried into
effect by Kant's methods.

Hegel's untimely attempt to construct a philosophy of
history had some unfortunate consequences. One of them

was the encouragement which it gave to theories of politics emphasizing the differences between peoples. The idea that the higher types of states were the creations of particular peoples gave support to the further idea that those peoples possessed political capacity which was superior to that of others. From this idea it was not a long step to the opinion that the peoples with superior political capacity had a right to extend the blessings of their sway over the inferior peoples. This opinion harmonized with the romantic notions of the nineteenth century. It helped greatly to give to modern nationalism and nationalistic imperialism the vitality which has made these political movements such mighty forces in the modern world. Fascism and Nazism stem from various roots, but the Hegelian political philosophy is surely one of the principal sources of their strength.

A second unfortunate consequence of the Hegelian political philosophy was the encouragement which it gave to the Communist dogma of the class struggle. Marx was correct in acknowledging that he did not originate the fundamental theories of modern Communism. Others before him had suggested (1) that all peoples have been divided into two major economic classes, the possessing and exploiting class on the one hand, and on the other the dispossessed and exploited, and (2) that all history has been largely a record of the struggle between these two classes. Marx merely added to these two broad and excessively vague generalizations three further propositions: (1) that successive stages in the progress of civilization are characterized by successive forms of the class-struggle; (2) that the present stage is characterized by the struggle between the capitalists and the proletariat, and will end in victory for the latter class; and (3) that the inevitable triumph of the proletariat will be followed by the establishment of a classless society and the cessation of struggle. These three propositions constitute the essence of Marxism.

Marx's debt to Hegel is obvious. He was captivated by the Hegelian logic. The conception of history as a progressive process of synthesizing on successively higher levels the conflicts between opposites seemed to Marx to provide a perfect explanation of the age-long struggles between the successive dominant economic classes and the subject masses of mankind. Deeply stirred by the plight of industrial wage-earners in the new capitalistic order, which a century ago was already well-developed in Great Britain, he sought a theoretical foundation for his passionate faith in the ultimate victory of the under-dog. The dominance of the capitalists constituted the thesis of the modern economic order in Marx's materialistic version of the Hegelian philosophy of history, the resistance of the proletariat was the antithesis, and the eventual establishment of the coöperative commonwealth, where class-struggle would be known no more, was the final synthesis, according to the Marxist dialectic.

The fatal dilemma of Marxism, regarded as a system of political philosophy, is also obvious. Marx rejected Hegel's explanation of the universe as the manifestation of a supreme spiritual power, but at the same time he clung to Hegel's belief that the world is ruled by law. He insisted upon a materialistic interpretation of history, but shared the repugnance to "the cheerless gloom of chance," which Hegel inherited from Kant. Precisely how a strictly materialistic world is to escape the dominion of chance and become a realm of law, has been a bone of perennial contention among the Marxian theorists. Neither Marx nor any of his disciples has ever succeeded in clarifying this essential link in the

Marxian dogmas. If the world is under the dominion of chance, the ultimate triumph of the proletariat is not inevitable. If the world is governed by law, it is not a strictly materialistic world, and those who would explain its history must look deeper than the Marxian dialectic.

Lenin, a more realistic thinker than Marx, saw through the logical fallacies of the traditional Marxism. He believed that masterful politicians, gifted with a better understanding of the circumstances of the age than the early Communists could possess, once having seized power by hook or by crook, might thereafter create the economic conditions which were indispensable for the ultimate triumph of a genuine proletarian political movement. He argued, not that the triumph of the proletariat was inevitable, but rather that a dictatorship of the proletariat was the one available instrument for the overthrow of capitalism. Armed with this knowledge, he proposed to destroy what Marxists called the dictatorship of the capitalists, when a disastrous war offered a favorable opportunity, and to create the economic basis of a durable proletarian state afterwards by using the power which his coup d'état would give him for the purposes which Communists alone would understand. Thus Lenin managed to rule in the name of Marx but on the ruins of Marxism. His little band of Communist conspirators succeeded in seizing the power, which others had failed to hold, and justified their sway on the tyrants' plea that the tools should go to those who are able to handle them. Instead of a proletarian dictatorship, they established a government over the masses by a new elite and became in fact, though not in name, the first of the contemporary Fascists.

To the American in search of a science of politics the

Hegelian logic seems the weakest part of the Hegelian philosophy of history. The gradual expansion of mankind's conception of liberty is doubtless one of the important signs of human progress, but it is not the only or the best sign. If political liberty be defined as the absence of human restraints upon personal behavior, except those imposed by authority of just laws,[19] it follows that the idea of political liberty is logically joined to the idea of political justice, and possesses no meaning except in terms of the latter. If the meaning of liberty is to expand, the meaning of justice must expand also. Since liberty is negative and justice positive, the expansion of the conception of justice is clearly the more important sign of human progress. It contributes no more to an understanding of history to suggest that the idea of liberty conflicts with the idea of authority than to suggest that the idea of justice conflicts with the idea of authority. Such a suggestion makes nonsense out of the whole idea of the state itself.

Marx's transformation of the Hegelian logic into the Marxian dialectic shifts the emphasis in the interpretation of history from the ideas of liberty and justice to the facts of class-consciousness and class-struggle. Marx's interpretation in terms of conflict between two economic classes depends for its validity upon the correctness of his assumption that every state is always divided into precisely two major classes, based upon man's mode of making his living. It is a matter of common observation, however, that the classification of economic society in modern states is more complex. There are many economic groups into which modern peoples are divided; and the question among observers of a

[19] See the author's *Foundations of the Modern Commonwealth* (New York, 1923), chap. vii, at p. 287.

reflective turn of mind is, does it serve any useful purpose, in explaining the processes of government, to arrange these groups in two grand divisions or would it serve a better purpose to arrange them in some greater number of divisions. The argument of this book is, that those who may be interested in discovering the best means of defending the American way of political life will find it more convenient and more profitable to arrange the various economic groups into three grand divisions than, like the Communists and Fascists, into no more than two.

John Adams, it will be recalled, when preparing his *Defence of the Constitutions of Government of the United States*, was uncertain whether to divide mankind for political purposes into two classes — he called them ranks or orders — or into three. His object was to devise the best method of insuring the stability of the state. The appropriate means, he believed, was to establish a balance between such classes of people as would naturally engage in the struggle for power. For this purpose he originally thought that a three-class system of politics would serve better than a two-class system. He referred to "the three natural orders in society," as if there could be no doubt concerning the existence of precisely three important classes, the upper, the middle, and the lower. He advocated, therefore, that all three should be represented in the government "and constitutionally placed to watch each other." [20] This idea of a three-class system seemed to fascinate him. "The triple balance is so established by Providence in the constitution of nature," he wrote on one occasion, "that order without it can never be brought out of anarchy and confusion. The laws, therefore, should establish this equilibrium as the

[20] Adams, *Works*, V, 90.

dictate of nature and the ordinance of Providence." [21]
But when Adams reached the point in the development
of his theory of government where he needed to reduce his
principles to practice, the three grand divisions of society
dissolved. In their place stood two grand divisions, the
upper and the lower, or as he preferred to say, the aristocracy and the common people. The middle class disappeared
from view, and instead of a middle class, as the balancing
agent in his scheme of a stabilized government, was an independent executive, representing not any particular class
but the state as a whole. The function of such an executive,
according to Adams, in a constitutional government of the
most approved type — what he called a monarchical republic — was to stand above all parties and to keep the two
important ones, the aristocrats and the common people,
in their proper places. When he became president of the
United States, he actually tried to govern in accordance
with this theory. Neither the aristocrats nor the common
people were satisfied with the place which he assigned
them. Whether the Hamiltonians or the Jeffersonians were
more annoyed at Adams' presidential policy may be debated. Adams' own course in his later years suggests that
he himself felt closer in his political philosophy to Jefferson
than to Hamilton.

The development of the American party system, as
analyzed in the second part of this volume, shows that
Adams would have been wiser if he had adhered consistently
to a three-class system of politics instead of going over to
the two-class system. The presidents have not been able
to hold aloof from partisan politics, but on the contrary
have been drawn into the midst of the struggle of parties.

[21] *Ibid.*, VI, 341.

The most influential presidents have been party leaders, and the presidents who have not been party leaders have had difficulty in maintaining the authority of their office. But the parties have not been clearly identified with particular classes of the people. No major party, since the definite establishment of the two-party system, has been exclusively an upper-class party or a lower-class party. All major parties have been more or less effectively dominated by the middle class. Thus through the party system, which Adams distrusted, the middle class has maintained a kind of political equilibrium, which Adams desired. In short, the middle class has succeeded in performing the function in American politics which Adams' political science assigned to the independent chief executive.

There is no good reason at this late day for trying to reconstruct Adams' political science upon a three-class instead of a two-class basis. Adams was absorbed in the task of stabilizing political institutions. The contemporary world needs a science of politics which will guarantee progress as well as order. Kant has created the vision of such a political science. The efforts of Hegel and Marx to give reality to Kant's vision have at least served the purpose of warning against some inviting but wrong roads. It may not be possible to demonstrate to an intelligent man that mankind possesses the ability to realize Kant's vision. Neither can it be demonstrated that the eventual realization of this vision is impossible.

III

Armed, therefore, with the faith that sound principles of government may be discovered and may also be intelligently applied to the problem of organizing a world for the purpose of establishing justice, securing the blessings of liberty, and enjoying peace and happiness, defenders of the American way can know what their task requires of them. It requires in the first place a clear understanding of what they mean by justice, upon which depend in the last analysis both the blessings of liberty and the enjoyment of peace. It requires, secondly, an understanding of the ways and means of establishing their kind of justice.

It is not excessively difficult to describe in general terms what Americans mean by justice.[22] A general description of the idea of justice must begin by recognizing that the need for justice arises out of the conflicting interests of the members of the state. It is not the clear conflict of right and wrong that gives vitality to the fundamental processes of government in a modern state, but rather the conflict of rights themselves and ultimately of the interests which lie behind the rights and give them specific meaning and practical importance. To establish justice is to adjust conflicts of interest, not by official force and violence merely, but also upon some principle which the members of the state can understand and to which they can give their rational consent. Political justice, in the general sense of the term, may be defined as such an adjustment of the conflicting interests of members of the state as will best promote, or least impair, the general interests of the state as a whole.[23]

The establishment of justice, therefore, consists, first, in ascertaining what is the public interest in a particular situation, and, secondly, in adopting the necessary measures for making the public interest prevail over all the private and special interests that may be involved in that situation. This

[22] See the author's *Foundations of the Modern Commonwealth*, chap. vi.   [23] *Ibid.*, p. 251.

is evidently an exceedingly complex undertaking. The laws of the United States are full of provisions authorizing public authorities of many kinds to do this or that as, in the exercise of a sound discretion, they shall judge to be in the public interest. Chief Justice Hughes has written that "this criterion is not to be interpreted as setting up a standard so indefinite as to confer an unlimited discretion." [24] In the last analysis, however, the only effective limit seems to be that provided by the judgment of the law-makers themselves. Under the American system of constitutional government the judgment of the law-makers is exercised by an elaborate and more or less obscure process. To the uncomprehending individual it must often seem that instead of justice what the member of the state actually gets is merely what the judges call due process of law.

Due process of law has received the sanction of public opinion because it has seemed to be in harmony with the principles of right in which the people have believed. It is necessary, therefore, in order to escape from a vicious circle of reasoning which can lead nowhere, to put some more solid content in the idea of justice than is afforded by its summary identification with due process of law. The nature of the public interest must be more precisely defined than it has been by the law-makers in many of the statutes which confer discretionary powers upon public authorities. These authorities themselves, notably such agencies as the Interstate Commerce Commission, the Securities and Exchange Commission, and the Department of Agriculture, have done much in recent years to put substantial content into the statutory concept of the public interest. The courts of law also, particularly the Supreme Court of the

[24] Federal Radio Commission v. Nelson Brothers, 289 U. S. 266 (1933).

United States, have contributed to a better understanding of this vital concept of American political science.

From the welter of discussion a variety of opinion emerges. In the first place, there are those tough-minded realists who assert that they see in the idea of the public interest nothing more than a pious pretense to cover the naked reality of a dominant private or special interest. According to this view, the adjustment of the conflicting interests involved in a particular situation, say, the abandonment of an unprofitable line of railroad which has been dedicated to the use of the public, or the transfer of a radio broadcasting station license from one corporation to another, or the reorganization of a bankrupt public utility, is determined by the relative strength of the different parties to the conflict. The victor in the struggle dictates the terms of peace and sanctifies his triumph by a figure of speech. His private interest is thereafter called the public interest and the vanquished interests make the best of the victor's terms.

In its crudest form this theory of the public interest serves to justify the use of power by the law-maker or his agent, the administrative officer, board, or commission, primarily with a view to keeping his power intact. The interstate commerce commissioner, for example, may be supposed to adjust the conflicts of interest between railroad executives, railroad labor, railroad investors, shippers, travelers, and competing transportation systems, primarily with a view to getting reappointed by the president at the end of his term and getting reconfirmed by the senate. A federal judge, charged with the protection of the public interest in a railroad reorganization case, may consider only the necessity of so using his power as to avoid impeachment.

One fatal objection to such a crude theory is obvious. Men with sufficient talent to reach such responsible positions may not be content to use their talent to so little purpose.

A more subtle and less pernicious form of the same realistic theory is that which holds the public officer to the duty of so using his power as to keep in good functioning order the whole political system of which he is a part. Realistic interstate commerce commissioners, engaged in adjusting conflicts of interest in the field of railroad transportation, would not be expected to think exclusively or even primarily of their chances of retaining their offices. They would be expected to think rather of the effect of their decisions upon the prestige of the government of the United States. They would be considerate, doubtless, of the more powerful special interests. But they would not be altogether indifferent to the opinion of their work entertained by the weak and humble.

If one could be content with a purely static order of society, there would be much to be said for such a theory of the public interest. But if the province of government be deemed to include a care for progress as well as for order, this form of the theory is also unsatisfactory. In a changing world the government itself must be capable of change, to the end that its services may continue to be adapted to the needs of the public. A truly realistic conception of the public interest must include a disposition on the part of public officers to be guided by a sense of the direction of change. This requires an effort on their part to apply a science of politics, such as Kant envisaged, which can give to public officers a suitable sense of direction.

A satisfactory theory of the public interest calls for an understanding by public officers, possessing important dis-

cretionary authority, of the scale of values with which the
public measures its interests. The public interest is more
than a particular private or special interest which is able to
prevail in the adjustment of a conflict with other special
interests. It is more than the sum of the special interests
which gain recognition in a particular process of adjustment.
It is more than the bare fact of a temporary balance between
a group of special interests. It is nothing less than such an
adjustment of conflicting interests as will produce an equilibrium which can give members of the state a feeling of confidence in the durability of the state itself.

The specific content of the idea of public interest depends
upon the nature of the particular state. In a thoroughly
militaristic state the adjustments of interest-conflicts which
could command general approval would be those which
were calculated to increase most or to diminish least the
strength of the state. In a thoroughly capitalistic state the
most satisfactory adjustments would be those best calculated to increase the material wealth of the members of the
state. In a thoroughly socialistic state the increase of the
wealth of the state as a whole and the promotion of equality
in sharing the wealth might be the supreme test of the
public interest. In the ideal state the most acceptable test
of the public interest would be the effect of a proposed adjustment of an interest-conflict on the virtue of its members,
as virtue might be understood by lovers of wisdom.

In actual states the different qualities which are of interest to the public seem to be variously distributed. If states
could be regarded as persistently static forms of community,
public officers might appraise the general interest which the
public deems important, and work out standards of measurement by which they could be guided in the adjustment

of conflicts between special interests. But if the idea of progress is to be accepted, the relative values of different general interests must be subject to continual alteration. It is true that change will not always proceed in a direction which can be reconciled with any intelligible conception of progress in a civilized world. At one time the need of preparation for national defence must weigh heavily in the balance against the desire to promote the general welfare. At another time there must be better appreciation of the need for greater material prosperity. At all times a sound system of politics will be inspired by a faith that in the long run changes in the scale of values will follow a trend towards the kind of state which can satisfy the ideals of the intelligent citizen.

In the United States prevailing conceptions of the public interest have responded to the traditions and the circumstances of the people. In the first place, a high valuation has always been placed on the personal dignity of the American citizen. When Jefferson wrote that all men were created equal and endowed by their Creator with certain inalienable rights, he meant more than the mere absence of hereditary titles and other legal privileges. He intended to express a positive faith in the natural nobility of mankind. This is the true significance of the revolutionary doctrine of natural rights and the primary characteristic of the American way of life.

Respect for the natural dignity of man has grown in America with the accumulation of political experience. American political institutions afford many illustrations of its practical consequences. The most significant of these lie in the field of popular education. The educational system of any country is in the long run the most characteristic feature of its constitution. The American system of public education, more than any other feature of the American political system, attests the widespread and deep-rooted respect for the dignity of man which distinguishes the American people.

The second leading characteristic of the American way is closely associated with the first. It is expressed in the revolutionary doctrine of the social compact. It means that governments are established for the service of the people, possessing such powers only as may be sanctioned by popular consent, and employing them for purposes to which reasonable persons may be supposed to agree. The acceptance of such a doctrine implies a generous measure of respect for reality in politics.[25] It implies also a firm disposition to favor sensible compromises in the adjustment of interest-conflicts, in short, a persistent preference for moderation in politics.

Realism and moderation are political traits which under favorable circumstances distinguish all the processes of American government. Their most important effects, however, are achieved through the operations of the political parties. The bipartisan system tends to minimize the differences between the major parties and to magnify the influence of those realistic and moderate voters who are free to throw their support to either side according to the nature of the paramount issues and the kind of leadership that is offered. Critics of the parties deplore the lack of principle which, they contend, characterizes the traditional partisanship in American politics. The criticism is superficial, since the members of all the major parties

[25] Cf. Gerald W. Johnson, "The Two Fundamentals" in *The American Way*, *Harpers*, 1938. See especially p. 153.

have been in agreement upon the fundamental principles of the American political system and the major party leaders have rightly emphasized the issues arising out of the details of policy over which reasonable men could properly differ.

These two characteristics of the American way lead to a third. This is a fixed determination to maintain what Americans understand as a republican form of government. The doctrine of natural rights culminates in the political principle of popular sovereignty. The doctrine of the social compact culminates in the political principle of the reign of law. The combination of the two is the essence of the republican form of government as established in the United States.

The republican form of government, as an aspect of the American way of life, reveals not only the kind of people who make America but also the kind of law which reigns over Americans. Americans reject the pernicious doctrine of absolute national sovereignty. They hold that the organized community, like the individual, is subject to a higher law than that made by politicians for the protection of immediate temporal interests. The state is not an end in itself with unlimited power to bind the individual, but merely one among several associations to which the individual may belong and which must be justified by their services to their members. Constitutional limitations upon the authority of public officers reflect the division of allegiance on the part of good citizens between the various kinds of communities to which they adhere.

This aspect of the American way has been illuminated by Chief Justice Hughes in a recent opinion which deserves more attention from the American people than it has received.[26] "Much has been said," the Chief Justice wrote, "of the paramount duty to the State, a duty to be recognized, it is urged, even though it conflicts with convictions of duty to God. Undoubtedly that duty to the State exists within the domain of power, for Government may enforce obedience to laws regardless of scruples. When one's belief collides with the power of the State, the latter is supreme within its sphere, and submission or punishment follows. But, in the forum of conscience, duty to a moral power higher than the State has always been maintained. The reservation of that supreme obligation, as a matter of principle, would unquestionably be made by many of our conscientious and law-abiding citizens. The essence of religion is belief in a relation to God involving duties superior to those arising from any human relation."

The fact that Chief Justice Hughes spoke in this case for a minority of the Court does not diminish the force of his statement. Americans are not only a nation with a right of self-preservation, but also, as he correctly pointed out, a people who accord to one another an equal right of conscience in matters of religious faith. They find an appropriate place among their leaders for churchmen as well as for statesmen. In the last analysis they seek in themselves the necessary adjustments between their conflicting loyalties. In short, the American way is a way which combines with the so-called law of the land the highest law known to the consciences of mankind.

It is evident that some important characteristics of the American political system are not essentials of the American way. Liberty, in the sense of a right to do as one pleases, has been in general an object of solicitude in the United

[26] United States v. Macintosh, 283 U. S. 605 (1931), at p. 633.

States. But the amount of respect accorded to that kind of
liberty by the laws of the land has varied greatly from time
to time. The nation which wrote the Eighteenth Amendment into the Federal Constitution can not boast of a tender
regard for freedom of choice in the selection of beverages.
In the light of experience greater consideration for a liberty
of personal taste was eventually deemed prudent, but there
was no surrender of the right of the people to protect the
public interest, as they might see it, in the control of commodities deemed injurious to health or safety.

Respect for equality, in the sense of a right to an equal
share in the power and perquisites of public office, is another American trait which has left its mark on American
politics but can not be regarded as an essential of the American way. Respect for equal rights to office in the Jacksonian era led to the paradoxical result that the victors in
partisan contests for elective offices claimed the privilege of
monopolizing all the appointive offices. To the vanquished
was denied not only an equal share in such offices, but also
any share whatever. The merit system of appointment to
administrative and judicial offices implies respect for equal
rights to office only on the part of those possessing suitable
technical and personal qualifications. The gradual establishment of the merit system of filling non-political positions
has introduced what is in principle an element of aristocracy
into the structure of the American democracy.

Democracy itself is a word which has undergone strange
vicissitudes in the history of American politics. Among the
founding fathers it was generally a term of disrespect. The
framers of the original state and federal constitutions did
not believe in a form of government dominated by the
weight of numbers regardless of differences in the degree of

interest which individuals might be supposed to feel in the maintenance of law and order. In the course of the nineteenth century the fashion in political terminology changed, and democracy became a word with highly acceptable connotations. Today democracy means to most Americans the kind of government which they think they actually possess, or, better, the kind they would like to possess. To the Greeks, who invented the term, it meant something roughly corresponding to what we now call a dictatorship of the proletariat. Our kind of democracy would have been called by Aristotle a mixture of democracy, oligarchy, and aristocracy. The relative portions of each element in the mixture have changed in the past, are changing now, and will doubtless continue to change in the future. What we will eventually do with the word is the future's secret.

A sound political philosophy requires a kind of government in which there shall be a harmony between the processes of law and the principles of right in which a people believes. Among a perfectly wise and enlightened people under a rightly constituted government justice and liberty and peace would be the necessary fruits of due process of law. It is doubtless too much to expect such great results from existing institutions or from any institutions mankind is capable of creating in a predictable future. But the ideas of justice and liberty, which tend to prevail among the American people, gain vitality from conceptions of the public interest, which seem to be consistent with a rational course of history. Americans may well have faith that the American way is a way leading towards the only goal which can be reconciled with an acceptable interpretation of the history of mankind.

IV

In the present period of urban expansion and growing class-consciousness new methods are needed for the purpose of maintaining the essential features of the American way. The test of their suitability will be their practical capacity to help accomplish the purposes of constitutional government, as set forth in the preamble of the Federal Constitution. To establish a tolerable kind of justice, which is the most important of these purposes, means to find effective instruments for making the public interest, as commonly understood, prevail over private and special interests. The details of such a project lie beyond the scope of this introductory essay.[27] It must suffice here to emphasize again the argument of this book, namely, that a sound system of American politics requires the preservation of a preponderance of power in the hands of the middle class.

This requirement is made more difficult by the circumstance that the composition of the middle class is constantly changing. The nature of the middle class remains in principle always the same, but its actual content is determined by the relations between the different economic and social groups within the state, which exist at a particular time. The term itself is comparatively new. John Adams, for instance, who, as we have seen, had a great deal to say about the class-structure of society and the importance of classes in politics, did not speak much of "classes" under that name nor at all of "the middle class." He preferred to say "the middling sort of people" or the "middle" one of the "three natural orders."

[27] For further discussion of the process of government from this point of view, see my *State Government in the United States* (3rd edition, 1931), Part IV, pp. 571–636, and also my *Government in a Planned Democracy* (New York, 1935), chaps. ii-v.

Adams never made altogether clear the precise content of his "middle order" or "middling sort of people." In one place he spoke of the "distinctions established by law" in North America between "laborers, yeomen, gentlemen esquires, honorable gentlemen, and excellent gentlemen." [28] But which of these groups would fall into the middle rank he did not say. His lack of clarity reflected the confusion in the minds of the earlier writers on the science of government whom he cited with an impressive show of learning. The idea, if not the name, of a middle class is as old as political science itself and is not greatly advanced from the state in which the Greeks left it.

Aristotle was the original author of the idea in the literature of political science. He defined the middle class in practical politics as that part of the people who lie between the very rich and the very poor.[29] The idea was appropriated by subsequent classical writers, seeking to explain the vicissitudes of Greek and Roman politics, notably by Polybius and Livy. From these writers the idea was taken over by political scientists in the Italian city-states of the Renaissance, notably by Machiavelli. But none of these writers could have given the term an application acceptable to John Adams, since they were thinking of states in which common laborers and the masses of mankind generally were excluded from citizenship.

Machiavelli, for instance, had a great deal to say about the importance of due consideration for the middle class in the government of Florence.[30] "I say then," Machiavelli concluded, "that those who model a Commonwealth must take

[28] *Works*, V, 488. Cf., VI, 123.
[29] Aristotle, *Politics*, Bk. IV, chap. xi, § 1295b.
[30] See Machiavelli's "A Discourse upon the Proper Ways and Means of Reforming the Government of Florence," in his *Works* (London,

such provisions as may gratify three sorts of men, of which all States are composed; that is, the high, the middle sort, and the low: and though there is a great equality amongst the citizens of Florence, as hath been said before; yet there are some there who think so highly of themselves that they would expect to have the precedence of others; and these people must be gratified in regulating the Commonwealth; for it was owing to the want of this that the last administration was ruined." [31] It was probably this theory of Machiavelli's which Shakespeare had in mind when he wrote the somewhat mystifying lines:

> For government, though high and low and lower,
> Put into parts, doth keep in one consent,
> Congreeing in a full and natural close
> Like music.[32]

Neither Machiavelli nor Shakespeare could have had in mind a modern notion of a middle class, when they urged the necessity for balancing the power of the upper and lower classes with an intermediate political force. The conception of active citizenship in even the most advanced of pre-Shakesperian commonwealths fell far short of the modern idea of democracy.

Modern political scientists can not simplify the problems of government by ignoring the existence of the elements which in earlier times were excluded from the state. Slaves and helots and metics had their place in the economic order of classical antiquity, but none in politics. In our time much of the work of slaves is performed by mechanical power,

---

1775), IV, 265–284, Ellis Farneworth, translator. This work was well known to John Adams.

[31] *Ibid.*, p. 274.

[32] Henry the Fifth, Act I, Scene ii, lines 180–183.

but unskilled and casual laborers remain, to say nothing of the technologically unemployed, and must be reckoned with in any system of politics compatible with the American way of life. The lower class, politically speaking, cuts deeper into the economic structure of modern society than in, say, Machiavelli's time, and the middle class, by definition, must also cut deeper. Whatever John Adams may have thought about the separation of classes for political purposes in a well-ordered state, the political classification of the members of contemporary society needs to be reconsidered in the light of the conditions of this neotechnic age.

The term, middle class, seems to have been introduced into English political terminology in the early part of the nineteenth century. Lord Brougham, speaking on parliamentary reform in 1831,[33] said: "Where the people — and by the people, I repeat, I mean the middle classes, the wealth and intelligence of the country, the glory of the British name — where this most important order of the community are . . . denied the constitution which is their birthright . . . etc." What Brougham really meant by the middle classes became evident a year later when the Reform Bill finally became law. He meant the businessmen and their more substantial employees, who were enfranchised by the Reform Act of 1832. He meant, in short, what was then coming to be known on the Continent of Europe as the *bourgeoisie*.

The identification of the British "Commons" and the Continental *bourgeoisie* with the middle class became an accepted part of nineteenth-century political terminology. John Stuart Mill, writing in his influential *Principles of*

[33] Henry Lord Brougham, *Speeches* (1838), II, 617.

Political Economy, referred to the kinship between "the Commons of England, the Tiers-Etat of France, (and) the bourgeoisie of the Continent generally." [34] The latter were originally the freemen of a borough or city, as distinguished from peasants on the one hand and gentlemen or landlords on the other, and came to be recognized as typical specimens of the commercial and industrial middle class of any country.[35] The term was introduced into English literature in the period of the Stuart Restoration, when French influence was strong in fashionable circles, and eventually became a familiar expression for describing middle-class characteristics of all kinds. In Germany Goethe and his contemporaries used in a similar sense the equivalent expression, *Mittelstand*.[36]

This is the sense of the term which the earlier Marxist writers adopted as their own. In their scheme of classification the *bourgeoisie* form the class to which the proletariat become the antithesis, and the existence of a landed oligarchy, between which and the peasantry the *bourgeoisie* had originally formed a genuine *Mittelstand*, is conveniently ignored. Modern American Marxists, Lewis Corey, for example, have followed a more up-to-date and realistic practice in the use of terms. Recognizing the altered importance of different elements of society in modern times, they distinguish between the greater and the lesser capitalists. The former are assigned to the *bourgeoisie*, and the latter with others to the middle class, which, they are forced

[34] J. S. Mill, *Principles of Political Economy* (London, 1848), 1876 ed., preliminary remarks, p. 12.
[35] See *Dictionnaire de l'Académie Francaise*, 6th ed., 1835. See also Pierre Larousse, *Grand Dictionnaire Universel du XIXe Siècle* (Paris, 1896), vol. IV.
[36] See Jacob Grimm, *Deutsches Wörterbuch* (Leipzig, 1877), vol. VI.

by the logic of circumstances to admit, does interpose between the greater capitalists and the proletariat in a country
like the United States.[37] The contemparary middle class,
it is evident, must be described in terms of the actual relationships obtaining between the different groups in modern
economic society regardless of the historical use of the term.

Discriminating social analysts find no use for the excessively simple and unrealistic Marxist social dichotomy. In
older countries there seem to be at least three important
elements in the middle class. These three elements are:
first, small farmers and businessmen, possessing some capital
of their own and controlling their own businesses, but
mainly dependent upon their energy and enterprise rather
than their money for their livelihood; secondly, the more
responsible and better-paid employees of capitalistic enterprises, who could hardly be expected to share the point of
view of the ordinary wage-earners, though dependent upon
capitalists for employment; and thirdly, the more or less
skilled independent workers of all kinds, who constitute
the contemporary successors of the medieval artisans, craftsmen, and small peasantry. These three groups may be called
the old middle class, the new middle class, and the transitional middle class. It is evident that upon a realistic view
of the economic order the middle class subdivides into the
middle classes.

The relations between the various sub-classes which compose the middle class vary from time to time and from country to country. In Germany, for example, a few years ago,
on the basis of a careful statistical analysis of the census
returns of occupations, it was estimated that forty-eight
per cent of the employed or employable population was

[37] See Lewis Corey, *The Crisis of the Middle Class* (New York, 1935).

assignable to the three groups composing the middle class.[38] Eighteen per cent of the total belonged to the old middle class; sixteen per cent belonged to the new middle class; and fourteen per cent belonged to the transitional middle class. Presumably the new middle class had been growing more rapidly than the old middle class. Presumably, also, both these sections of the middle class had been enjoying a relatively more satisfactory position in the economic order than the transitional middle class.

In the United States all three of these middle-class elements must be reckoned with by the political analyst. The old middle class, as represented by the bulk of the professional men, small merchants, and independent farmers, have played a leading role in American politics. The rapid growth of large-scale capitalistic industry has produced a correspondingly rapid development of the new middle class. The transitional middle class, on the other hand, the tenant farmers and independent craftsmen, can never have possessed the importance in the economic order which it formerly possessed in older countries such as Germany. The relative proportions of these three elements would certainly be very different in Germany and in the United States.

Estimates of the total size of the middle class in the United States are dependent upon occupational statistics which have been inferior to those formerly available in Germany. It is not possible to make calculations with the precision feasible for the German statisticians. The best available estimates are noted elsewhere in the second part of this volume.[39] It is enough to note here that the middle class, including all its several elements, is at least as large

---

[38] See Theodor Geiger, *Die Soziale Schichtung des deutschen Volkes* (Stuttgart, 1932).   [39] See pp. 200–209.

in the United States as in Germany, and presumably larger. But it varies considerably in size in different sections of the country. It is largest in the states with a comparatively large population of independent farmers. It is relatively smaller in the more highly industrialized urban states.

It is easy to exaggerate the importance of objective measurements of the middle class. From the viewpoint of the political analyst and the politician, the important fact about the middle class is not its size, according to any system of objective measurement, but rather the state of mind which makes its existence possible. Politically speaking, the middle class is significant, not because it is logically an economic category or a social order, but because its members are conscious of their special position in politics and disposed to act self-consciously and energetically. It is well to recall Aristotle's definition of the middle class as that portion of the community which is neither very rich nor very poor. But what is less than very rich and more than very poor is a matter of opinion. There is no middle class, politically speaking, but thinking makes it so. By due process of thought any wage-earner can promote himself into the middle class.

The fact is, as will be shown in the second part of this book, that a substantial part of the wage-earning population of the United States has promoted itself into the middle class. Consequently, the American middle class is materially greater than any statistician would suppose from the available information concerning the nature of the economic order and the distribution of wealth and income. Its size is determined by the persons who compose it under the influence of tradition, education, and personal reflection. Agitators, propagandists, publicists, and leaders of opinion of all kinds contribute toward the result. In short, the middle class in American politics is essentially a subjective phenomenon, and is radically different from the middle classes of European countries.

Changes in the composition of the middle class, as will also be shown in the second part of this book, are not likely to diminish the influence which it has exerted in the practical operation of the American political system. Its preponderant power has been due, not only to the number of its members, but also to the intensity of their convictions and to their firmness of purpose. The members of the middle class have been the most ardent and vigorous believers in the essentials of the American way of life. They have demanded order; they have had faith in the possibility of progress; they have held in the highest esteem the fundamental traits of the specifically American political character, that is, respect for the natural dignity of mankind and for realism and moderation in politics. They have been the most determined that the American Commonwealth should serve the best interests of the whole body of people and not be perverted into an instrument of special privilege for a particular class, neither the elite nor the proletariat nor even the middle class itself.

These are facts which Fascists and Communists seem to be unable to understand. Fascists have little respect for the dignity of man. They boast of their contempt for the opinions and the aspirations of the masses. Communists have little respect for realism and moderation in politics. They boast of their determination to destroy a dictatorship of the capitalists, which does not exist in the United States, in the interest of a proletariat, which also does not exist in the United States. Fascism and Communism are fantastic creeds for Americans, in the name of which unrealistic agitators try to pursue immoderate policies. Such effort is thoroughly un-American in the strictest sense of the term; if the future is to grow out of the past, it can not succeed.

In the past the development of the essential traits of the American way in politics has been fostered by the advance of natural science. The demand for order was stimulated by the universal acceptance of the Newtonian laws of motion and the general comprehension of the idea of equilibrium. The belief in progress was encouraged by the persuasiveness of the Darwinian theory of organic evolution. The continued advance of natural science in the present century seems capable of further strengthening the fundamental articles of faith underlying American political science. Among the recent contributions to scientific thought, one of the most significant from this point of view is Dr. Walter B. Cannon's doctrine of organic homoeostasis.[40]

Cannon's researches in human physiology led him to emphasize a striking biological phenomenon. "Organisms, composed of material which is characterized by the utmost inconstancy and unsteadiness, have somehow learned the methods of maintaining constancy and keeping steady in the presence of conditions which might reasonably be expected to prove profoundly disturbing." [41] Thus, to take a simple illustration, the bodily temperature of man may be maintained at a uniform and constant level in all kinds of weather despite extraordinary fluctuations of heat and cold. Likewise, the temperature of the body is kept at normal during the most intense muscular activity, which might

[40] Walter B. Cannon, *The Wisdom of the Body* (New York, 1932).
[41] *Ibid.*, pp. 21–22.

be expected to produce so much heat from internal combustion of tissues as to stiffen some of the bodily substances like a hard-boiled egg. The coördinated physiological processes, which maintain most of the steady states in the organism, are so complex and so peculiar to living beings that Cannon suggested a special word for them, homoeostasis.

The concept of organic homoeostasis suggests the inquiry, may there not be general principles of stabilization, applicable to bodies politic as well as to the higher vertebrates? [42] Political and social philosophers have often drawn comparisons between the human organism and the organization of mankind in civilized society, in which arguments by analogy have not infrequently been pressed much too far. Bluntschli's comparison of the state to a masculine and of the church to a feminine organism is a sufficient warning against the dangers of such methods of reasoning about politics. Cannon, as a natural scientist, proposed to approach the problem of political homoeostasis from the viewpoint of a physiologist rather than from that of a metaphysician or historian. May not the new insight into the devices for stabilizing the human organism, he asked himself, offer new insight into defects of social organization and into possible modes of dealing with them?

At the outset, Cannon noted,[43] the body politic itself exhibits some indications of crude automatic stabilizing processes. "A certain degree of constancy in a complex system is itself evidence that agencies are acting or are ready to act to maintain that constancy. And moreover, that when a system remains steady it does so because any tendency toward change is met by increased effectiveness of the fac-

[42] Ibid., "Epilogue: Relations of Biological and Social Homoeostasis," pp. 287–306.   [43] Ibid., pp. 293–294.

tor or factors which resist the change. Many familiar facts prove that these statements are to some degree true for society even in its present unstabilized condition. A display of conservatism excites a radical revolt and that in turn is followed by a return to conservatism. Loose government and its consequences bring the reformers into power, but their tight reins soon provoke restiveness and the desire for release. The noble enthusiasms and sacrifices of war are succeeded by moral apathy and orgies of self-indulgence. Hardly any strong tendency in a nation continues to the stage of disaster; before that extreme is reached corrective forces arise which check the tendency and they commonly prevail to such an excessive degree as themselves to cause a reaction. A study of the nature of these social swings and their reversal might lead to valuable understanding and possibly to means of more narrowly limiting the disturbances. At this point, however, we merely note that the disturbances are roughly limited, and that this limitation suggests, perhaps, the early stages of social homoeostasis."

Any application of Cannon's theory to the problems of political science must go beyond the structure of the body politic and reach the political processes which reflect the essential vitality of the modern state. Among these processes the most important seem to be those associated with the activities of political parties. A political party is something more than a mere combination of politicians for the purpose of influencing elections and appointments to public office. It is something less than a body of people, such as Burke described, united for the purpose of promoting the national interest upon some principle in which they are all agreed. It is through the operations of parties, apparently, that the phenomenon of homoeostasis must largely be realized in such a political organism as the United States.

The following part of this book is devoted primarily to studies of the shifting and incidence of power in the government of the United States with a view to discovering their effects upon the stability of the American political organism. The underlying causes of the major political disturbances seem to have lain chiefly in the unequal rates of growth of different sections of the country and different classes of the people. Throughout the greater part of the history of American politics the unequal growth of different sections exerted a greater influence on the process of stabilization than the unequal growth of different classes. Recently the relative importance of these two factors has been reversed. At all times the most important single force in the process of stabilization has been the membership of the middle classes operating through the major political parties. Some of the evidence in support of this thesis is set forth in the following studies. They deal also with the manner in which the process of stabilization operates and with some of the implications of this stabilizing function of the middle classes.

The American way includes a belief in progress as well as a demand for order. Whether the middle classes can perform the function of promoters of progress, as effectively as they perform that of guardians of order, depends upon the relations between order and progress. The concept of homoeostasis implies more than the maintenance of static stability. Organisms are capable of growth as well as of balance. The possibilities of growth in the natural organism seem to be limited by the nature of the organism. In a political organism the achievement of homoeostasis might open the way for endless growth in harmony with the Kantian conception of progress. The capacity to believe in such a future may well prove to be one of the greatest sources of political strength to the middle classes and one of the principal securities for progress in a middle-class state.

V

The studies in the second part of this volume have been produced in response to the stimulus of different occasions. They deal with various aspects of American politics, regarded both as a course of action and as a system of thought. But they relate to a common subject. That subject is the shifting and incidence of political power in the United States under the changing conditions of our time. That political power is shifting from elements of the American people, which have long possessed it, to others to which its possession is a novel experience, is a fact which is easily demonstrated. The significance of these changes in the incidence of power, their implications for the future of the American way of life, are matters more difficult to interpret and explain.

The first of these studies was designed to set forth some noteworthy facts concerning the transition from a predominantly agrarian to a predominantly urban economy in the United States and to state the political problem which such a transition poses. The growth of the factory system of capitalistic industry and the political effects of the resulting transfer of influence from farmers and planters to industrial capitalists and wage-earners have brought American politics to the crossroads. The tangible effects of the rise of modern capitalism upon the distribution of political power at Washington may be roughly measured. The intangible effects are more obscure and elusive. These various effects, however, are radically transforming the economic basis of national politics.

The time has come for an attempt to investigate more thoroughly the implications of these economic changes, and to formulate a tentative answer to the resulting political problems. This answer is, in brief, that the urban middle class is likely to play a part in American politics in the years ahead similar to that played by the rural middle class in the years already behind us. The rural middle class has generally held the balance of power in the struggle between the sections, which has given vitality to American politics throughout the period of national independence, and for the greater part of this period this class has exerted its decisive influence largely through the medium of the independent farmers in the grain-growing regions of the country. Thus the ascendency of the grain-growers has been the essential factor in an economic interpretation of American politics under the Federal Constitution. For many years the average American might appropriately have been personified in the form of a typical farmer from the Corn Belt.

The recent change from a predominantly agrarian to a predominantly urban economy has changed also the comparative importance of sectionalism and of class-consciousness in American politics. As long as the American economy remained predominantly agrarian, the sectional aspects of the ascendency of the grain-growers tended to obscure its significance with reference to the relations between the different classes of the American population. But the rise of an urban economy has brought with it a growing self-consciousness on the part of the different classes into which the industrial population is divided. The urban middle class, like the upper and lower classes in the urban population, has become increasingly conscious of its special interests at the same time that it has become increasingly aware of the great opportunities in national politics offered to it by the changing circumstances of the present age. Class-consciousness waxes as sectionalism wanes among the underlying forces in American politics, and the struggle of classes in some form threatens to become as important in the years ahead as the intersectional struggles in the years behind. Because the rivalry of the sections produced a civil war in the nineteenth century, it does not follow that the class-struggle will necessarily produce another civil war in the twentieth. But there can be little doubt that the future course of American politics will largely depend upon the relative strength of the different classes of the urban population and that the insurance of domestic tranquillity will be bound up with the practical capacity of the urban middle class to maintain the balance of power.

The second of the studies in the second part of the volume is devoted to an attempt to trace the development of middle-class influence in national politics and to estimate its prospects for the future. How the structure of the American political system and the processes of government under the Federal Constitution have conspired with the economic circumstances of the people in the different sections of the country to favor the ascendency of the middle class in the actual conduct of national affairs forms an illuminating chapter in the story of American politics. It furnishes convincing evidence in support of the thesis that the rural middle class was on the whole the dominant factor in national politics during the period of intersectional rivalry.

In the nature of things the evidence can not be equally clear in support of the belief that the urban middle class will be able likewise to dominate the political scene in the coming years. But the possibility of such a development is plainly indicated.

The instrument by means of which the conflicting interests of the different sections have been expressed in the political struggles of the past has been the political party. Some of the intersectional conflicts have been adjusted within the ranks of the parties by the skillful leadership of practical politicians. The adjustment of such conflicts, the record shows, has been one of the most important and most useful functions of the major parties in national politics. Other intersectional conflicts have been adjusted as an incident of the struggles between the parties. At all times a major clue to the vicissitudes of the parties has been the unequal rate of growth of the different sections the interests of which the parties have sought to represent. Unequal rates of sectional growth disturb the equilibrium of interests within the party which prudent party leaders try to preserve. They tend to destroy the balance of interests in the nation which it is a function of the party system in a democracy to maintain.

The leaders of the major parties under the changing conditions of the present age must concern themselves more and more with the consequences of class-consciousness in national politics and of unequal rates of growth of different economic classes. Unequal rates of growth of different economic classes in the urban areas will disturb the equilibrium of the established parties in the future as the shifting of power between the sections has done in the past. A disproportionate rate of growth among any one class will tend to destroy the balance of class interests and thereby threaten the stability of the democratic republic itself. Communists, or similar agitators of extreme measures, will try to organize the lower classes by promising to promote their material interests regardless of the effect on the members of other classes, and Fascists, or other advocates of special privileges for the elite, will seek to seduce the upper classes by offering the prospect of spirited leadership regardless of its effect on the masses. Thus arise both the need and the opportunity for the balanced measures and the judicious leadership of the spokesmen for the middle class.

The outlook for a stable democratic republic is the subject of the third of the following studies. A half-century ago a learned British political scientist, James Bryce as he then was, concluded his monumental treatise on the government and politics of the United States, *The American Commonwealth*, with some observations on the future of democracy in America. The American Political Science Association, of which Lord Bryce was once president, celebrated the fiftieth anniversary of the first publication of Bryce's epochal work by devoting one of its meetings to an appraisal of Bryce's views and opinions. The study which is reprinted in the present volume was originally prepared as a contribution to a book that grew out of the Bryce celebration. Bryce's confidence in the future of democracy in America, it appeared, was not as great as has commonly been supposed, and could not have been greater in the light of the principles of political science which Bryce accepted.

Confidence in the future of democracy in America requires something more than the technique of political science, the purposeful and systematic study of political structures and political processes. By such a technique it can be shown, I believe, that a stable and progressive democratic republic may be maintained in the United States, provided that the ascendency of the middle class can be preserved under a predominantly urban economy as well as under a predominantly agrarian economy. It can also be shown that the ascendency of the urban middle class is possible, provided that no cataclysm destroys the established economic order and that the further development of its character proceeds along the lines indicated by the trend of recent economic changes. But the methods of science do not enable the political scientist to demonstrate that the survival of the democratic republic in America is inevitable, because they do not enable him to predict with certainty that the urban middle class will repeat the achievement of the rural middle class in determining the essential character of American politics. The fact, that Communists and Fascists are no less incapable of proving that their favorite solutions of the outstanding political problem of the present age are certain to be adopted, affords inadequate consolation for the deficiencies of scientific method in the study of contemporary politics.

Confidence in the future of the American democratic republic requires a sound political philosophy. The character of such a political philosophy is the subject of the fourth and last of the following studies. A sound political philosophy, I believe, will condemn the Communist and Fascist theories which divide mankind into two sharply differentiated classes, called by the former, capitalists and proletarians, and by the latter, elite and masses. It will recognize that the classes into which the people of a modern state may be divided are more numerous, less clearly defined, and more interdependent. It will recognize particularly the decisive political function of the middle classes in a body politic possessing a good constitution. One of the great merits, indeed, of a sound political philosophy is its power to strengthen the position of the middle classes in the organization of the state and to extend their influence in the actual processes of government. Such a political philosophy will thereby help to defend the American way itself.

PART II

I

The Economic Basis of National Politics

THE most striking characteristic of the two great parties in American politics is their longevity. The Democrats have now been operating under their present name and with a continuous organization for more than a century; the Republicans, for more than eighty years. The present is the twenty-first consecutive campaign which the presidential candidates of the major parties have waged against each other.* The issues which originally divided Republicans from Democrats have long ceased to hold the attention of the voters. Even the campaign orators now show little interest in them. But the parties continue on their way.

Another striking characteristic of the major parties is their ability to divide the bulk of the nation's voters between them and to exclude independent political organizations from any but a minor role in national politics. In the electoral college, where Presidents are officially chosen, the general rule is that all the votes are divided between the candidates of the two great parties. The latest exception was the election of 1924, when an independent candidate, the elder LaFollette, carried one state, his own state of Wisconsin. In 1912 the Progressive party carried half a dozen states, but the circumstances were peculiar. The "Bull Moose" candidate, Theodore Roosevelt, had been the most popular contender for the regular Republican nomination, and preferred to split the party rather than submit to

* Written in 1936.

what his followers believed to be intolerable injustice at the national convention. Though he carried more states than the regular candidate, the Republican party, after the smoke of battle cleared away, was found substantially intact. It is necessary to go back to the election of 1892 to find a durable independent party making serious inroads into the electoral college vote. The Populists carried several Far-western states, but were ruined by their success. In the next campaign the Democrats took over their leading issue, and they accepted the Democratic candidate for the Presidency. Though the Populists maintained an independent organization through several campaigns, they never again won a place in the electoral college. Altogether, among the twenty campaigns in which Republicans and Democrats have jointly participated heretofore, there have been only five in which the candidates of minor parties obtained electoral votes.

The record of the popular voting in presidential elections points to the same characteristic of the American party system. At every election minor parties solicit the support of the voters for their candidates. In 1932 there were five candidates of minor parties who carried on more or less active campaigns. Their combined popular vote, however, was less than three per cent of the total. In a majority of the twenty campaigns which the two great parties have waged over the Presidency, the minor parties have polled less than five per cent of the total popular vote. With the exceptions of 1856, 1860, 1892, 1912 and 1924, the Republicans and Democrats have succeeded in polling at least ninety per cent of the popular vote. Their general predominance in the political scene is indisputable.

A third outstanding characteristic of the major parties is

their ability to maintain through the years a not-too-unequal division of the bulk of the voters. Neither party has ever gained for its presidential candidate the support of more than sixty per cent of the total popular vote. The record was made by Harding in 1920 and has been closely approached only by Hoover in 1928 and by Roosevelt in 1932. Ordinarily, the winning candidate has received less than fifty-five per cent of the total vote. In seven of the twenty campaigns he has received less than fifty per cent. On the other hand, the losing candidate has usually made a respectable showing. No Republican candidate since 1856, if the split in the party during the "Bull Moose" campaign of 1912 be disregarded, has polled less than forty per cent of the total vote. The Democrats have fared worse in several of their campaigns. Neither Judge Parker in 1904, nor any of the candidates in the three campaigns following the World War, was able to poll as much as forty per cent of the total popular vote. But these apparently crushing defeats have not destroyed the character of the bipartisan system in national politics.

A survey of the record of elections since the present major parties began to dominate the political scene in 1856 shows three clearly defined periods in the relations between the parties. The first was the period of Republican supremacy, which began with the election of Lincoln in 1860 and ended with the loss of control over the House of Representatives in the election of 1874. During this period of fourteen years the Radical Republicans controlled all the political branches of the federal government and were able to give effect to their policies. A period of twenty-two years followed in which the two great parties were so evenly matched in strength that neither of them could control for long both the Presidency and the Congress. Except for two years in the Harrison administration and for the same length of time in the second Cleveland administration, effective party government was impossible. Then, following the exciting free-silver campaign of 1896, came another period of Republican supremacy in Washington. For fourteen years the Conservative Republicans were in the saddle. The split in the party and the bolt of the Progressives in 1912 cleared the way for the Wilson administration, but this interlude of Democratic ascendency was ended by the return to "normalcy" in 1920 and the resumption of control by the Conservative Republicans. This period of Republican supremacy continued until the collapse of the Hoover administration under the strains and stresses of the great depression.

It is evident that on the whole the Republicans have been the stronger party. They have controlled the Presidency and the Congress together for forty-two of the eighty-two years since the foundation of the party in 1854.* During the same period the Democrats have controlled the political branches of the federal government for fourteen years, two under Buchanan, two during the second Cleveland administration, six under Woodrow Wilson, and the past four.† During twenty-six of these eighty-two years neither party has held full control of the political power in Washington. Periods of Republican supremacy have alternated with shorter periods of partisan deadlock or Democratic ascendency.

It might be expected that such alternations of power would continue in accordance with the normal changes in the moods and temper of the voters. The Radical Republi-

* Written in 1936.   † Now, of course, the past eight years.

cans lost control of the federal government in the first
election following the panic of 1873. The Conservative
Republicans came into power at the congressional and presidential elections following the panic of 1893. The Democratic victory in 1912 might seem to break the rule that
political crises are closely associated with economic crises.
But the Democratic victory in 1912 was not brought about
by a shift of voters from the Republican to the Democratic
party. The Conservative Republicans lost control of the
federal government when they lost control of their party
through their dissensions with the Progressives. They regained control of the government when they regained
control of their party. The latest revolution of the business cycle caught the Republicans unprepared. Will they
recover their former authority after an interlude of Democratic ascendency? Or does the present setting of the political scene presage a permanent change in the relations
between the two great parties, or even, perhaps, a new
realignment of the parties?

On the face of the latest election returns there is little
to indicate that the future of the major parties will be
greatly different from their past. Yet there are signs of
impending changes in their relationship to each other and
to the country. The most significant is the increasing
volatility of the electorate. The voters have shown themselves more disposed to change sides in recent campaigns
than in those of earlier years. From 1860 to 1908 the Republicans never polled more than fifty-six per cent of the
popular vote, nor less than forty-three per cent. But in
1912 a majority of them temporarily left their party and,
though most of these dissatisfied Republicans drifted back
during the Wilson administration, their adherence has been

much less firm than in the years from Lincoln to the elder Roosevelt. The LaFollette campaign in 1924 revealed the growing instability of the Republican party, and the desertions to the Democrats since 1930 have surpassed those of any previous crisis in the party's history. The Democrats also have shown distressing symptoms of increasing instability. Cox in 1920, still more Davis in 1924, and Smith in 1928, proved unable to hold the party lines. The triumph of 1932 demonstrated the party's power of recuperation, but enhanced the general impression of partisan instability. Certainly, party ties rested more lightly on the voters than they did a half-century earlier. The habit of party regularity was plainly declining. In the present campaign the signs of the times point more strongly than for many years toward fundamental changes in the alignment of the major parties.

Why, young men and women inquire of their elders and of one another with growing frequency, should a new voter become either a Democrat or a Republican? It is not easy — indeed, it is not possible — to give a convincing answer, if the reply is based upon no better evidence than is afforded by the planks of the party platforms and the declarations of the party candidates. Party platforms have tended to grow longer with the passing years, and less intelligible. Often they seem designed rather to conceal the differences among the members of the party than to expose those between the party as a whole and its opponent. Platforms may speak out boldly on unimportant or incontestable issues, but in dealing with the paramount problems in the minds of the voters they are apt to be verbose, deceptive and obscure. Political critics fill the ears of the public with complaints about the emptiness of the official declarations of party policy. The party leaders do little to render them more explicit and thus to abate the grounds of criticism. To find more satisfactory answers to the riddle of the parties, it is necessary to look below the surface of partisan contention. It is necessary to pursue the verbal controversies to their origins among the underlying forces which influence the setting of the political scene.

Political analysis of the major national parties begins with the record of the popular voting in presidential elections. In 1932 the Democrats carried forty-two of the forty-eight states and elected their candidate with 472 of the 531 electoral votes.* The Republicans carried only six states with 59 electoral votes. But in 1928 the Republicans carried forty of the forty-eight states with 444 votes, while the Democrats carried only eight states with 87 votes. Six states went Republican at both elections, four in New England (Maine, New Hampshire, Vermont and Connecticut), together with Pennsylvania and Delaware. Eight states went Democratic at both elections, two in New England (Massachusetts and Rhode Island) and six in the Lower South (South Carolina, Georgia, Alabama, Mississippi, Louisiana and Arkansas). The other thirty-four states supported the Democratic candidate in the election of 1932 and the Republican in 1928. On the face of the returns not much more is indicated than the fickleness of a great many voters. If a longer view, however, be taken of the political scene, there emerges from the election statistics a durable pattern of voting behavior which gives real character to the national political parties.

The firmest figure in the partisan pattern is the Solid

---

* In 1936 the Democrats carried all but two states, Maine and Vermont, and gained 523 of the 531 electoral votes. The election was an emphatic repetition of 1932.

South. The ten states extending along the South Atlantic and Gulf coasts from Virginia to Texas, and including Arkansas in the back country, have regularly for many years, cast larger majorities for the Democratic presidential candidates than any group of states in any other section of the country. These ten states, together with Tennessee, formed the Southern Confederacy in 1861. Though most of them were carried by the Republicans one or more times during the period of reconstruction after the Civil War, they never failed to support the Democratic presidential ticket in all the campaigns between 1876 and 1928. In the "Al" Smith campaign of 1928 four of these states, Virginia, North Carolina, Florida and Texas, cast their presidential votes for the Republican candidate. But they returned the Democratic candidates for Congress by the usual majorities, and in 1932 all were back again in the fold. It is an unequaled record of party regularity in American national politics.

The solidarity of the Solid South is not an altogether natural phenomenon. In the early years of the Republic, partisan distinctions were as conspicuous there as in any other portion of the Union. The owners of the great plantations along the coast were generally arrayed against the small farmers in the back country and the pioneers on the frontier. The plantation owners were also far from united among themselves, since the tobacco planters of the Old Dominion had interests somewhat different from those of the sugar and rice planters of the Lower South. The development of cotton as the staple crop of the larger part of the South brought greater unity of interests, but popular leaders like Jefferson and Jackson always made a stronger appeal to the smaller farmers and frontiersmen than to the great planters. Important partisan divisions persisted throughout the Upper and Lower South down to the period of the Civil War. It was the war and the unintelligent, though intelligible, process of reconstruction after the war that created the Solid South.

The growing diversification of interests in the Solid South threatens its traditional solidarity. The states which compose that section have been the states with the largest percentages of Negroes. The density of the Democratic vote has been apparently a direct function of the density of the Negro population. But the migration of Negroes to the cities, especially to those in the North, has disturbed the normal relationship between Negroes and whites. Moreover, in the mountainous regions of western North Carolina and Virginia, as in eastern Tennessee and Kentucky, where the Negro population is sparse, there are large blocks of Republican voters. The poor mountain whites still cherish ancient grievances against the great planters and their followers on the fertile plains. On the plains, also, new divisions of interest have sprung up with the development of cotton manufactures and other urban industries. In one of the states of the Solid South, Florida, the urban population has come to outnumber the farmers and planters and other inhabitants of the open country, though in the rest of that section the rural population still holds sway. It is clear that even in the South "the old order changeth."

A second major figure in the partisan pattern is the Northeast. On the ordinary maps this is the section of the country which contains the six New England states and the three adjoining states on the North Atlantic coast. On the maps of the political analyst it may be identified as that section of the country in which the Democratic party gained more than it lost in the "Al" Smith campaign. Outside of the nine Northeastern states there was only one state in the whole Union, Illinois, in which Smith clearly brought net gains to the Democratic party. In that state Smith's strength lay in Chicago, and in the Northeastern states likewise it was his strength in the great cities which chiefly explains his superiority at the polls over other Democratic presidential candidates. But it was not alone in the great cities of the Northeast that Smith ran well in 1928. Although he carried only Massachusetts and Rhode Island, where the urban population is densest, he cut into the regular Republican majorities even in Maine and Vermont, which are still predominantly rural. Smith's popularity in the Northeast was a definitely sectional phenomenon.

The political character of the Northeast is less easily described than that of the South. New England and New York became strongly Republican when the party was first organized, but Pennsylvania was not carried by the Republican party in a presidential election until 1860, and in that election New Jersey was divided between the Republicans and the Douglas Democrats. While Pennsylvania presently became a strong Republican state, New York soon became a doubtful one and remained doubtful until the Bryan campaign in 1896. New Jersey also remained a doubtful state during most of this period, and at times the Democrats even broke the ranks of the New England states by carrying Connecticut. Beginning in 1896, the Northeast was almost solidly Republican down to 1928. The split in the Republican party in 1912 enabled Woodrow Wilson to carry most of the Northeast by a plurality of the votes, but the only Northeastern state to desert the Republican party at any other presidential election between 1896 and 1928 was

New Hampshire in 1916. While the Northeast was the only section of the country in which Smith proved to be a strong candidate in 1928, it was also the section in which Roosevelt encountered the most opposition in 1932. In fact, he lost five of the nine Northeastern states while carrying every other state in the country except Delaware. It is evident that the Northeast, like the Solid South, is different from the rest of the country.

The political character of the Northeast is not only more difficult to describe than that of the South but also more difficult to explain. In the early years of the Republic the Northern and Eastern states contained many small farmers and frontiersmen, and, like the Upper and Lower South, furnished many electoral votes for the parties of Jefferson and Jackson. But the maritime and commercial interests of the seaboard towns, and later the manufacturing interests which sprang up in the vicinity of the numerous water-power sites, preferred to coöperate in national politics with the great planters of the more prosperous parts of the South, forming the sectional coalitions known as Federalist and Whig. Today the farmers are reduced to a small minority of the voters in the Northeast. In Massachusetts, Rhode Island and New Jersey less than five per cent of the population lives on farms, in Connecticut and New York not much more than five per cent, and in Pennsylvania not over ten per cent. Even in rural states like Vermont less than a third of the inhabitants actually live on farms. Urban interests dominate the political scene and give character to both of the major parties.

The distribution of the urban voters in the Northeast between the two great parties has been complicated by differences of class, race and religion. It is evident that the

popularity of "Al" Smith in 1928, not only in New York
but also in the other Northeastern states, cannot be explained solely by the general policies to which he was
pledged or the particular measures which he advocated.
But the strength of the opposition to Roosevelt in 1932
clearly reflected the special economic conditions which
distinguish this section from the rest of the country. Except in New York City, the leading business men have been
generally affiliated with the Republican party for many
years and have sought through its instrumentality to frame
the policies and promote the measures which their interests
have seemed to require. Even in New York City the commercial and financial leaders have tended to be strongly
Republican since the struggle over "free silver" in 1896.
The Republican party in this section of the country has
reflected more definitely than any other group in national
politics the special interests of urban industry and of modern capitalism. It is this specialization of interests which
seems chiefly to explain the solidarity of the by no means
thoroughly solid Northeast.

The third major figure in the partisan pattern is the
West. "West" is a convenient expression which has had
many different meanings in American history. Regarded
as a geographic area, it began in the western portions of the
seaboard states. Pennsylvania was the most typically "western" of the original states. With the westward movement
of population the "West" shifted over the Appalachian
mountains and across the prairies and plains of the Mississippi valley to the Rocky-mountain region, the intermountain plateaus, and the Pacific coast. Its progress has
left numerous landmarks in local nomenclature. Western
Reserve University is located in Cleveland, Ohio. North-

western University flourishes in Chicago and Evanston, Illinois. Occidental University is established in Southern California. Traces of the "West" may be found in all sections from the Atlantic to the Pacific.

In American politics the "West" is rather a state of mind than a definite geographical area. It is a state of mind which has reflected the conditions of life in newly settled regions and on the frontier. It has been more hospitable to what have been believed to be liberal and progressive ideas than have the older portions of the country. It has been more sensitive to the vicissitudes of agriculture and of industry. It has been less tenacious of habitual partisan preferences than has been the Northeast or the Solid South. It is more national than the Northeast or the South, being in some measure a mixture of both. Yet it is intensely conscious of its sectional individuality.

However the West may be defined on the map, not all its parts are equally "western." California has become a state with a predominantly urban population, like the great states of the Northeast. In both the other Pacific-coast states the city dwellers outnumber those who live in the open country, though by less wide a margin than in California. In Colorado and Utah, also, large cities impart a more urbane character to the politics of those states than would be natural amidst the rusticity which prevails in most of the Mountain states. But while most of the Western states are predominantly rural, they are not equally agrarian. In Arizona the percentage of the population living on farms is as low as in New Hampshire or Delaware, which are classed as urban states, and in Nevada it is not much higher. In the Dakotas, on the other hand, the farm population is as dominant as in Arkansas and Mississippi.

The contemporary political West begins with Wisconsin. It extends across the Mississippi to Minnesota, Iowa, Kansas, Nebraska and the Dakotas. It includes all but one of the Mountain states and all the states on the Pacific coast. It accounts for more than a third of all the states in the Union. This is a section which was solidly Republican in 1920 and in 1928, but it is the section in which the reaction against the Hoover administration was most decisive in 1932. It is the section in which Senators LaFollette and Wheeler, running on the Independent Progressive ticket in 1924, made the greatest inroads into the normal strength of the major parties. It is the section in which, in 1916, the appeal on behalf of Woodrow Wilson to keep the country out of war played the greatest havoc in the Republican ranks. Clearly, this section, as the Northeast and the Solid South, is different from the rest of the country.

Perhaps the most characteristic expression of the political traits of the West in recent years was manifest in the election of 1924. LaFollette's Independent Progressive party developed strength enough to take his own state away from the Republicans and to put the Democrats down into third place in a dozen of the Western states. The Democrats ran behind both the Republicans and the Progressives in every state along the Canadian border from Wisconsin to the Pacific coast, down the coast to California, and back through Nevada, Idaho, Wyoming and South Dakota, to Iowa. In Nebraska the Democrats barely held second place through the influence of the Bryan brothers, and in Kansas, Colorado, Utah and Arizona they were hard pressed by the Progressives. In 1912, also, this was the section of the country in which the Roosevelt Progressives made their best showing, though they actually carried only four of the

Western states, Minnesota, South Dakota, Washington and California. Earlier still, the Populists scored their chief victories in this section. But it is not necessary to multiply instances of the hospitable disposition of the West toward independent political movements. It is evident that the leading trait of Western politics, compared with the politics of the Solid South, or even of the Northeast, is its partisan instability.

Besides the three major sections in American politics there are three intermediate sections lying between the major sections. The first of these, in political importance, lies between the Northeast and the West, and for lack of a better name may be called the Middle States section. The original Middle States in American politics lay on the Atlantic coast, but the Middle States, politically speaking, have gone westward steadily, following the political "West." This section now consists of four states, Ohio, Indiana, Illinois and Michigan, which mingle Northeastern conservatism with Western liberalism and progressivism in fairly balanced portions. They are states in which the industrial and urban population predominates, though not to the extent of its predominance in most of the Northeastern states. The percentage of the population actually living on farms is low, though not so low as in most of the Northeastern states. Modern capitalism, as in the Northeast, tends to dominate the political scene. Agrarianism, however, as in the West, has not altogether lost its former sway.

The role of these mid-western "Middle States" in national politics is complicated by their position close to the border between North and South. Virginia, Kentucky and other states of the Upper South contributed largely to their original population, as well as did New England and the

Middle Atlantic states. The early settlers from these different sections brought their characteristic sectional attitudes with them and gave to the political campaigns in the present mid-western Middle States, particularly the three immediately north of the Ohio River, a uniquely intersectional character. Michigan, which was originally settled chiefly by Northerners, was formerly more definitely Northwestern, like Wisconsin, Iowa and Minnesota. It did not become a typical Middle State until in recent years the growth of automobile manufacturing and other great capitalistic industries created a predominantly urban population and compelled a new adjustment between Western and Northeastern political attitudes. In the other Middle States also the development of urban industry in recent years has tended to strengthen the characteristic Northeastern political attitudes at the expense of those reflecting the character of the Upper South and West.

The partisan record of the Middle States reflects their peculiar situation at the center of equilibrium between Northeast and West, and also for many years, though not recently, at the center of equilibrium between North and South. Generally Republican in presidential elections, they have been less stable than the Northeast and, at least since the Bryan campaigns, more stable than the West. Solidly Democratic in 1932, they were solidly Republican in the three preceding elections. The defection of Ohio to the Democrats in 1916 was as decisive of the result in that closely contested campaign as the more notorious defection of California. In 1912 the Bull Moose Progressives carried one state in this section, Michigan, with a degree of success attained in no Northeastern state except Pennsylvania. Prior to that election Michigan had been Republican, generally strongly Republican, in every presidential election since the organization of the party. Ohio, Indiana and Illinois, on the other hand, had always been closely contested down to the Bryan campaigns, and often doubtful, if not Democratic.

The second of the intermediate sections is the border between North and South. Five states, Delaware, Maryland, West Virginia, Kentucky and Tennessee, belong in this section. They were originally slave states and possessed important interests in common with the other states of the South. In none of them could the Republican party originally obtain any considerable support. Only one of them, Tennessee, actually joined the Southern Confederacy; the people of West Virginia, indeed, broke their connection with the mother state rather than attempt to leave the Union. In all of them the small farmers were too conscious of their traditional opposition to the great planters to follow willingly in so desperate an enterprise as secession. The "poor whites" in the Appalachian mountain valleys were particularly hostile to the political leadership of the dominant slaveholders of the Lower South. It was from this class of mountain whites that Lincoln picked Andrew Johnson to run with him on the Union ticket in 1864. Around them the Republican party leaders gradually built up, in the border states, a substantial following which survived the abortive effort to found a new Republican party in the South with the support of Negro votes.

At the present time the political character of these border states is very different from what it was in the period of Radical Republicanism. Delaware has become predominantly urban and industrial, and seems to be almost as strongly Republican as Pennsylvania. In Maryland, which has also become a predominantly urban state, the influence of the South has persisted more strongly, though the Republicans carried the state twice for McKinley against Bryan, and three times in the 1920's. In West Virginia, Republican influences have strengthened with the economic transformation of the state following the development of the soft-coal industry. Its political orientation tends to turn toward Pittsburgh and the Northeast rather than toward Richmond and the Upper South. Kentucky and Tennessee have remained more agrarian and have been more consistently Democratic. The Republicans, however, carried the former state in 1896 and again in 1924 and 1928, while Tennessee went Republican in 1920 and 1928.

The last of the intermediate sections is the border between South and West. Three states, Missouri, Oklahoma and New Mexico, belong in this section. The first and second of these, though not situated in the South, were originally settled chiefly by farmers and planters from the South and were endowed with the Southern political traits. Missouri, being a grain-growing state with many settlers from Kentucky and Tennessee, naturally tended to follow the Upper South in its politics, while Oklahoma, lying partly within the cotton belt and being settled more largely from the Lower South, tended to follow the Lower South more closely. Further political complications have followed the growth of manufactures in Missouri and the discovery of oil in Oklahoma. Kansas, which was originally a bone of contention between the sections, finally fell under the control of the free-state men and became definitely "western." Many of its early settlers came from strongly Republican New England, and after the Civil War many Union veterans were attracted there by the liberal terms of settlement under the Republican Homestead Act. Since many Kansans mingled with the early settlers in Oklahoma, the northern part of that state, which happened to lie in the wheat-growing region, acquired a distinctly different political character from that of the more southerly portions of the state. New Mexico has always possessed a peculiar political character on account of the large Spanish-speaking population, and remains uniquely Southwestern.

The confusion resulting from the mixture of ancestral political habits and conflicting economic interests is better illustrated in the Southwestern border section than in any other section of the country. Missouri, which was carried by Douglas in 1860, and then became Unionist for two elections, went over to the Liberal Republicans in 1872, and thereafter was Democratic until the end of the century. From 1904 to 1928 it was carried by the Republicans, except in 1912 and 1916 in the two Wilson campaigns. In 1932 it went Democratic, as did most of the rest of the country. Oklahoma has regularly been Democratic except in 1920 and 1928. New Mexico has been more closely contested, the Spanish-speaking population apparently holding the balance of power between settlers from the South and those from the North and West. In short, the political character of the Southwestern border is more mixed than is that of either of the other intermediate sections.

The relations between the sections furnish the key to American national politics. As Frederick J. Turner has wisely observed: [1] "Statesmanship in this nation consists not only in representing the special interests of the leader's own section, but in finding a formula that will bring the different

---

[1] Frederick J. Turner, *The Significance of Sections in American History* (Henry Holt and Company, New York, 1932).

regions together in a common policy." The conditions of the problem which American statesmen — that is, the party leaders — have to solve are revealed by the distribution of electoral votes among the sections. This distribution is shown in the accompanying table:

SECTIONALISM IN AMERICAN POLITICS, 1936

Sections	Number of States	Representa-tives	Electoral Votes
1. The Northeast	9	122	140
2. The North-South border	5	31	41
3. The South	10	93	113
4. The South-West border	3	23	29
5. The West	17	86	120
6. The Middle States	4	80	88
Total	48	435	531

It is evident that no one of the three major sections holds the balance of power between the other two. There are too many votes in the intermediate sections. But any two of the major sections can gain control of the federal government by forming a combination which includes the intermediate section. (If the combination were formed between the South and the West, it would be necessary not only to carry the Southwestern border states but also to pick up an additional state in the border section between the South and the North.) The Northeast section is the only one which can theoretically win a presidential election without help from either of the other major sections, but to do so its candidate would have to carry every one of the Middle States and also the states in the border section between North and South. Thus, the balance of power lies in the intermediate sections.

Under these circumstances, finding a formula that can bring a winning combination of sections together in a common policy can be no easy task. In the earlier years of the Republic the former "Wests" did for a long time hold the balance of power between Northeast and South, but neither the Northeast nor the South was then as nearly solid as it became in later years. At present the West together with the Middle States can theoretically hold the balance between Northeast and South, but these two sections can not be united as easily as the earlier "Wests." The problem of national statesmanship, as defined by Turner, has always been one which has exercised to the utmost the powers of the great party leaders.

There have been many different solutions of this basic problem of American politics. The Federalists tried to build a majority by a combination of Northeast and South against the West, but this proved to be an unstable combination and could not maintain its hold on power without the strong hand of Washington. Jefferson, who from the political point of view was a Western, not a Southern, leader,[2] and later Jackson, built up victorious sectional combinations by organizing the bulk of the West and attracting to the main body of their supporters a sufficient following in both Northeast and South to gain firm control of the federal government. Clay, Webster and Calhoun tried to form a sectional combination to rival that of the Jacksonian Democrats, but their Whig coalition never possessed the solidarity of the Democrats, and could not be as effective an instrument of national statesmanship. On the whole, down to the Civil War period partisan strategy favored sectional combinations drawing their strength from all three major sections, though relying more heavily upon the West than

[2] Charles A. Beard, *The Economic Origins of Jeffersonian Democracy* (The Macmillan Company, New York, 1915).

upon either of the others. It was no accident that the Federalist party, which paid little attention to the West, was one of the less successful of the major parties.

The anti-slavery Republican party was founded upon a combination of Northeast and West against the South. This combination, though strong enough to win the Presidency, did not possess the strength needed to control the Congress under normal conditions. Hence the frantic efforts of the Republican leaders, first to extend their power into the South by means of Negro votes and later to strengthen themselves in the West by the admission of new states and the cultivation of Western interests with appropriate measures. But Populism ruined Republican hopes in the West as the failure of Negro suffrage had ruined them in the South, until the bold attempt of the Democrats under Bryan's leadership to repeat the achievements of Jefferson and Jackson under less auspicious circumstances solidified the Northeast and Middle West and gave the "sound-money" Republicans under more conservative leadership a less precarious supremacy in national politics than the anti-slavery Republicans had ever had. Woodrow Wilson came into power through the accidental division of his opponents rather than through any special strength of his own, and retained power through the accidental intrusion of European affairs upon the American political scene. Now, at last, Franklin D. Roosevelt leads against the Republican lines a new assault which apparently carries a greater threat to the old order in national politics than any of the earlier campaigns since the present party alignment was first established.

The real character of sectionalism in American politics, and hence of the major political parties also, does not appear from a superficial inspection of the election returns. The politician who knew no more about the political attitudes of the people of the different states than was revealed by the results of the latest presidential elections would be at a loss to explain their apparent fickleness. The shifting of thirty-four states from the Republican to the Democratic side between 1928 and 1932 does not show what really happened. Maine, New Hampshire, Vermont, Connecticut, Pennsylvania and Delaware, which voted Republican at both elections, are not the only states in which Republicanism flourishes. Nor are Massachusetts and Rhode Island, which voted Democratic at both elections, with South Carolina, Georgia, Alabama, Mississippi, Louisiana and Arkansas, as solidly Democratic as the company which they kept would suggest. In uneven contests, like those of 1928 and 1932, tidal waves of popular votes may wash particular states far away from their usual moorings, while others hold out against the tide or drift sluggishly with it. In states where the results are close, pluralities of the popular vote fall in favor of one candidate or the other in the most casual manner; and a state where the margin of victory over defeat is less than ten per cent of the total vote is in a very different category from one in which the victorious candidate receives two or three times as many votes as his defeated rival.

Fruitful analysis of the election returns begins when the states are arranged in accordance with the extent of their deviation from the average. In 1932 Roosevelt polled over fifty-seven per cent of the total popular vote in the forty-eight states, while Hoover polled barely forty per cent. States in which the popular vote for the candidates of the two major parties was distributed in approximately the same way as in the whole country may be described as average states at that particular election. States in which the vote for the Republican and Democratic candidates deviated from the average by a considerable amount — let us say by at least five per cent — may be described as states with a Republican or Democratic deviation. When all the states are assigned to their proper places in accordance with such an arrangement, the pattern of national politics begins to emerge from the obscurity of the ordinary voting statistics.

The pattern for 1932 is interesting. There were ten states with a Democratic deviation in the Solid South. There were four others (Tennessee, Missouri, Oklahoma and New Mexico) in the two border sections. There were six more (Wisconsin, the Dakotas, Nebraska, Nevada and Arizona) in the West. There were seven states with a Republican deviation in the Northeast (all but New York and Rhode Island), one (Ohio) in the Middle States section, and one (Delaware) on the North-South border. The nineteen remaining states fell into the category of the average. A majority of the nineteen lay in the West. Three others (Illinois, Indiana and Michigan) lay in the Middle States section, three (Maryland, West Virginia and Kentucky) in the North-South border section, and two (New York and Rhode Island) in the Northeast. There was no state with a Republican deviation in either the South or the West, and none with a Democratic deviation in either the Northeast or the Middle States. The border between North and South was the only section with one or more states in each of the three categories. The Solid South and the South-West border were the only sections with all their states in one category.

The differences between this pattern and that for 1928 are significant. In 1928 three of the states in the South

(Virginia, North Carolina and Florida) were among the average states. Three of the Northeastern states (New York, Rhode Island and Massachusetts) were among the states with a Democratic deviation, and three others (New Hampshire, Connecticut and New Jersey) were among the average states. Only Maine, Vermont and Pennsylvania were among those with a Republican deviation at both elections. In the West no state was among those with a Democratic deviation in 1928, and six appeared among those with a Republican deviation. In the Middle States section there is no difference in the location of three states, while one (Michigan), an average state in 1932, was one of those with a Republican deviation in 1928. In the border between North and South there is no difference, and in the South-West border there is a general preference for the Republican instead of the Democratic side. Altogether, twenty-six states shifted their position between 1928 and 1932, while twenty-two remained in the same category at both elections.

By constructing a series of such patterns for presidential elections, it is possible to determine what may be called the political climate of the United States. This may be defined as the average deviation of the individual states from the average distribution of popular votes for the whole country over a considerable period of time. If the average distribution of votes between the two major parties at the four elections since the World War be taken as normal, the political climate will measure the extent to which the states depart from this normal. By assigning to each state its proper number of electoral votes, a simple table may be prepared which will serve to illustrate how party leaders make the calculations upon the basis of which the party strategy in presidential campaigns is determined.

Section	Number of Electoral Votes				
	I	II	III	IV	V
1. The Northeast	...	..	51	45	44
2. The North-South border ...	...	30	8	3	..
3. The South	113	..	..	..	..
4. The South-West border ...	...	29	..	..	..
5. The West	...	26	52	42	..
6. The Middle States	...	..	14	55	19
Total	113	85	125	145	63

Number of electoral votes which may be cast by states which show (I) an average deviation on the Democratic side of more than 10 per cent, (II) an average deviation on the Democratic side of less than 10 per cent but more than 2½ per cent, (III) an average deviation of less than 2½ per cent in either direction, (IV) an average deviation of more than 2½ per cent but less than 10 per cent on the Republican side, and (V) an average deviation of more than 10 per cent on the Republican side.

Since 266 electoral votes are necessary for the election of a President, the problem of the national party leaders may be clearly stated. It is, to carry enough states in the third or average-state category to supply at least fifty-eight electoral votes, if the candidate be a Republican, or enough to supply at least sixty-eight electoral votes, if he be a Democrat. With a theoretically normal distribution of the popular vote, carrying these states should insure the victory in the presumably more reliable states of categories IV and V, or I and II, as the case may be. In practice, of course, prudent party leaders will not calculate so closely as is suggested above, since a margin of safety is desirable to cover losses from abnormal deviations among the presumably reliable states.

The character of the major parties compels the party leaders to distinguish sharply between the choice of policies and measures and the choice of candidates. In choosing general policies, as well as the specific measures for carry-

ing them into effect, it is necessary to suit them to the
special interests of the major sections from which the party
ordinarily derives the bulk of its support in the Congress.
If clearly defined measures and policies can not be suited
to the partisan sectional interests, then it becomes necessary
to effect compromises that will be acceptable to the interests
concerned, or else to evade the issues by glittering general-
ities and equivocation. If this is not done, the campaign
will be ineffective in the very sections where the party
should be strongest, and the leaders, if successful, will have
difficulty in carrying out their program after the election.
Hence the vagueness and ambiguity of many planks in the
national platforms, and the apparent lack of principle and
the insincerity so often denounced by the critics of American party politics. On issues of minor or only local importance the platforms of the two great parties may speak
out boldly, but on the major issues there must often be obscurity and confusion. This is a part of the price which the
American people pay for the services of national parties in
a country where sectionalism prevails.

In choosing their candidates, however, the party leaders
have to be mindful of considerations that are very different.
If the platforms are properly constructed, the interests of
the party in the states with a strong party deviation can be
safely left to the local leaders. In fact, in states with a
strong party deviation, as in the Solid South from the Democratic point of view, the management of the campaign can
be left entirely to the local leaders, and neither platform nor
candidates need give much attention to the special interests
of these states. After the election, of course, in case of success the local leaders can demand much more consideration
from the Congress for their special sectional interests. But

in the choice of candidates little regard need be paid to their popularity in the comparatively reliable states. It is to the doubtful states that the appeal of the candidates must be mainly directed.

It is evident from the characters of the major political parties that the tests of availability for presidential candidates must be different. Party leaders on both sides are well aware that the largest blocks of doubtful votes under "normal" conditions are in the Northeast (particularly in New York) and in the West. But the circumstances which shape the character of the Republican party compel its leaders to make their basic appeal to the Northeast and the West. Hence, they must seek to embody in the national platform the formula which will bring those two major sections together in a common policy. Hence, also, the candidate must be selected with an eye particularly on his vote-getting ability in the intermediate section. It is not surprising, therefore, that eight of the eleven men who have been elected to the Presidency on the Republican ticket should have hailed from the Mid-western Middle States. Two of the other three, Theodore Roosevelt and Calvin Coolidge, were originally nominated for the vice-presidency and owed their availability for the subsequent presidential nominations to the accidents which first brought them into the White House. Herbert Hoover is the only real exception to the rule of availability among successful Republican candidates. The unsuccessful candidates (apart from candidates for a second term who failed of reëlection), namely, John C. Fremont, James G. Blaine and Charles E. Hughes, were also exceptions to the rule.

Availability for the Democratic presidential nomination has likewise reflected the circumstances which have shaped the character of that party. Unlike the Republicans, the Democrats have sought to build their party upon a combination of all three major sections. Since the Civil War their strategy, except in the Bryan campaigns, has been based upon the hope of adding to the Solid South enough votes in each of the other two major sections to give their candidate the necessary electoral majorities. The nature of the American political climate makes it practically impossible for them to win a close election without carrying doubtful states in the Northeast, the Middle States section and the West. If they lose New York, they must carry, in a close election, every other doubtful state in the whole country. Under the circumstances the Democratic party leaders have logically sought their presidential candidates in New York. It is not surprising that eight of the twelve men who, since the Civil War, have run for the Presidency on the Democratic ticket, have hailed from New York. Pursuing the same strategy, the Democrats have often taken their vice-presidential candidates from the Mid-western Middle States. Once, in 1920, they reversed their tactics and took their presidential candidate from Ohio and their vice-presidential candidate from New York. But they have never sought presidential candidates in the border sections. Those sections, like the Solid South, could safely be left to shift for themselves if the ticket made a strong appeal to New York and the Middle States.

William Jennings Bryan, the only real Westerner among these Democratic candidates, rejected the customary party strategy. He directed his campaigns toward a combination of South and West, regardless of the opposition of the Northeast. But his leadership never brought success. Woodrow Wilson, who in 1916 made the Bryan strategy succeed without perhaps really intending to do so, was originally brought forward as a candidate with a special appeal to New York, though not himself a New Yorker. It is now clear that Wilson's victory in 1916 was the product of an accidental union of South and West resulting from the intrusion of foreign issues into domestic politics. It did not signify a permanent realignment of the two great parties on the basis of a new combination of the sections. It is equally clear that the nature of the American political climate compels the Democrats either to concentrate upon the capture of New York in presidential elections, or, as Bryan desired, to effect a realignment of parties upon the basis of a new sectional combination.

The nature of the political climate compels the Republicans likewise to carry New York as well as some of the doubtful states in the Middle States section or in the West. This explains the Republican propensity to choose their vice-presidential candidate from New York or to nominate for the vice-presidency a man from some other Northeastern state who can make a strong appeal to New Yorkers. Theoretically the Republicans might elect their candidate without carrying New York by winning the bulk of the doubtful states in other sections of the country. Actually that has not been accomplished since 1876, and was not accomplished even then without carrying some states in the South. The Republicans have lost one election, that of 1916, when they did carry New York, and they can not hope to win again under the existing circumstances without carrying that state. Thus the power of the Republican party seems to depend upon the preservation of the existing party alignment. The Democrats, on the other hand, might continue to flourish under a different alignment. They might even increase their power if they adopted a partisan strategy designed to appeal more strongly to either New York or the West.

It is such possibilities that lend interest to the study of national politics. But it is clear that the analysis of the election returns must go beyond the voting statistics of the various sections or even of the individual states. It is necessary to analyze the forces within the states which influence the responses to the appeals of the national party leaders. In general, the leading economic interests in any section are associated with the party which is dominant in that section. But when no party can dominate a section, the distribution of sectional interests between the two great parties is more complicated. The political analyst is thus primarily concerned with the identification and measurement of "interests" and with tracing their influence upon the character of the parties. Critics of American politics deplore the importance of the "interests" in the major parties, but it is the influence of the "interests" that gives the parties their individuality and much of their character.

The most important influences, within the states, which affect the calculations of the party leaders are those which result from the division of population between city and country. American politics was originally agrarian politics. The people of the original states lived for the most part in the open country and were chiefly occupied in the cultivation of the soil. In eight of the original states the first census reported no city or town with as many as eight thousand inhabitants. Ninety-six per cent of the entire population of the United States lived in smaller towns or on the land. New York and Philadelphia were the only cities large enough to elect each a Congressman of its own. Boston,

Charleston and Baltimore were the only other places that might have dominated a congressional district. At least one hundred of the 105 Congressmen in Washington's time may fairly be assumed to have represented rural rather than urban interests.

The nature of agrarian politics insured a deliberate preference for rural over urban interests. "The inhabitants of the commercial cities," declared Jefferson in a letter to one of his correspondents, "are as different in sentiment and character from the country people as any two distinct nations, and are clamorous against the order of things established by the agricultural interest." Jefferson added that "though by command of newspapers they make a great deal of noise, [they] have little effect on the direction of policy." Jackson's testimony confirms that of Jefferson. "The agricultural interest of our country," he declared in his first annual message to Congress, "is so essentially connected with every other and so superior in importance to them all that it is scarcely necessary to invite to it your particular attention. It is principally as manufactures and commerce tend to increase the value of agricultural productions and to extend their application to the wants and comforts of society that they deserve the fostering care of Government." As late as 1840, when a more careful census of occupations was taken than in any previous enumeration of the population, agriculture was still the leading occupation in every state except Rhode Island. In the country as a whole, persons engaged in agriculture outnumbered those engaged in manufactures almost five to one.

The century which has passed since Jackson lived in the White House has witnessed an astonishing growth of urban industry and of urban population. By 1900 there were 545 cities of eight thousand inhabitants or more in the United States. Yet two-thirds of the people still resided in smaller places or in the open country. The World War marked the final passing of the rural districts as the dwelling-place of a majority of the American people, and the rise of the urban population to the first place. By the census of 1930 the rural population was estimated at under forty-four per cent of the total. Over twelve per cent of the people lived in cities of more than one million inhabitants; over seventeen per cent, in cities of less than one million but more than one hundred thousand; and nearly eighteen per cent in smaller cities with populations exceeding ten thousand. If all the inhabitants of incorporated places with a population of as much as five thousand are counted as rural, the rural part of the American people is still in a minority.

Time was when such a development was viewed with grave alarm. Jefferson's opinions are well known. Writing in 1787 from Paris to his friend Madison, he predicted that "when we get piled upon one another in large cities, as in Europe, we shall become as corrupt as they." Later, writing from Monticello to another friend, he declared: "I view great cities as pestilential to the morals, the health, and the liberties of man. True, they nourish some of the elegant arts, but the useful ones can thrive elsewhere, and less perfection in the others, with more health, virtue, and freedom, would be my choice." This predilection for life in the country continued to characterize the dominant opinion among the American people throughout the nineteenth century. It continued to demand the use of political power for the purpose of favoring the agricultural interests over those of commerce and manufactures.

The traditional prejudice against the cities and against

urban interests in national politics seemed to be sanctioned by the best authorities of the period. In Jackson's time a discerning French writer, Alexis de Tocqueville, made a careful study of American politics and returned to his native land to write a book filled with discriminating praise of American institutions. Though he found much to admire in America, he viewed the growth of cities with unconcealed alarm. Among the principal causes which, he believed, tended to maintain the republican form of government, he listed the absence of a great capital city. Then he added a memorable warning: "The United States have no metropolis; but they already contain several large cities. . . . The lower orders which inhabit these cities constitute a rabble even more formidable than the populace of European towns. . . . I look upon the size of certain American cities, and especially on the nature of their population, as a real danger which threatens the future security of the [Republic]; and I venture to predict that [it] will perish from this circumstance, unless the government succeeds in creating an armed force, which, while it remains under the control of the majority of the nation, will be independent of the town population, and able to repress its excesses." A half-century later, in Grover Cleveland's time, another discerning foreign observer, James Bryce, made another careful study of American politics, and, like de Tocqueville, recorded his opinions in an immortal book. Bryce also was distrustful of the influence of cities. "The growth of cities," he wrote, "has been among the most significant and least fortunate changes in the character of the population of the United States."

It is not surprising that the spirit of agrarian politics continued to be suspicious of the urban population and hostile

to its peculiar interests. As the influence of the urban population in national politics grew, the conflict between rural
and urban interests became sharper. American politics
ceased to be almost entirely agrarian and sectional; it became
increasingly urban and class-conscious. Now, at long last,
the urban population actually outnumbers the rural, and the
struggle between city and country, and among different
classes in the cities, threatens to become as important a factor in national politics as the traditional struggle between
sections. Already the states in which the urban population
is more numerous than the rural possess a majority of
the votes in the electoral college. But the distribution of the
urban population among the states is so unequal that the
urban states do not yet possess a majority of the votes in
the Congress. A revolution in American politics is manifestly in process, but it has not yet been completed.

The ability of the rural population to maintain an influence in national politics greatly disproportionate to its numbers is one of the anomalies of the American political
system. It results from the capital fact that a large majority
of the urban population is situated in a minority of the
states. Though a substantial majority of the whole population of the United States is urban, according to the census of
1930, in only twenty-one of the forty-eight states is a majority of the population urban, and in several of these the urban population exceeds the rural by no more than a slender
margin. Hence, a majority of the Senators of the United
States are dependent for their election upon bodies of voters
which are still predominantly rural in composition. The
urban states, however, include a disproportionate number
of the more populous states. Therefore, although the Senators from the urban states are outnumbered by the Senators

from the rural states, there are more presidential electors from the former than from the latter. Under the latest apportionment the twenty-one urban states have 310 votes in the electoral college, a clear majority of the total. The urban states, by forming a combination among themselves against the rural states, could seize the Presidency and hold it indefinitely, but they could not dominate the Senate.

The disproportionate power of the rural population in national politics is increased by the unequal distribution of urban and rural voters among the congressional districts. If the seats in Congress could be distributed exactly in accordance with the distribution of population between city and country, the urban population would now have 244 seats, while the rural population would have only 191. But so great a portion of the urban population is concentrated in the largest cities where there are no rural voters, and so many other urban voters are scattered over the countryside in small cities where they are outnumbered and politically submerged by the rural population, that the urban population cannot hope to dominate a number of districts corresponding to its numerical importance. The over-representation of the rural population is further magnified by the retention in many states of obsolete districting laws designed to favor the rural population at the expense of the urban. The consequence is that the number of districts dominated by the urban population, though not easy to estimate with accuracy, is certainly much less than a majority of the whole.

In order to understand how the distribution of population between city and country and among different classes in the cities affects the calculations of the party leaders, it is necessary to estimate the voting strength of the states and districts which may be dominated by the urban population as accurately as possible. For this purpose the distinction which the census for 1930 makes between metropolitan and other urban areas is useful. The former term is designed to show the magnitude of each of the principal areas of urban population, regardless of the actual city limits, by including in a single total both the population of the central city itself and that of the suburbs or urbanized areas surrounding it. In some cases the population of two or more cities located in close proximity, together with that of their suburbs, is combined in a single metropolitan area. Ninety-five such areas were reported, each having an aggregate population of one hundred thousand or more and containing one or more central cities of at least fifty thousand inhabitants. Without the District of Columbia, which is not represented in Congress, these metropolitan areas contained approximately fifty-four million inhabitants. The total rural population of the United States, including that of incorporated places with less than 2500 inhabitants, was very nearly the same. There remained about fourteen and a half millions residing in urban areas outside the metropolitan areas.

The voting strength of the urban population, in the Senate and in the electoral college, may be roughly estimated without difficulty. All the states in which the population of the metropolitan areas forms a clear majority of the total may be put down as predominantly urban in politics. The other states in which a majority of the total population are reported as urban may be put down as doubtful, though more probably urban than rural. The remaining states may be put down as predominantly rural. The rural states are not, of course, necessarily agrarian in politics. The population of such states actually living on farms may be outnumbered by the rural population engaged in mining or other non-agricultural pursuits. In fact, such is apparently the case in West Virginia, Arizona and Nevada. The results of such a classification are shown in the accompanying tables. All the Northeastern states except Maine, New Hampshire

NUMBER OF SENATORS

Section	Metropolitan	Other Urban	Rural	Total
1. Northeast	12	2	4	18
2. North-South border.	4	0	6	10
3. South	0	2	18	20
4. South-West border .	0	2	4	6
5. West	2	10	22	34
6. Middle States	6	2	0	8
Total	24	18	54	96

NUMBER OF ELECTORAL VOTES

Section	Metropolitan	Other Urban	Rural	Total
1. Northeast	128	4	8	140
2. North-South border.	11	0	30	41
3. South	0	7	106	113
4. South-West border .	0	15	14	29
5. West	22	35	63	120
6. Middle States	74	14	0	88
Total	235	75	221	531

and Vermont, fall in the metropolitan division. All the Middle states except Indiana fall in the same division. Delaware and Maryland in the North-South border section also fall in this division. In the three other sections only California can be classed among the metropolitan states. Most of the other urban states are small Western states. The South is solidly rural except Florida, and the Southern border sections are predominantly rural. The section with the largest number of rural Senators, however, is the West. The extraordinary inequalities between the representation of the sections in the Senate and in the electoral college are brought out strikingly by these tables.

The voting strength of the urban population in the lower branch of the Congress cannot be so easily estimated. It is a fair assumption, however, that all congressional districts which are situated wholly within a metropolitan area, or which contain a metropolitan area of at least a quarter of a million population, are predominantly urban in politics.

NUMBER OF CONGRESSIONAL DISTRICTS

Section	Metropolitan	Other Urban	Rural	Total
1. Northeast	62	35	25	122
2. North-South border.	4	9	18	31
3. South	7	10	76	93
4. South-West border .	5	2	16	23
5. West	19	14	53	86
6. Middle States	26	17	37	80
Total	123	87	225	435

Other congressional districts, containing a smaller metropolitan area or lying partly within a larger metropolitan area, may often, though not necessarily always, be dominated by the urban population. Congressional districts, which neither lie wholly or partly within a metropolitan area nor contain a metropolitan area of any size within their own limits, will generally, though certainly not always, be subject to domination by the rural population. Upon these assumptions the congressional districts, including states in which Congressmen are elected at large, may be distributed among the urban and rural population as shown in the accompanying table. The congressional representation of the Northeast is predominantly metropolitan, and metropolitan and urban districts dominate the Middle States. The other four sections are predominantly rural. It is clear that the distribution of population between city and country is much more fairly reflected in the House of Representatives than in the Senate, where the country population is greatly over-represented. But it is less fairly reflected than in the electoral college, where the operation of the general ticket system of choosing presidential electors compensates for discrimination against cities in laying out congressional districts.

The final step in the analysis of the present partisan alignment is to classify the various types of districts in accordance with the distribution of the popular vote between the major parties. For this purpose it is not enough to divide the districts into Democratic and Republican upon the basis of the results of the latest congressional elections. The elections of 1934 were too one-sided to give a true picture of the distribution of party strength among the different types of districts in the various sections of the country. A less distorted picture is presented by a further division of the Democratic districts into the strongly Democratic, where the Democratic vote was at least twice as great as the Republican, and the comparatively close districts. The results of the 1934 congressional elections are set forth upon this basis in the accompanying tables. The Republicans hold less than one-fifth of the rural districts, nearly one-fourth of the metropolitan districts, and more than one-third of the urban districts. More than a third of the rural districts were strongly Democratic, a third of the metropolitan districts, and less than one-fifth of the other urban districts. The largest blocks of close districts lay in the rural West and Middle States and in the metropolitan Northeast. Altogether, 144 districts were strongly Democratic, 187 were close, and 104 were Republican. A majority of the strongly Democratic districts were located in the South or in the

METROPOLITAN DISTRICTS

Section	Republican	Close	Strongly Democratic	Total
1. Northeast	18	21	23	62
2. North-South border ..	0	2	2	4
3. South	0	0	7	7
4. South-West border	0	3	2	5
5. West	6	11	2	19
6. Middle States	5	16	5	26
Total	29	53	41	123

OTHER URBAN DISTRICTS

Section	Republican	Close	Strongly Democratic	Total
1. Northeast	19	15	1	35
2. North-South border ..	2	5	2	9
3. South	0	0	10	10
4. South-West border ...	0	1	1	2
5. West	3	9	2	14
6. Middle States	7	10	0	17
Total	31	40	16	87

RURAL DISTRICTS

Section	Republican	Close	Strongly Democratic	Total
1. Northeast	14	11	0	25
2. North-South border ..	2	11	5	18
3. South	0	6	70	76
4. South-West border ...	1	10	5	16
5. West	15	31	7	53
6. Middle States	12	25	0	37
Total	44	94	87	225

adjacent border sections. Nearly one-fifth were located in the metropolitan Northeast and Middle States. The rest were scattered. Approximately half of the Republican districts were located in the Northeast. The rest were mostly

scattered over the Middle States and West. The Republican
strength in the border states lies in the mountain districts of
eastern Tennessee and Kentucky and in the Ozarks. Close
districts were situated in western Virginia and North Carolina and on the South-West border. The Democrats made a
poor showing in the Northeastern rural districts except in
the mining regions of Pennsylvania. The Democrats were
weak also in the rural districts of the Middle States. The
distribution of party strength in the rural districts of
the West follows a more complex pattern, but in general
the Republicans made their best showing on the Pacific
coast.

The explanation of the distribution of party strength in
the rural districts awaits a further inquiry into the nature of
rural interests. The agricultural area of the United States
may be divided into an eastern and a western half — the
former characterized, broadly speaking, by a sufficient and
the latter by an insufficient amount of rainfall for the successful production of crops by ordinary farming methods.
The eastern half is further divided by the influence of temperature and topography. The cooler and hillier portions
of the East are better suited for pasturage than for the cultivation of staple field crops. Dairying is consequently the
most profitable rural industry, and the dairy belt constitutes a major influence in the politics of the region. The
warmer and more level portions of the humid East and
South seem to have been especially designed by nature for
the production of cotton, except for the region close to the
South Atlantic and Gulf coasts, where climatic conditions
are less hospitable to cotton but well suited to the production of subtropical fruits, sugar and rice. Between the dairy
and the cotton belts lies the great region in which the

dominant form of agriculture is the growing of corn and wheat and other grains, although in certain localities tobacco furnishes the major crop.

The western half of the agricultural area of the United States is also subdivided into special regions by the influence of temperature and topography. The plains and intermountain plateaus, where water is not available for irrigation, have furnished the basis for a great livestock industry, chiefly cattle raising but in some localities sheep raising. Where water is available and the land is sufficiently level for irrigation, various crops may be grown, dependent upon the elevation and the temperature, ranging from apples and sugar beets to citrus fruits and long-staple cotton. On the North Pacific coast there is an area of abundant rainfall and a cool climate where dairying flourishes as in the Northeast and northern Middle West. Lumbering and fishing help to set off this region from the arid portions of the West. California, too, with its Mediterranean climate and agricultural productions joins in giving the Pacific coast a distinct character of its own. In the mountainous regions the mining industry challenges the supremacy of agriculture and grazing, and further complicates the interests of the rural West.

It is evident that the rural districts possess a great diversity of interests and cannot easily be united in national politics. The regions where the leading money crops are produced in excess of domestic requirements are vitally interested in the development of foreign markets, and will normally support a political party which proposes to use the constitutional powers of the federal government for that purpose. Cotton has been a great export crop for many years, and it is not without reason therefore that the cotton belt constitutes one of the principal special interests in American politics. Tobacco, corn (chiefly in the form of pork and beef), and wheat (in the natural state or in the form of flour) have also been leading exports throughout the years, and it might be supposed, therefore, that the tobacco, corn and wheat belts would also form a leading special interest in national politics. In fact, the tobacco belt has been closely allied with the cotton belt in national politics for many years, but the grain growers have pursued an independent course. Dairy farmers, on the other hand, and also the producers of subtropical fruits, sugar and rice, have not been able to satisfy the demands of the domestic market. This circumstance logically dictates a different attitude toward the use by the federal government of its constitutional powers. It must be expected that the dairy belt of the Northeast and Northern Middle West, therefore, as well as the Pacific coast, will form a separate special interest. On the Great Plains of the West and in the mountainous areas, the attitudes of the rural interests in national politics are naturally more complex, making of those regions a convenient battleground for parties which appeal primarily to the special rural interests in other sections.

The strength of the parties in the principal agricultural regions may be roughly measured by the distribution of the rural districts in the congressional elections of 1934. The results of these elections are shown, as before, in the accompanying table. The partisan pattern revealed by this classification of congressional districts is much more significant than that presented by the classification of rural districts according to sections. The agricultural regions correspond more closely than do the geographical sections to the diversity of agricultural interests, and the election returns consequently throw a good deal of light upon the puzzle of the parties. It is evident that the Republicans are not only relatively weaker than the Democrats in the rural districts as a whole but also derive the bulk of their agricultural support from the dairy belts. The close districts which appear to lie in the dairy region actually are situated chiefly in the coal-mining areas. The Republicans hold a number of districts in the grain-growing regions, chiefly, in fact, in

RURAL DISTRICTS

Agricultural Regions	Republican	Close	Strongly Democratic	Total
1. The grain-growing regions	13	57	10	80
2. The cotton belt	0	0	61	61
3. The Eastern and Northern dairy belts	24	24	0	48
4. The Western Plains and inter-mountain plateaus	3	11	8	22
5. The rural Pacific Coast ..	4	2	2	8
6. The Southeastern sub-tropical coast	0	0	6	6
Total	44	94	87	225

the corn belt and in the wheat belt, but are relatively stronger in the districts on the Pacific coast. On the plains and in the mountain area there is some fighting ground where the parties may struggle on fairly equal terms under normal conditions, but in the cotton belt and Southeastern subtropical coast region the Democrats have the field entirely to themselves.

The truth is that the agricultural regions hold the answer to the riddle of the parties. It was in the agricultural regions that the strength of the major parties originally lay, and it is in terms of their respective special interests that their characteristic differences must be largely explained.

The largest block of close districts lies in the grain-growing regions, and it is the grain growers who have dominated American politics throughout the greater part of the history of the nation. This they have done, at first by overpowering their opponents, and later by holding the balance of power between the cotton planters and the dairymen. It was the organization of the bulk of the grain growers into a solid party that gave the Jeffersonian Democratic-Republicans their early supremacy in national politics. It was the repetition of this achievement by the Jacksonian Democrats which secured for them their ascendency over the ineffective Whigs. It was the success of the Anti-slavery Republicans in capturing the bulk of the grain growers north of Mason and Dixon's line and the Ohio River that put an end to the ascendency of the Democratic party. The cotton belt and the dairy belt were bound to oppose each other as long as the agricultural interests remained leading factors in national politics, and the corn and wheat belts were bound to hold the balance of power as long as the cotton and dairy belts remained fairly equal contenders in the struggle for supremacy.

It is the growth of cities and of special urban interests that tends to upset the traditional alignment of parties. In the smaller cities, especially in those where commercial interests are more important than manufactures, the politically dominant elements have usually reflected the political complexion of the surrounding rural area. This is still the case in the cotton belt. But in the larger cities, and in most cities where the population has grown as much or more from foreign immigration as from the movement of people in from the surrounding countryside, urban politics has become more complex. This is most strikingly the case in the great cities of the Northeast and Mid-western Middle States. In the smaller cities in these sections Republican ascendency still reflects the ascendency of the Republican party in the adjoining rural areas, but in the great cities a radically different, and peculiarly urban, alignment of parties has come into existence. The character of the parties in these metropolitan districts no longer reflects the traditional divisions among the early farmers and planters. The metropolitan party character seems to be dominantly the result of independent economic and social forces. The investigation of these forces should make possible the completion of this description of the present-day character of the major political parties.

The distinctive characteristic of urban politics is the development of new forms of class-consciousness. There have always been class divisions among the American people, but in the earlier periods of national politics the principal classes were derived from the conditions of agriculture in the different sections of the country and class-consciousness tended to merge into sectional consciousness. To be sure, the great planters of the Upper and Lower South carried their local conflicts with the small farmers and frontiersmen into national politics, and there were localities in the North where tenant farmers and agricultural laborers tended to take opposite sides, in national as well as local politics, from the owners of the great estates. But the predominant agricultural type was the independent small farmer, and so numerous were the members of the independent small-farmer class in most sections of the country that they succeeded in establishing their supremacy in national politics under such leaders as Jefferson and Jackson, without developing an acute sense of class-consciousness. They constituted, in fact, a great middle class which tended to even the temper and moderate the tone of American politics. Merchants and manufacturers as well as great planters had to adjust themselves as best they could to the political combinations effected by the dominant interests in American life. But representatives of northern merchants and manufacturers such as Daniel Webster, and of great planters in the Lower South such as John C. Calhoun, were far less effective national leaders than middle-class politicians like Jackson and Clay.

The growth of great cities brought new types upon the political scene. Captains of industry and great financiers tended to segregate themselves on the right, the proletarian masses on the left. But both within the ranks of the industrial wage-earners and among their capitalistic employers the traditional American middle-class point of view tended to persist, despite the advent of crowds of alien immigrants, and the characteristic class-consciousness of modern capitalism has grown much more slowly than have the cities. Even in the present century it was still possible for Theodore Roosevelt, when writing his autobiography, to identify "the interests of the people as a whole" with "the interests of the average men and women of the United States," and for Woodrow Wilson, when campaigning for the Presidency, to describe "the great problem of government" as that of knowing "what the average man is experiencing and is thinking about." Moreover, consciousness of class among the industrialized masses of the urban population has been complicated by consciousness of grave differences in race and religion. Americanism, by emphasizing the importance of tolerating such differences, has tended also to belittle the significance of the economic and social differences which might otherwise have been more destructive to the middle-class traditions of American politics.

But the influence of the new economic and social forces in the cities upon the character of the major parties cannot be ignored. Naturally, it is in the metropolitan areas of the Northeast and Middle States that this influence has been greatest. In these areas the number of strongly Democratic and close districts is far out of proportion to the Democratic strength in other parts of the North and West, and forms a special interest in the Democratic group of interests second in importance only to the cotton belt. It is not only in New York City that the effect of this influence is manifest, though the large delegation of Tammany Congressmen is one of the striking exhibits in contemporary national politics. Across the Hudson in northern New Jersey, and also in Boston, Chicago, Cleveland and Detroit, similar political developments must be noted. This development, as observed in Chicago, has been carefully studied by Professor Gosnell of the University of Chicago.[3] His analysis of the 1932 election returns in that city leads him to the conclusion that the major party which enjoys the least success over a period of years "tends to atract to it those elements which have the least social prestige and economic security." Noting that the Republican party was the one which had normally held the reins of government in national and state politics for a considerable period of time, he added: "The men of wealth, the scions of the older Protestant families, the women with money and leisure, were attracted to the Republican party. On the other hand, the foreign born,

[3] Harold F. Gosnell and Norman N. Gill, "An Analysis of the 1932 Presidential Vote in Chicago." in *The American Political Science Review*, vol. xxix, no. 6 (December, 1935). See especially p. 983.

those who happened to emigrate recently from Catholic countries, those who had difficulty in getting jobs in this country, naturally gravitated to the Democratic party." These conclusions seem to be generally applicable to the alignment of parties in the great cities of the Northeast and Middle States.

With the continued growth of cities, the ability of the grain growers to hold the balance of power in national politics is increasingly jeopardized. At the same time the importance of the elements in the great cities which might hold the balance between the rising forces on the left and on the right is magnified. This element is neither the capitalist class nor the proletarian masses. As the capitalist economy evolves, it employs decreasing proportions of unskilled factory workers. Other groups have come to the fore. Technicians, engineers, professional men and women, civil servants, skilled and "white collar" workers, provide the ingredients for a new middle class. As proletarian and capitalistic class-consciousness increases, that of the urban middle class will surely increase also. The leaders of the socialistic and communistic minor parties, like the would-be leaders of special capitalistic or Fascist parties, are quick to deny the possibility of an effective class-consciousness for the urban middle class. But nothing would be more consistent, under the new conditions of a city-dwellers' world, with both the traditions of American politics and the interests of the urban middle class itself, than the development of precisely such a class-consciousness.

It is such considerations as these that give rise to the belief that important changes in the alignment of national parties may be approaching. No radical reconstruction of parties may take place in the present campaign, but the way is apparently being cleared for a change in the old partisan pattern. It was foreshadowed by the Smith campaign in 1928. The Democratic party has frequently nominated a New York governor for the Presidency, but Smith was the first who definitely represented the new urban spirit of revolt against the dominant agrarian traditions in national politics. Smith's success would have meant a profound change in the character of the Democratic party, and hence also eventually in that of the Republican party. But Smith failed, and the agrarian elements in the Democratic party remained in control. Yet the urban elements in both major parties are manifestly impatient under the present party alignment.

The agrarian forces in national politics will not easily be dislodged from their strategic positions in the two great parties. The cotton belt and the dairy belt seem unlikely to lose their partisan complexions as long as the grain growers continue to hold an important share in the balance of power. The waning strength of the grain growers has been reinforced by the rising strength of the agrarian interests in the Farther West, that of the cattlemen and wool growers, the sugar-beet producers and the orchardists. Their influential position in national politics seems likely to remain intact, at least for another decade. An exclusively urban movement in national politics could only have the result of driving the various agrarian interests together into a unified agrarian party. Such a party could hold the Senate for a greater number of years than any urban politician likes to contemplate. Whatever realignment of parties proletarian or capitalistic leaders might like to bring about, the urban middle classes are not likely to become willing tools for the execution of their designs. Rather will they probably prefer to maintain a partisan alignment consistent with the preservation of the middle-class spirit in American politics. This does not mean necessarily the preservation of the existing alignment, but it does mean great obstacles in the way of those who wish to transform American politics by building new major parties on the basis of proletarian or capitalistic class-consciousness.[4]

What seems most likely as the next phase in the development of the character of the major political parties is the rise of the middle class in the great cities of the Northeast and Middle States to a more influential position in national politics. Such a position does not imply the definite affiliation of the urban middle class in a body with either of the major parties. It implies merely such a division of that class between the two great parties as will enable a portion of them, by swinging from one side to the other in response to the ebb and flow of the circumstances, to exert a disproportionate effect upon the results of elections. In short, it means sharing the balance of power with the grain growers. The establishment of such a balance of power is a much more promising enterprise than an attempt to organize a new party in the name of the new majority, who live in the cities, for the purpose of dominating the political scene. After all, the success of national party leaders does not depend upon victory in presidential elections. Such victories do sometimes make new national leaders, but the lack of such victories does not necessarily destroy old party leaders. Party leadership ultimately depends upon the ability to hold the leadership in the states, and in the sections which leading states represent. National leadership may

[4] See A. N. Holcombe, *The New Party Politics* (W. W. Norton and Co., New York, 1933), chap. v.

often be found in the White House. It will always be found in the Capitol, particularly in the Senate.

The rise of the urban middle class to a more influential position in national politics does not even necessarily involve any radical shift in the existing partisan pattern. This pattern is woven from the materials which are afforded by the existing distribution of interests among the whole body of people. The established major parties are coalitions of sectional and class interests. New parties which might be created by means of a realignment of the established parties would still be coalitions of the same interests. They could only be the product of new combinations of the existing materials. Short of an economic cataclysm, they could not be greatly different from those which now exist. The existing parties are going concerns which possess valuable assets in the guise of great traditions, associated with former leaders who left their mark on American history, campaign slogans, and the inertia of large numbers of voters who have formed the habit of taking a certain side in the party battles. They are going concerns which are strongly fortified by primary laws, ballot laws, patronage laws and other legal privileges. It will not be easy to make radical changes in them, despite the animosity of many critics who denounce their alleged irrationality, and the skepticism of many voters who deplore their lack of principle.

The higher strategy of party leadership is founded upon the calculation of the durable forces which are capable of dominating the behavior of voting majorities in districts, states and sections. These are not exclusively economic. Social, racial and religious forces also must be considered. But in the long run the economic forces seem to be most effective. In other words, there is more rationality in na-

tional politics than many of the critics have been willing to
admit. There are sound reasons why a cotton planter
should be a Democrat and a wool grower a Republican.
To be sure, the number and the variety of special interests
are so great that it is idle to expect all of them, or even many
of them, to be effectively represented by a major political
party. Most special interests must utilize special-interest
organizations or the ordinary lobby to secure the special
representation which they desire.[5] There is always the possibility of partisan raids on either side by directing special
appeals to particular interests that are unattached to either
major party or that might be detached from the opposing
coalition, as the present Roosevelt administration has obviously sought to detach soft-coal miners from a traditional
preference in certain localities for Republicanism. Such
tactics may change the result in a few pivotal states. Except
for these minor operations, ordinary party leaders are likely
in general to try to hold the established lines, hoping to get
into power, when out, by taking advantage of the cyclical
ups and downs of affairs, rather than by trying to bring
about fundamental changes in the character of the parties.
Extraordinary leadership will be required to accomplish any
radical partisan realignment.

During a recent presidential campaign a well-known
newspaper offered a prize for the best answer to the question, "What is the difference between a Democrat and a
Republican?" The winning answer, which happened to be
submitted by a woman, was as follows: "A Republican is a
person who thinks a Democratic administration bad for
business; a Democrat is a person who thinks a Republican

[5] See A. N. Holcombe, *Government in a Planned Democracy* (W. W.
Norton and Co., New York, 1935), chap. ii.

administration bad for business." This answer, which at
first sight seems frivolous or cynical, contains an essential
truth concerning the nature of the major parties. This
truth is concealed in the ambiguity of the word "business."
It begins to emerge in the light of the answers to the further
inquiries, "For whose business may a Democrat think a
Republican administration bad?" and, "For whose business
may a Republican think a Democratic administration bad?"
In short, the character of the parties is determined chiefly
by the nature of the special interests which are associated
with them.

The latent causes of partisanship, as Madison sagaciously
remarked in the celebrated tenth number of *The Federalist*,
are sown in the nature of man. "So strong is this propensity
of mankind to fall into mutual animosities," he wrote, "that,
where no substantial occasion presents itself, the most frivolous and fanciful distinctions have been sufficient to kindle
their unfriendly passions and excite their most violent conflicts. But the most common and durable source of factions
has been the various and unequal distribution of property.
. . . A landed interest, a manufacturing interest, a mercantile interest, a moneyed interest, with many lesser interests,
grow up of necessity in civilized nations, and divide them
into different classes actuated by different sentiments and
views. The regulation of these various and interfering
interests forms the principal task of modern legislation, and
involves the spirit of party and faction in the necessary and
ordinary operations of the government." Since the causes
of partisanship cannot be removed, Madison's conclusion
was that the protection of the public interests is best to be
sought by controlling its effects. The greater the number
and variety of the special interests, he believed, the greater

the difficulty of forming a combination among them dangerous to the general welfare. Hence his conviction that a new and more nearly perfect union must be superior to the individual states or any lesser union.

The same course of reasoning leads to the conclusion that the two great parties are superior to the minor parties which would exist if the major parties could be broken down into the special-interest groups of which they are composed. The leaders of minor parties often display an unbalanced devotion to a particular interest and a vexatious disregard for all other interests, which would be ruinous on the part of the rulers of the country. But the leaders of the major parties are compelled to take a broader view. The wider extent and more diversified interests of the major parties are the best guaranty which the people possess that power will be used with moderation. If the practical business of government consists largely in the adjustment of the conflicts of interest arising among the people, politicians, who understand the nature of the people's interests and are responsible for their treatment of them to powerful and durable parties, may well be the most serviceable rulers that the people can reasonably expect to obtain.[6] The American system of bipartisan politics is subject to just criticism at many points, but lack of character in the major parties is not a just ground of criticism.

The vindication of the character of the existing major parties depends ultimately upon the serviceability of the particular combinations of interests by which they are constituted. Woodrow Wilson in his campaign speeches used

[6] See A. N. Holcombe, *The Political Parties of Today* (Harper & Brothers, New York, 2nd ed., 1925), p. 384. See also T. V. Smith, *The Promise of American Politics* (The University of Chicago Press, 1936), chap. vi, "Americanism," especially pp. 247 ff.

to claim superiority for the Democratic party, regarded as an instrument of the popular will, over the Republican combination of interests, for the reason that, resting on an appeal to all three of the major sectional interests, it must come nearer to representing the general interest of the whole body of people than a party which, like the Republican, rests upon an appeal to only two of the major sectional interests. There is manifestly some merit in this claim. The Republicans might have replied that a good working combination of two major sectional interests forms a more serviceable instrument of government than a more nearly universal combination which does not work so well. As long as the two wings of the Republican party did work well together while the Democrats were torn by such dissensions as were revealed in the Smith campaign, there would have been some merit in this reply.

Certain conclusions are clear. The failure of the Republican party to obtain any substantial support in the South has been a grave defect in the constitution of that party. On the other hand, in the past the Tammany wing of the Democratic party seems to have been attracted to that party less by the prospect of obtaining a due influence in the conduct of national affairs than by the hope of securing a freer hand in local affairs than under Republican rule. Indeed, the solidarity of the Solid South was originally brought about by precisely such considerations. The Republicans might plausibly have argued that the Democratic party was less an instrument of national government than a group of instruments of sectional and local government. To this the Democrats might have replied that the charge was not altogether inapplicable to the Republicans also. On both sides the possibility exists of creating a more serviceable instrument of popular government than either of the major parties in its traditional form.

The adjustment of conflicting sectional and class interests is not enough to justify the function of major party leadership. In many cases, as Madison pointed out long ago, such an adjustment cannot be made "without taking into view indirect and remote considerations, which will rarely prevail over the immediate interest which one party may find in disregarding the rights of another or the good of the whole." It is necessary, as Turner said, that statesmen not only should represent the special interests of their own section—or, it may now be added, class—but also should find a formula that will bring together the different sections, and classes, in a common policy. It is necessary, too, that statesmen should be able to appeal to more general interests than those of any particular combination of sections or classes. Herein lies the essential difference between successful party leadership and true statesmanship. Major parties, reflecting in their characters the dominant traits of independent small farmers and even-tempered middle-class city-dwellers, may offer the closest approach to ideal instruments of government that modern democracy can reasonably expect to obtain. But the ideal party would be devoted to the common good regardless of section or class.

There can be no such party, in reality. All the more important is it that party leaders should cherish proper political ideals. This obligation seems to be recognized by many politicians. Both the Republican and the Democratic parties profess their devotion to ideals. But they are devoted to the same ideals. They are both Democratic-Republican parties. Hence the temptation to fall into the wearisome repetition of truisms and platitudes which so tries the patience of many well-wishers of popular government. The history of our times reveals the widespread craving for more inspiring leadership. The apparent popularity of single-party systems of government in certain foreign countries challenges the pretensions of double-party systems like our own, which seem to many citizens to subordinate principle too much to expediency. Interests, as has been shown, play an indispensable part in the political scene. But the drama cannot satisfy the spectators unless, somehow, principle also can play a major role. The great party leaders must be able to rise above the characters of their several parties and assume the character of the whole people — or what may be cherished as the character of the people — for whom the parties hold their vast powers in trust. The popular instinct is sound which insists that there is a real difference between the mere politician and the statesman. The American people rightly demand that there be more statesmanship in national politics.

II

The Influence of the Middle Classes in National Politics

1. Their Influence in the Federal Convention of 1787

THE history of the human race, viewed as a whole, may be regarded as the realization of a hidden plan of nature, to bring about a perfect political constitution, as the only state in which all the capacities implanted in mankind can be fully developed. This proposition we owe to a great German philosopher, who, as it happens, is not held in high esteem by the present rulers of Germany. It is a proposition which appeals strongly to Americans, believing, as they do, that the development of their political institutions falls into line with the fundamental trend of history. The American way of life, as manifested in the political institutions of the United States, we call democratic republicanism. We have believed, or perhaps it is more accurate to say we would have liked to believe, that democratic republican institutions were destined to spread over all the earth and eventually to unite all mankind under a single reign of law sustained by the universal consent of the governed.

Now we are bound to admit that all is not well with democratic republicanism. It is obviously not at the present moment spreading over the earth. On the contrary, it is violently challenged by powerful enemies who loudly declare their profound contempt for democratic republicanism and their invincible purpose to establish political systems incompatible with it, at least in principle, and to extend their sway as far as possible. Communists strive to propagate the view that democratic republicanism, as developed in the United States, is merely an arrangement to maintain a dictatorship of the capitalist class, and Fascists of various kinds, though conceding that dictatorial power should belong to a governing class, insist that membership in the governing class must be determined by superior capacity for the actual exercise of power rather than by the consent of the governed or by the accidental possession or non-possession of wealth. Communists and Fascists may quarrel bitterly with each other over the alleged principles of their various creeds, but they agree in affecting to despise the principles of the democratic republican creed, particularly the principle that governments derive their just powers from the consent of the governed.

From the democratic-republican point of view, the resemblances between the political theories of Communists and of Fascists are more important than the differences. Communists and Fascists alike found their theories of politics upon the assumptions that the peoples of modern states are divided into clearly defined classes and that these classes are precisely two in number. Communists contend that the basis of the division into classes is economic and that the consequence of class-division is a struggle for supremacy between the two classes. Fascists contend that the basis of division is psychological and that the consequence is a natural subordination of the subject class to their rulers. In either case there is a simple dichotomy of the body politic into two sharply differentiated classes, whether superciliously called the elite and the masses, according to the Fascist style, or more harshly, as is the mode among the Communists, exploiters and exploited.

The Communist and Fascist theories of the class structure of modern states are more alike than they seem. According to the Communists the class struggle leads inevitably to a dictatorship of the proletariat, if one accepts the Marxist version of the Communist theory, or, if one prefers the Leninist version, one may say that the inevitable means of overthrowing a dictatorship of capitalists is a dictatorship of the proletariat. In either case the proletariat must submit in practice to the dictatorship of its most vigorous and resolute elements, namely, the leaders of the Communist party. They form the elite of the exploited class and must necessarily seize power in its name, according to the Communist view, if there is to be any change in the composition of the governing class. The significant fact is, that the power passes to the Communist leaders, not to the proletarian masses.

This is also precisely what must happen, according to the Fascists, if the ruling class in a modern capitalistic state loses its capacity for domination, and power is to pass to a new ruling class. The Fascists, more clever than the Communists, make their revolutions in the name of all the people rather than in the name of a part, or at least in the name of all those who may be supposed to possess the qualities requisite for membership in the state. In a capitalist state the capitalists are the elite as long as the capitalists can remain in power, and the Communists are the elite, if they are strong enough to put the capitalists out. Likewise the Fascists are the elite, if they happen to be the masterful politicians who succeed in seizing power. In any event the elite are the rulers and the masses remain the masses.

Both these theories of politics depend for their validity on the truth of the assumptions on which they rest. Is it true that the people of modern states are divided into clearly defined classes, and that these classes are precisely two in number? More explicitly, is it true that the American people are divided into two classes, on the relations between which the structure and processes of government wholly or largely depend? Whether the principle of classification be derived from the economic conditions which characterize the production of wealth in the United States, as Communists argue, or, as contended by Fascists, from the psychological conditions characteristic of human nature as revealed in American politics, is a question of secondary importance. The primary questions are: first, what in fact have been the principal divisions in American politics? secondly, what kind of system of classes, if any, can be discovered which will explain the political divisions that may be found to exist? and, finally, to what extent do the political ideas which may be derived from such findings and discoveries animate the constitutional government of the United States, giving it efficient force and practical effect?

The purpose of these chapters is to set forth the answers to these questions which seem in the light of available evidence to be most nearly correct. The execution of such a purpose involves an inquiry into the basic political struggles which have given rise to organized parties and largely determined the general pattern of national politics. For the pursuit of such an inquiry American politics first acquired sufficient unity when the members of the Federal Convention of 1787 assembled with a view to framing a new Constitution of the United States. In this first chapter, therefore, I shall examine the proceedings in the Constitutional Convention in order to find what divisions actually occurred among the delegates. I shall then consider what light these divisions throw upon the main question, that of the class structure of the American people.

Let us begin with a view of the class structure of the Federal Convention itself. Fifty-five delegates from twelve states attended the Convention at one time or another during its deliberations. Of these, forty-two were present on the last day and thirty-nine actually signed the finished Constitution. Most of these delegates stayed in Philadelphia for a period of nearly four months, but none received a salary from the United States for his services. Although reasonable expense accounts were generally allowed to the delegates by the states which sent them, it is clear that persons without independent means of support were practically excluded from the Convention. In fact, no wage-earner of any kind was a delegate, nor any member of the artisan class, nor any independent handicraftsman, nor was there among the delegates any person from what was then by far the most numerous class in America, the small independent farmers who outnumbered all other classes of white people in every state from New Hampshire to Georgia. There can be no doubt how a Marxian theorist would classify such an assemblage.

The Federal Convention was as superior in political experience as in economic status. Thirty-nine of the delegates had already served in the Continental Congress or in the Congress under the Articles of Confederation. Eight had served in state constitutional conventions, and a much larger number had served in the state legislatures and judiciary. Seven had been chief executives of their states. Twenty-one were veterans of the Revolutionary War. About half of the whole number were college graduates, and nearly two-thirds were practitioners of some profession, chiefly law. The commanding general of the Revolutionary armies, the financier of the Revolution, and the most popular philosopher of the age gave the Convention prestige and dignity. A Fascist theorist would surely classify this body of men as fairly representative of the elite of the United States.

Democratic republicans, however, will wish to know more about the individual members and the general character of the delegations from the several states before subscribing to the view that there were two well-defined classes of people in the United States in 1787, and that only one of these was effectively represented in the Federal Convention. The facts concerning the social origins and dominant interests of the members of the Convention are in almost all cases well known. They seem to show, contrary to the views of Fascists and Marxists, that there were three principal classes of people in the United States at that time, and that two of them were well represented in the Convention. These three classes may be most conveniently described as the upper class, the middle class, and the lower class. The existence of at least the first two of these classes was never forgotten by members of the Convention, and the debates reveal clearly the characteristic attitudes of upper and middle-class delegates, respectively, on the various issues arising out of the interests of the different classes of people.

The upper-class members of the Convention were divided

into three parts. The first consisted of those who belonged
to the landed interest, as men used to call it in the eighteenth
century, either by birth, adoption, or marriage. There were
twenty-two of these, including not only the great land-
holders, but also the members of land-holding families who
were trained for the professions, notably the law. Some of
them were eminent practitioners at the bar, but professional
success could not divest them of their family connections
or, as the modern Marxist would say, of their class-consciousness. Alexander Hamilton, who practiced law in
New York when not playing politics somewhere else, was
the son-in-law of one of the greatest land-holders in America, and a member in spite of himself of the landed interest.
So were Gouverneur Morris, who practiced law and high
finance in Philadelphia, Edmund Randolph, who practiced
law and not-so-high finance in Richmond, and the two
Pinckneys in South Carolina. Among the leading members
of the landed interest were Washington, who presided over
the Convention and whose firm determination to bring its
deliberations to a satisfactory close was more important
than other delegates' speeches; Washington's neighbor,
George Mason, an uncompromising advocate of the rights
of man and of the interests of Virginian tobacco planters;
and James Madison, political scientist by profession and
master-spokesman for the Virginia delegation.

The second group of upper-class members consisted of
the commercial interest, as the phrase ran at the time,
gentlemen engaged in trade or navigation and possessors
of substantial fortunes derived from long-established businesses, including professional men belonging to successful
mercantile and shipping families. There were an even
dozen of members in this group, including five delegates

from New England sea-ports, Boston, Marblehead, Newburyport, and Portsmouth, and four leading merchants from Philadelphia. The Massachusetts delegates, belonging to this group, Gerry, Gorham, and King, took an active part in the debates, but the Philadelphia merchants, headed by Robert Morris, at whose house Washington stayed while attending the Convention, preferred to leave the talking to their lawyers. The most talkative of these, Gouverneur Morris of the New York Morrises, who had been included in the Pennsylvania delegation, was one of the leaders among the younger element in the Convention, a brilliant group of able young men, the "brain-trusters" of their time. He, with King, Hamilton, and Madison, of whom Madison, the oldest, was only thirty-six, made four of the five delegates on the Committee of Style, which prepared the final draft of the Constitution at the close of the Convention. At all stages of the proceedings, these "brain-trusters," to whom should be added the youthful Charles Pinckney of South Carolina, were leading advocates of what men then called a "high-toned" Constitution. Happily they were unable to persuade the Convention to adopt all their "high-toned" theories, but they did succeed in making a solid contribution, not only to the debates, but also to the substance of the Constitution.

The third group of upper-class members consisted of professional men, who were the sons of successful professional men, and whose professional activities brought them into close contact with the great land-owners and merchants. There were four of these, three lawyers and one physician. One of them, John Rutledge of South Carolina, was chairman of the important Committee of Detail, which prepared the first draft of the Constitution. Another, Dr.

Johnson of Connecticut, who served as chairman of the Committee of Style, was the son of the first president of King's, now Columbia, College, and was himself elected president of Columbia in the very year of the Convention. Rutledge was the most vigorous representative of his class and of South Carolina; Dr. Johnson, one of the most cultivated and respected "characters," as his contemporaries would have said, in North America.

Altogether more than two-thirds of the delegates belonged to the upper class. They controlled nine of the twelve state delegations. When they were united, they could control the Convention itself. But it was difficult for them to unite, because the interests of their class were constantly complicated and confused by the conflicting interests of the various sections to which they belonged. Three state delegations, those of Virginia and the two Carolinas, were dominated by the landed interest. Three other delegations, those of Massachusetts, New Hampshire, and Pennsylvania, were dominated by the commercial interest. In three others, those of New Jersey, Delaware, and Maryland, the upper-class delegates were in a majority, but were divided between the landed and commercial interests. Since the conflicts of interest between agriculture and commerce caused some of the sharpest struggles in the Convention, the solidarity of the upper-class delegates was often greatly disturbed.

The other seventeen delegates are apparently assignable to the middle class. The most doubtful case is that of a businessman from Georgia, William Pierce, about whom little is known, though his pen sketches of his fellow delegates furnish the most entertaining commentary we possess on the personal aspects of the Convention's proceedings. Pierce was absent from the Convention at one time for the purpose, according to one report, of engaging in a duel. Duelling is rather an upper-class than a middle-class activity, but the failure of Pierce's business not long after the Convention adjourned and the absence of information concerning his family suggest a middle-class background and career. In any case Pierce contributed nothing of importance to the work of the Convention.

Another delegate, whose classification Marxists might consider doubtful, was Benjamin Franklin. Franklin was one of Philadelphia's richest men. A long life, marked by uncommon industry, thrift, and practical sagacity, had enabled him to accumulate a substantial fortune, and in his old age he could not unfairly be described as a capitalist. To later generations indeed his name has symbolized the virtues and the rewards of the successful big businessman. But in his active business life, while his fortune was in the making, he was not recognized by the upper class as one of themselves. Born in poverty and apprenticed to a trade, he had to make his own way in the world without the aid of money or influential friends. Leaving Boston, when a very young man, for Philadelphia, which was then the heart of the American West, he worked his way up to a position of leadership in Colonial America. In Pennsylvania politics he led the opposition to the Proprietary interest at the local state house, and in national politics he led the opposition to the British Crown at the Court of St. James and later at the Court of Versailles. He was America's first great Nationalist. But always he remained a plain man of the people. His material success makes it impossible to leave him permanently in the lower class, where he began life, but his political career makes it impossible to put him definitely in the upper class, where he ended life. Franklin, the statesman, was a man of the middle class. He is the supreme expression of middle-class personality in early American politics. His character and career afford the final and conclusive answer to those who doubt the existence of a middle class in American life. Clever young aristocrats, "brain-trusting" in the Federal Convention, might show scant respect for the opinions of this wise old man. Outside the walls of Independence Hall he was widely recognized as the perfect representative of the largest single class in America.

Fifteen of the middle-class delegates were professional men, all but one of whom were lawyers. A few of them could boast of origins as humble as Franklin's. Roger Sherman of Connecticut, the next oldest delegate, was one. He, like Franklin, had been born in Massachusetts and had left home in early manhood to seek his fortune. James Wilson of Pennsylvania, who often read Franklin's speeches for him on the floor of the Convention, was another. Wilson had been a charity scholar in Scotland, and, coming to Philadelphia much as Franklin had come a generation earlier, had worked his way up to the leadership of the Pennsylvania bar. Like Franklin, he never permitted his material success to spoil his understanding of and sympathy for the common people. Several other delegates, notably Oliver Ellsworth, a typical Connecticut Yankee, and Luther Martin, the stubborn advocate of states' rights from Maryland, were sons of small farmers, but their families managed somehow to send them to college and get them started on their way up in the world.

Most of the middle-class lawyers exerted little influence in the Convention. Some of them might have been capable of greater achievements, but, like Yates and Lansing of New York, were recalled from Philadelphia before the proceedings ended because of opposition on the part of those whom they represented to what the Convention was believed to be doing. Others, like Martin and Mercer of Maryland, friends of paper money and considerate of debtors, were out of sympathy with the plans of the Convention leaders, and, guessing that the result would be unpopular among their constituents, abandoned the Convention in mid-term. Eight of the middle-class delegates left Philadelphia before the Convention finished its work, while only five of the upper-class delegates left. A few of these middle-class lawyers, however, took a leading part in the work of the Convention and put their mark on the Constitution. Most noteworthy among them were James Wilson, the canny Scot, and the two Connecticut Yankees, Sherman and Ellsworth. Ellsworth and Wilson made two of the five delegates who served on the important Committee of Detail. All three were among the most active delegates and took leading parts at every crisis of the Convention. These able middle-class lawyers were inferior in numbers to the spokesmen of the upper-class delegates, but they were not inferior in parliamentary skill or aptitude for the business of politics.

The middle-class members of the Convention controlled the delegations of three states. One of these was the Connecticut delegation, which succeeded at more than one crisis of the Convention in holding the balance of power between contending factions and thereby exerted a disproportionate influence upon the making of the Constitution. This meant a disproportionate influence also for the middle class. Another delegation, generally controlled by its middle-class members, was that of Georgia. Georgia was a frontier state in 1787, and its delegation was divided between middle and upper-class members. The leading delegates were two adventurers, a Connecticut Yankee, named Abraham Baldwin, and a native son, named William Few. Few was a self-made man of pioneer stock, but Baldwin had been a tutor at Yale before the Revolution and after the war went South in search of his fortune, becoming first a college president and later a lawyer-politician. In the Convention Baldwin extended the influence of the other Connecticut Yankees in unexpected directions. The third middle-class delegation was that of New York. As long as Yates and Lansing remained in the Convention, they out-voted Hamilton, and, when they left, both the state and Hamilton lost their votes. The Connecticut delegation stood out, therefore, as the unauthorized but none the less effective champion of the middle class in the Convention.

The influence of middle-class views was not measured by the number of delegations controlled by middle-class delegates. All the delegates knew that their work would come to nothing unless ratified by the states. The state legislatures contained large numbers of representatives of the middle class. Though the qualifications for voting and for office-holding in 1787 excluded all but property-owners and tax-payers from the legislatures, under the conditions of the time the small independent farmers and pioneers could generally qualify for election, at least in the northern states, and many of them were actually elected. They controlled the lower houses in most of the states with bi-cameral legislatures and might even dominate the whole legislature, especially in states like Pennsylvania with a single chamber. The small farmers were in control in

Rhode Island, and refused to send any delegation to the Convention, although the merchants of Providence and Bristol were eager for representation. In other states the small farmers could easily prevent the ratification of the Constitution, if dissatisfied with the work of the Convention, and in fact did prevent it in North Carolina. The consciousness of the latent power of the small farmers was never absent from the debates at Philadelphia, and lent invisible but powerful support to the pleas of Franklin, the arguments of Wilson, and the parliamentary maneuvers of the Connecticut Yankees. The Federal Convention might seek to circumvent the dubious state legislatures by arranging for ratification by a special convention in each state, but it could not safely offer a new Constitution which was certain to offend the great middle class. The voices of the middle-class delegates in the Federal Convention might be in a minority, but they spoke with the strength of a multitude.

The middle-class delegates played their hand shrewdly. They were in general as keenly aware as the upper-class delegates of the evils flowing from the excessive issue of paper money and the unwise enactment of laws designed to protect the indigent debtor against his creditor. No delegate was more hostile to wild inflation and to arbitrary stay laws than the two Connecticut Yankees, Sherman and Ellsworth. Most of the middle-class delegates readily joined those of the upper class in prohibiting the states from issuing paper money and making laws which would impair the obligation of contracts. But they took an independent course in dealing with certain problems which arose when the framework of the national government was under consideration. The most important of these problems concerned the direct election of the members of at least one branch of the Congress by the people, the qualifications of voters for the election of members of the more popular branch of the Congress, and the qualifications of members of both branches. These were the features of the Constitution the discussion of which brought out most clearly the conflicting views of the upper and middle-class delegates.

The exclusion of the public from the galleries and the members' pledge to preserve the secrecy of the debates encouraged the utmost freedom and candor in the expression of opinion. The delegates from South Carolina were most outspoken in opposition to the direct election of representatives by the people and in advocacy of property qualifications for voting and office-holding, and received strong support from upper-class delegates in other sections of the country. Franklin and Wilson of Pennsylvania were the strongest champions of democratic principles, but even upper-class delegates supported for various reasons a limited application of democratic principles to the framework of government. The aristocratic "brain-trusters," for example, favored the direct election of representatives by the people on the theory that the new government was to be a balanced government, in which the "people" would be represented in the lower house and "property" would be represented in the upper house. They hoped to secure an agreement upon a "high-toned" senate by conceding to the "people" the control of the other branch of the Congress. But they were divided among themselves over the question of property qualifications for voting and for office-holding. Gouverneur Morris thought that the franchise, even for the popular branch of the Congress, should be limited to freeholders, that is, owners of land, while Madison was convinced that the small farmers, who could qualify under such a franchise, were not more responsible voters than artisans and handicraftsmen, who would generally be unable to qualify. He therefore favored a more popular franchise which would include in the electorate both the urban and the rural middle class. Other upper-class delegates, notably Gorham of Massachusetts, favored a democratic franchise on the more practical ground that some of the leading states would not accept the new Constitution, unless the common people could have at least a minor part in the government. The Connecticut Yankees favored the compromise which was finally adopted, namely, that the Convention should not attempt to write a uniform rule of voting into the Constitution, because conditions varied greatly in different states, but should leave the choice of suffrage qualifications in national elections to each state. This happy decision greatly facilitated the progressive democratization of the national government as democratic principles gradually came into favor in the separate states.

The variety and intensity of opinion with respect to these issues over which upper and middle-class delegates tended to divide can be readily illustrated by a few selections from the debates. Gouverneur Morris, speaking in favor of a property qualification for the franchise, declared: "The time is not distant when this country will abound with mechanics and manufacturers [that is, factory workers], who will receive their bread from their employers. Will such men be the secure and faithful guardians of liberty — the impregnable barrier against aristocracy? The ignorant and the dependent can be as little trusted with the public interest as children." John Rutledge, who spoke next, strongly endorsed these views. "The gentleman last up," he said, "has spoken some of my sentiments precisely. Property is certainly the principal object of society." Rutledge's colleague from South Carolina, Pierce Butler, presently added: "Property is the only just measure of representation. It is the great object of government." On another occasion Butler condensed his upper-class political philosophy into the laconic phrase: "Money is power." Gouverneur Morris elaborated the same thought, when he said: "Give the votes to the people who have no property and they will sell them to the rich, who will be able to buy them." Another upper-class delegate, John Dickinson of Delaware, shared Morris' misgivings concerning the future, if the vote were extended to poor workingmen. "The freeholders of the country," he declared, "are the best guardians of liberty, and the restriction of the right to them is a necessary defence against the dangerous influence of those multitudes without property and without principle, with which our country, like all others, will in time abound."

The middle-class delegates expressed greater confidence in the masses of mankind. James Wilson, who wished to give what he called "the Federal pyramid" as broad a basis as possible, said that he considered popular elections "not only as the cornerstone but as the foundation of the fabric." His metaphors seem mixed, but his trust in the people is clear. "He wished for vigor in the government," Madison reports, "but he wished that vigorous authority to flow immediately from the legitimate source of all authority. The government ought to possess not only, first, the force, but also, secondly, the mind or sense of the people at large. The legislature ought to be the most exact transcript of the whole society." Retorting to the animadversions of Gouverneur Morris against the plain people without property, Wilson declared: "He could not agree that property was the sole or the primary object of government and society. The cultivation and improvement of the human mind was the noblest object." Ellsworth added: "The rule should be that he who pays and is governed should be an elector; virtue and talents are not confined to the freeholders."

Another strong advocate of confidence in the plain people was Benjamin Franklin. "It is of consequence," he pleaded, "that we should not depress the virtue and public spirit of our common people. . . . This class possess hardy virtues and great integrity." Franklin was in fact the foremost advocate of democratic principles in the Convention. During the discussion of Charles Pinckney's motion that the president of the United States should be required to own one hundred thousand dollars' worth of property, and other national officers corresponding amounts, Franklin expressed his dislike of everything, as he put it, "that tended to debase the spirit of the common people." "If honesty was often the companion of wealth," he continued, "and if poverty was exposed to peculiar temptations, it was not less true that the possession of property increased the desire for more property. Some of the greatest rogues he was ever acquainted with were the richest rogues. . . ." He added a far-sighted observation. "This Constitution," he said, "will be much read and attended to in Europe, and if it should betray a great partiality to the rich will not only hurt us in the esteem of the most liberal and enlightened men there, but discourage the common people from removing into this country." Pinckney's motion, so Madison relates, was rejected by such a chorus of noes that the roll of the state delegations was not called.

The greatest achievement of the middle-class delegates in the Convention was a triumph of indirection. The so-called Connecticut Compromise is commonly supposed to have resulted from a struggle between the large and the small states. It is true that the struggle had been originally one between the large states, which wanted representation in the Congress adjusted to the population and wealth of the states, and the small states, which wanted equal representation for all states, regardless of differences in population and wealth. But as the issues involved in the struggle came to be better understood, it was evident that there were not two, but three, sides to the controversy. The delegates on these three sides may be called the Nationalists, the Federalists, and the Confederationists. The eventual victory of the Federalists spelled defeat for both the original combatants. But it was a defeat for the upper-class delegates on all sides as well as for the delegations from the large states. How the middle-class delegates, who controlled only a minority of the delegations, could have won a victory against such apparently overwhelming odds, is one of the most interesting stories in American politics. The upper-class delegates controlled the delegations of all the largest states. They controlled a majority of the small-state delegations. Yet they lost the battle. The middle-class delegates were not fighting in the name of middle-class interests. Yet they won a great victory for the middle class. It is not only one of the most interesting, but also one of the most important, chapters in the history of American politics.

The leadership of the Nationalists in the Convention was

taken by the delegation from Virginia. The spirit of the Virginia delegation was vigorously expressed by Washington in a letter to Madison, dated March 31, 1787. "My wish is," he wrote, "that the Convention may adopt no temporizing expedients, but probe the defects of the Constitution to the bottom, and provide a radical cure." What Washington meant by a radical cure is made clear in a letter of Madison's, written a few days earlier to Jefferson in Paris. In this letter Madison stated four principles which he believed essential for a satisfactory national government. First, the new constitution should be ratified by the people themselves rather than by the state legislatures. Secondly, the national legislature should have power to veto any act of a state legislature which in its judgment might trespass upon the proper authority of the national government. Thirdly, the people should be represented proportionately in the national legislature in accordance with some suitable rule without regard to their distribution among the states. Fourthly, the national government should be constructed upon the principle of the separation of legislative, executive, and judicial powers. The Virginia delegates, who reached Philadelphia ahead of the other delegations and conferred together daily while awaiting the arrival of the others, were united in support of this program. It meant to them not merely an effort to establish a strong highly centralized national government, but also an opportunity to secure for the upper class a dominant position in the conduct of such a government.

The alignment in the early struggle over the equal representation of the states in the national legislature reveals the true nature of the conflict between them. The six states whose delegations originally supported the Nationalist program were Massachusetts, Pennsylvania, Virginia, North Carolina, South Carolina, and Georgia. The first three were the largest states in the Union, much larger in fact than any of the others. Together they contained nearly half of the total population of the United States. They boasted more than their share of the leadership of the American people, whether leadership be measured by the number of eminent statesmen or by their importance in public affairs. The two Carolinas were considerably smaller than the three great states, and Georgia was then one of the smallest. But these three southern states possessed excellent prospects for future growth in wealth and population. South Carolina was dominated by a class of wealthy planters who had developed a capitalistic system of agriculture, based upon the employment of large stocks of slave-labor, and looked forward to a great expansion of their prosperity and power. North Carolina and Georgia possessed extensive vacant lands on their frontiers, which were plainly destined to attract new settlers in large numbers. They were not yet large states, but they expected to be large states in the future.

The five states which originally opposed the Nationalist program were in order of size, New York, Maryland, Connecticut, New Jersey, and Delaware. Their relative political importance at that time was measured by the assignment of representatives in the first Congress of the United States, which was determined in the Constitutional Convention. New York and Maryland received six times as many congressmen as Delaware, the smallest state. Connecticut received five times and New Jersey four times as many. New Hampshire, which was not represented in the Convention at this stage of its proceedings, was rated at three congressmen, and Rhode Island, which was not represented at any time, at two congressmen. New York and Maryland were rated above three of the Nationalist states, the two Carolinas and Georgia, and Connecticut was rated as equal to any of these three. New Jersey fell clearly into the class of small states along with Delaware and the two absent states of New Hampshire and Rhode Island. It is evident that a majority of the so-called small states in the Convention were really not small states but middle-sized or average states. New York indeed was already one of the wealthiest states, with an assured future of rapid growth in both wealth and population. Maryland and Connecticut did not possess such good prospects as New York, but on the other hand they were capable of a much more vigorous political life than Delaware or Rhode Island.

The alignment of the states on the question of proportionate or equal representation in the national legislature could not have been wholly determined by their differences in size. New York's opposition to proportionate representation was manifestly prompted by local interests, which had no relation to the state's existing or prospective importance in the Union. Governor Clinton had consistently opposed the measures of the Congress under the Articles of Confederation, which had been designed to strengthen its authority. The port of New York handled much of the foreign trade of Connecticut and New Jersey, and the state profited by the levy of customs duties on the commerce of its neighbors. The rural population dominated the government of the state, and its leaders thereby were enabled to control the patronage of the port. They desired no aggrandizement of the Congress which would diminish their patronage or threaten their power to exploit the possibilities of their strategic position. The New York merchants might take a longer view of the requirements of their situation, but they could not impose their view upon the people of the state who lived up the Hudson River. In other states there were similar conflicts between the interests of the merchants in the seaports and the farmers in the interior. In Rhode Island such a conflict prevented the merchants, who would have gladly sent delegates to the Philadelphia Convention, from taking any part in its proceedings. In New York the merchants were strong enough to put Hamilton on the delegation, but the majority of the delegates were representatives of the up-state agrarian interests. Everywhere adverse local interests complicated the political scene, but nowhere outside of Rhode Island and New York did they prevent the selection of delegates honestly devoted to the cause of a new and more perfect Union.

The course of the great debate in the Convention, which resulted in the so-called compromise between the large and small states, shows not only that there were in fact, not two, but three sides in the struggle, but also that these sides were apparently related to the division of the states into three classes, the large, the medium-sized, and the small. The Confederationists, who were the genuine small-state faction in the Convention, wished to revise the Articles of Confederation without altering their essential character. They favored additional powers for the Congress of the United States without any change in the equal representation of the states in the Congress. Their views were set forth in the New Jersey plan, which was debated in the Convention in the latter part of June and finally rejected by a majority of the delegations. This plan was supported in part by the delegations from the middle-sized states of Maryland and Connecticut as well as by those from the small states of New Jersey and Delaware. But when it was finally defeated, Ellsworth of Connecticut frankly confessed that he did not regret its defeat, since the plan did not really represent what he believed to be the best solution of the problem of representation.

The Connecticut delegates were in fact the first leaders of the Federalists. After the defeat of the New Jersey or small-state plan, they brought forward the Connecticut, or, as we might now more aptly say, the middle-sized state plan. This plan embodied the essential feature of the great compromise, the proportionate representation of the people in one branch of the Congress and the equal representation of the states in the other. The leading Nationalists never approved it, and the Pennsylvania, Virginia, and South Carolina delegations voted against it to the bitter end. But the Massachusetts, North Carolina, and Georgia delegations weakened in their opposition at critical moments. At one such moment the Georgia delegation was divided by the desertion of one of its middle-class delegates, Abraham Baldwin, to the Federalists. Baldwin, though originally a Connecticut man, seems to have been a convert to the Connecticut plan on its merits. At the final crisis the Massachusetts delegation was divided and lost its vote because Caleb Strong, a middle-class delegate from the Connecticut Valley, joined Elbridge Gerry in going over to the compromisers. The North Carolina delegation, in which Hugh Williamson, another middle-class delegate, took the lead at this time, switched its vote from the large-state to the middle-sized state side. Thus both the large states and the small states lost the leadership of the Convention, and the triumph of Federalism was definitely a triumph also for the middle-sized state point of view.

This point of view was determined less by considerations of size than by more fundamental principles of political science. The people of the middle-sized states would have exerted about the same relative influence in the government of the United States under either the Nationalist or the Confederationist program. Under the Nationalist program the peoples of the middle-sized states would have been represented in proportion to their numbers and could have exerted an influence in national affairs equal to the average of the large-state and the small-state peoples. Under the Confederationist program all the states would have been average states, politically speaking, regardless of differences in population and wealth. Federalism, as understood by the middle-class delegates from Connecticut, meant something more substantial than a mere compromise between states of different sizes.

The Connecticut and other middle-sized state delegations eventually supported the Federalist program, because they strongly preferred a form of government for the new and more perfect union in which the state government, regardless of size, would occupy an independent and important position. They recognized the force of the Nationalist argument in favor of a strong central government operating directly upon the people of the United States in matters of general concern. But they could appreciate much better than the Nationalists the wisdom of the Confederationists in insisting upon the preservation of local self-government in matters of local concern. The representatives of the middle-sized states, which on the whole were the best-governed states during the critical period after the Revolution, understood more clearly than the large-state delegates that the best security for local self-government was the maintenance of the state governments in the full vigor that only complete independence within their proper sphere could ensure. Federalism, as designed by the Convention of 1787, was a contribution to political science of inestimable value, which was recommended with compelling force by the experience of the peoples of the middle-sized states.

Federalism possessed another important advantage over Nationalism in the framing of the Constitution. The Nationalist program required the inclusion in the Constitution of uniform rules, governing such matters as the right to vote and the qualifications for office-holding. The great differences in the social and economic conditions of the states in the different parts of the country made agreement upon uniform rules in such matters difficult and, if agreed upon, would have made them very inconvenient in practical operation. The Connecticut delegates argued consistently that the determination of such matters of detail should be left as much as possible to the separate state governments. In order that the state governments might be competent to attend to such matters, it was necessary to leave them as much as possible in vigorous independence.

The greatest merit of the Federalist program was of a different kind. If the states had not been utilized as units of representation in the senate of the United States, there would have been a sharp contest between the aristocratic and the democratic members of the Convention over the basis of representation in the senate. Most of the Nationalists and many of the Confederationists would have favored a senate designed to give special protection to the interests of the rich and well born. They would have advocated comparatively high property qualifications for senators and for voting in senatorial elections. Democratic-Republicans, notably Franklin, would have stoutly opposed such an aristocratic senate, but almost certainly without success. The owners of property, particularly in land and slaves, would have received a highly privileged position under the Constitution, which would have made it a much less satisfactory instrument of government from the standpoint of a majority of the people. The election of senators by the state legislatures, as arranged by the Federalists, doubtless tended to make the upper house a more aristocratic body than the house of representatives, but much less aristocratic than the upper-class delegates wished to make it. Under the Connecticut plan the progress of democracy in the state governments would gradually democratize the federal senate also. It was a great achievement of the Federalist program that it gave to wealth the special recognition demanded by the aristocratic spirit of the times without putting excessive obstacles in the way of a more democratic system of federal law-making when the states themselves should become more democratic. It is more than a coincidence that the delegates from Connecticut, the most democratic of the middle-sized states in 1787, took the lead in the development of the Federalist program. In short, Federalism was not only a middle-sized state program, but also a middle-class delegates' program. It was unconsciously a program for the middle class.

The merits of the Federalist program cannot be obscured by the fact that the inequalities among the states have increased with the passage of time to a degree which the delegates from the middle-sized states could not have expected. At present the largest state has forty-five times as many congressmen as the smallest. It has more congressmen than the eighteen smallest states combined. States possessing less than five per cent of the total population of the United States can defeat an amendment to the Constitution and states possessing less than ten per cent of the total population can defeat a treaty in the Senate. States with less than twenty per cent of the population can defeat any act of Congress. The large states are relatively larger, and the small states are relatively more numerous, now than in 1787. The effect of time on the utility of the states, regarded as organs of local government, is perhaps even more disturbing to the reflective student of contemporary government and politics in the United States than its effect upon them as units of representation in the federal senate. The average state of today is less competent to meet the problems of contemporary civilization than the average state of a century and a half ago. The small states are much more inadequate. The demands upon the modern state governments can not be satisfied with reasonable efficiency by states so deficient in taxable resources and skilled administrative officers as are many of the small states. It is greatly to be deplored that the prospect of combining small states into larger states in the near future is much darker than that for dividing large states into smaller states a century and a half ago.

The record of votes in the Federal Convention reveals the progressive development of middle-class opinions as the middle-class delegates gradually acquired their proper influence. At the beginning the leadership was taken by the delegation from Virginia, and the Virginia plan naturally reflected an upper-class point of view. The struggle between the large and the small states diverted attention from the other issues raised by the Virginia plan, and the fight against that feature of the plan which would have made the senate an organ for the special representation of property waited upon the determination of the fight for equal representation of the states in the senate. The defeat of the Virginians in that fight destroyed the opportunity to establish special property qualifications for voting in senatorial elections, but it did not end the effort to establish such qualifications for membership in the senate. When first a vote was taken on the motion of George Mason of Virginia, to establish property qualifications for membership in both branches of the Congress, only three states, Connecticut, Pennsylvania, and Delaware, voted against property qualifications. Eight states favored such qualifications. A month later, when the issue was finally settled, the South Carolina delegates, the most aristocratic in the Convention, stood almost alone. The eventual rejection of a uniform rule of voting for congressmen, and of property qualifications of all kinds for membership in Congress, gave the finished Constitution a far more middle-class complexion than the upper-class delegates had planned at the beginning of the Convention. The success of the Connecticut Yankees in the fight for equal representation of the states in the senate involved, not only the defeat of the plan for a specially privileged upper-class senate, but also the ultimate collapse of the whole effort to frame a "high-toned" Constitution which would have been unacceptable to the middle class.

The triumph of middle-class views in the process of making the framework of the national government reflected a growing consciousness in the Convention of the importance of the middle class in the country. What this class actually was, or how it was composed, was never explained in the Convention itself. In 1790 the first census of the United States showed that more than ninety-six per cent of the population lived in places of less than eight thousand inhabitants. The bulk of the people were cultivators of the soil, planters, farmers, pioneers, and frontiersmen. The differences between the great planters of Virginia and the Carolinas and the small farmers of the back country, and between the merchants and artisans of the North and East and the small farmers outside the towns, were important. But these planters and farmers and pioneers and frontiersmen and townsmen were not sharply divided into two mutually antagonistic classes. The fact that there are only two sides to a question, when it is put to a vote, is misleading. The class-structure of American society in 1787 was already complex, and the Constitution can not be understood, if it be regarded as the product of a Convention acting as the agent of a dominant upper class.

A different view of the dominant class in the United States, when the Constitution was adopted, was offered by Richard Henry Lee, the Anti-Federalist leader, in a letter written shortly after the close of the Convention. In this letter he declared that there were two parties in the United States, "between which," as he put it, "the honest and substantial people have long found themselves situated. . . . One party is composed of little insurgents, men in debt who want no law and who want a share of the property of others; these are called levellers, Shaysites, etc. The other party is composed of a few, but more dangerous men, with their servile dependents; these avariciously grasp at all power and property; you may discover in the actions of these men an evident dislike to free and equal government, and they will go systematically to work to change essentially the forms of government in this country; these are called aristocrats, etc. Between these two parties is the weight of the community, the men of middling property, men not in debt on the one hand, and men on the other, content with republican governments, and not aiming at immense fortunes, offices, and power." This is the letter of a politician, writing in a moment of exasperation, and doubtless bears down too hard on the members of the upper and lower classes, whom he was counting as lost to his cause. But he was not so far wrong in his description of the middle class.

The true nature of the middle class appears more clearly from the proceedings in the state ratifying conventions. The debates in several of these conventions, notably those of Massachusetts, New York, and Virginia, were carefully reported. In all three conventions discussions of the relative influence of aristocratic and democratic principles in the proposed constitution led to some consideration of the interests behind the principles. A particularly significant debate grew out of a proposal in the New York convention that the size of the federal house of representatives should be increased in order that membership might not be monopolized by the aristocracy. The proposal was offered by a delegate from one of the up-state rural counties, Melancton Smith by name, and drew fire from the heaviest guns in the convention, Alexander Hamilton, John Jay, and Chancellor Robert R. Livingston.

The argument of Delegate Smith was, "that, in order to have a true and genuine representation, you must receive the middling class of people into your government." And who were the middling class of people? His answer was definite and illuminating. They were "such as compose the body of this assembly," that is to say, farmers, independent but not wealthy, and lawyers, dependent for professional success mainly upon the patronage of that description of farmers. This was the class which supplied the bulk of the delegates in all the state ratifying conventions. It formed the most numerous and most characteristic element in the middle class throughout the United States. It made the middle class what it was in American politics at the time of the adoption of the Constitution, the class without whose consent the new and more perfect union could not have been established.

This is the class of people who are unknown or forgotten by Communists, Fascists, and others, who seek to explain the fundamental processes of modern politics by a division of the people into two antagonistic classes. These men of middling property, as Richard Henry Lee put it, men who were content with a republican form of government and did not cherish immoderate aims, were the typical Americans of 1787. They furnished the principal part of the population in every state, if only the white population be taken into account, and the principal part in most of the states, if the colored population be also included. In the states where slaves were numerous in 1787 the presence of the slaves stimulated the development of middle-class consciousness on the part of all whites except the great planters. In the other states there was a lower white class, consisting of indentured servants and casual laborers, but the abundance of unsettled lands in the back country and the ease of escape to the frontier hindered the development of a permanent sense of inferiority. The line of division between lower and middle classes among the white population was obscure and easily crossed.

Lower-class consciousness could not be an important factor in politics. Without lower-class consciousness there could be no true middle-class consciousness. The great planters and merchants were definitely class-conscious, as the debates in the Federal Convention clearly show, but the barrier between the upper and middle classes was low. In the back country and on the frontier all men really seemed to have been created equal. They did not think of themselves as members of any class, but simply as people, endowed with inalienable rights. These were the common people of whose existence the members of the Convention were always mindful. The skill of the middle-class delegates in voicing the opinions of these common people explains largely their disproportionate influence in the framing of the Constitution.

The first conclusion which emerges from a study of the conflict of class interests in the whole process of framing and ratifying the Federal Constitution is that a theory of politics based upon a division of the people into three classes is more useful in explaining this great historical event than theories based upon the assumption that there are only two classes of primary importance. A second conclusion is, that class divisions of any kind are less important than the Communists and Fascists would have us believe. This conclusion is supported by a casual remark of George Mason's, uttered during the course of the debate on the election of members of the house of representatives by the people. It was a remark which reflected an attitude not confined to members of the upper class, to whom Mason was particularly directing his argument. "We ought to attend," he declared, "to the rights of every class of people. He had often wondered at the indifference of the superior classes of society to this dictate of humanity and policy; considering however affluent their circumstances, or elevated their situations might be, the course of a few years not only might but certainly would distribute their posterity throughout the lowest classes of society. Every selfish motive, therefore, every family attachment ought to recommend such a system and policy as would provide no less carefully for the rights and happiness of the lowest than of the highest of citizens." Every vote in which a delegation subordinated their private views for the sake of general agreement — and there were many such votes in the Convention — attests the force of this appeal to the consciousness of common interests transcending those of any special class.

Class-consciousness certainly existed in the Convention and influenced votes. So did that peculiar sense of social solidarity which in the last analysis holds together in a common union all the various classes within the state. This sentiment of social solidarity rather than any particular kind of class-consciousness was the firm foundation of the original Federalism in American politics. It was the middle-class delegates in the Federal Convention who best understood the true nature of this foundation. They understood it as it was, not as a special kind of class-consciousness but rather as that positive spirit of participation in the common welfare which is celebrated in American politics as the spirit of the average man. This is the spirit which eventually animated the Constitution of the United States and gave it its peculiar character and vitality. The Federal Constitution was not a triumph of capitalistic interests or of oligarchical principles, as is often alleged by Communists and Fascists. It was the supreme instance in history up to 1787 of the triumph of the average man.

2. The Influence of the Rural Middle Class under the Constitution

The influence of the middle class in the Federal Convention of 1787 was strengthened by the conflict of interests between different sections of the country and by the effects of sectionalism in the Convention. Two-thirds of the delegates, as was shown in the last chapter, were members of the upper class. Nevertheless the middle-class delegates exercised a decisive influence upon the organization of the federal government. Middle-class politicians also exercised a decisive influence upon the organization of political parties under the Constitution. This resulted from the nature of the economic interests which were dominant in the United States in the early years of the Republic and from the manner of their distribution among the several sections into which the country was then divided.

The leading economic interests of the United States in 1787 were agricultural. A majority of the delegates in the Convention were landholders or professional men mainly dependent for their livelihood upon the patronage of the landed interests. But these landed interests were divided against themselves and the balance of power among them happened to fall into the control of the delegations which were most responsive to middle-class interests. The possession of the balance of power in intersectional controversies by sections in which middle-class interests were most influential was decisive at one of the great crises of the Convention. From that time on the control of the balance of power by the leading middle-class sections has been a characteristic feature of national politics. For the greater part of our national history agricultural interests have been predominant in most of the states and the balance of power has been held chiefly by the rural middle class. How this has been accomplished and with what consequences are the subjects of this chapter.

The principal division among the delegates to the Federal Convention of 1787 with respect to their economic interests is commonly supposed to have been that between the two great sections of the country, the North and the South. Madison's remark in the course of the debate on the Connecticut Compromise has often been quoted. "The states are divided into different interests," he said, "not by their difference in size, but by other circumstances the most material of which results partly from climate, but principally from the effects of their having or not having slaves. These two causes concur in forming the great division of interests in the United States. It does not lie between the large and the small states. It lies between the Northern and the Southern." This division between North and South was undoubtedly a fact, a very stubborn fact. It profoundly affected the attitude of the Convention toward some of the most important questions. Notable among these was the question of the basis of representation in the popular house of the Congress, and that of the extent of the federal powers to impose taxes and to regulate commerce, particularly the trade in slaves.

This simple division between free and slave states, however, like the simple division between large and small states, fails to give an adequate explanation of the struggles in the Convention over issues arising out of the differences between different geographical sections of the country. In the first place, the distinction between free states and slave states was by no means as clear in 1787 as it had become by the time of the Missouri Compromise a third of a century later. Slavery had existed in all the states at the beginning of the Revolution. By 1787 it had been abolished in Massachusetts and was in process of extinction in the rest of New England. Gradual emancipation had been provided for in New York and Pennsylvania, and the importation of slaves from abroad had been prohibited in New Jersey, Delaware, Maryland, and Virginia. The manumission of slaves was encouraged by leading slave owners as far south as Virginia, and the rapid decline of the institution of slavery was anticipated by public opinion everywhere except in the Carolinas and Georgia. Where then was the boundary between North and South? Certainly few, if any, could have foreseen that Mason and Dixon's line was to attain the importance in national politics which has been assigned to it by history. The division between the slave-holding and the free-labor interests, which Madison pointed out and all delegates recognized, could neither be definitely located nor generally regarded as of permanently major importance.

A more familiar geographical division in 1787 was that between three sections, the Eastern, Middle, and Southern. In the previous year Dr. Benjamin Rush of Philadelphia, a well-informed contemporary professional man, writing to his friend, Dr. Richard Price, in London, commented on a recent manifestion of sectionalism of this kind. "Some of our enlightened men," he observed, "who begin to despair of a more complete union of the States . . . have secretly proposed an Eastern, Middle, and Southern Confederacy, to be united by an alliance offensive and defensive. These Confederacies, they say, will be united by nature, by interest, and by manners, and consequently they will be safe, agreeable, and durable. The first will include the four New

England states and New York. The second will include
New Jersey, Pennsylvania, Delaware, and Maryland; and
the last, Virginia, North and South Carolina, and Georgia.
. . . This plan of a new Continental Government is at
present a mere speculation. Perhaps necessity, or rather
Divine Providence, may drive us to it." By the time the
Federal Convention met, the newspapers were openly dis-
cussing the possibility of three separate confederacies.

Several proposals inspired by the recognition of three
major sections in the United States were submitted to the
Federal Convention. In the course of the debate upon the
organization of the executive branch of the national government, both Randolph and Mason of Virginia advocated
a plural executive consisting of three persons. Mason urged
as a special advantage of such a form of executive that the
jealousies between the different sections might be allayed
by giving one of the three executive magistrates to the
Northern states, one to the Middle States, and one to the
Southern. He evidently had in mind a division into sections
similar to that mentioned by Dr. Rush. When the organization of the senate was under consideration, Charles Pinckney of South Carolina suggested that the states be divided
into three groups for the choice of senators, a Northern, a
Middle, and a Southern, in order to establish a proper balance between the principal sections of the country. Though
these proposals failed to receive serious consideration, they
were objectionable on other grounds than lack of realism
in the description of the sections.

At about the same time the French Chargé d'Affaires at
Philadelphia, who was following the proceedings in the
Convention with a keen professional interest, noted the
menace of sectionalism in one of his reports to the Foreign

Office in Paris. Some delegates were convinced, he wrote, that it would be impossible to unite all the states in a single strong Confederation. These delegates, he added, urged a division of the country into three separate confederacies, a Confederation of the North, including the states east of the Hudson, a Confederation of the Center, including the states between the Hudson and the Potomac, and a Confederation of the South, including Virginia, the Carolinas, and Georgia. "Their political interests," he wrote, "their commercial views, their customs, and their laws are so divergent that there is not a resolve of Congress which is equally useful and popular in the South and in the North. . . . The inhabitants of the North are fishers and sailors; those of the Central states, farmers; those of the South, planters." The French diplomat's description of the leading sectional interests leaves a good deal to be desired, but his main point is clear, namely, that the existence of three major sections was one of the vital facts in the political situation.

Intersectional jealousy, whether founded on differences in the material interests of the sections or on prejudice, was much stronger in the eighteenth century than can be easily imagined in the twentieth. John Adams, when attending the second Continental Congress, wrote from Philadelphia: "We can not suddenly alter the temper, principles, opinions, or prejudices of men. The characters of gentlemen in the four New England colonies differ as much from those in the others as that of the common people differs, that is, as much as several distinct nations almost." He added that the "gentlemen of other Colonies were habituated to higher notions of themselves and of the distinction between them and the common people than we are. . . ." In the Federal Convention Pierce Butler of South Carolina remarked that he considered the interests of the Southern and Eastern states "to be as different as the interests of Russia and Turkey." General Pinckney of the same state, speaking in favor of the compromise over the power to regulate commerce, which was engineered by the delegates from New England and South Carolina, handsomely confessed that "he had himself prejudices against the Eastern states before he came to the Convention," but he wished to acknowledge that "he had found them as liberal and candid as any men whatever." Evidently he had formerly supposed that the Yankees were naturally illiberal and uncandid.

The complexity of the sectional interests represented in the Federal Convention is most clearly revealed by the debates over the powers of the federal government. The great tests of sectionalism came over the proposals to give the Congress power to levy taxes and to regulate foreign commerce. The struggle over the tax and commerce powers caused a sharp alignment of sections in the Committee of Detail, which prepared the first draft of the Constitution, and culminated in the second great compromise, which was adopted by the Convention near the close of its proceedings. The alignment of sections in the Committee of Detail revealed that both North and South were divided against themselves, and the second great compromise demonstrated the amazing possibilities of permutations and combinations in the adjustment of conflicting sectional interests. The adjustment of these interests by the formation of suitable combinations among them has in fact proved to be the principal task of national politics under the Constitution.

The leading sectional interests likely to be affected by the exercise of the federal tax and commerce powers were described by Charles Pinckney of South Carolina in one of his speeches against the proposed compromise. New England, he declared, was interested in the fisheries and in the carrying trade; the Middle States, in the export of wheat and flour; Maryland, Virginia, and North Carolina, which may be termed the Upper South, in the export of tobacco; and the Lower South, that is, South Carolina and Georgia, in the export of rice and indigo. All the advocates of a strong general government were bound to favor broad powers over foreign commerce, but none of the sections dependent for prosperity upon the export of staples, such as tobacco or rice, could fail to view with alarm the possibility of a general government, which they might not be able to control, levying export taxes upon its principal money-crop. The most valuable American export at that time was tobacco, and a combination of sections in the Congress to impose an export tax on the money-crop of the Upper South might hope to pay all the costs of the general government with the proceeds and thus avoid the necessity of submitting to any taxation of their own products. Other sectional combinations might seek to finance the general government largely with taxes on the export of rice and indigo and thus impose an unfair and possibly ruinous share of the burden of federal taxation on the Lower South. New England and New York would surely seek special favors for their shipping interests, and if able to secure a navigation act, which would give them a monopoly of the carrying-trade in the other sections of the country, would be able to exploit those sections and win an undue share of the profits of American industry for themselves. These possibilities furnished the materials for one of the most important struggles over economic issues that has ever taken place in American politics.

The clash of sectional interests over commercial policy was well understood by practical politicians at this critical period in American history. Madison, for example, had written as early as 1785, that "the giving Congress a power to legislate over the trade of the Union would be dangerous in the extreme to the five Southern or staple states, whose want of ships and seamen would expose their freightage and their produce to a most pernicious and destructive monopoly. With such a power eight states in the Union would be stimulated by extreme interest to shut close the door of monopoly, that by the exclusion of all rivals, whether for the purchasing of our produce or freighting it, both these might be at the mercy of our East and North." He added: "The spirit of commerce throughout the world is a spirit of avarice, and could not fail to act as above stated." By 1787 Madison had become convinced that the power to tax exports was necessary in order to render the general government financially independent and strong enough to protect the national interests, but his colleagues from Virginia, Randolph and Mason, continued to adhere to the Southern point of view.

Most determined in their opposition to export taxes were the delegates from the Lower South. Early in the proceedings of the Convention General Pinckney of South Carolina had warned the Convention that, unless the Southern states received some security against the emancipation of slaves and the taxation of exports, he should be bound by his duty to his state to vote against the proposed draft of a Constitution. Other delegates from the Lower South made it clear that the adherence of South Carolina and Georgia to the "new and more perfect Union" would depend upon their ability to obtain protection for these special plantation interests. At the same time the Pennsylvania delegates made it equally clear that the commercial interests of Philadelphia would cause them to side with New York and New England in support of broad powers over commerce for the general government. Gorham of Massachusetts declared flatly that to obtain such powers was a principal object of Massachusetts in promoting the Convention, and that without them the Massachusetts delegates would be little interested in the new constitution.

The conflict of interests over the taxation and regulation of commerce was further complicated by differences of interest within the Southern sections over the regulation of the trade in slaves. The Upper South produced more slaves than were really needed on the tobacco plantations, while the rice and indigo plantations of the Lower South could not get enough slave-labor to meet the demand. Prohibition of the importation of slaves from abroad would assure to the planters of the Upper South a profitable market in the Lower South for their surplus slaves, but the protection of the domestic slave-raising industry would increase the cost of production of rice and indigo in the Lower South and perhaps blight the prosperity of that section. The great South Carolina planters wanted free trade in slaves, or at least some assurance that the slave-trade would not be ruinously restricted by hostile legislation. Thus the South was sharply divided against itself, and four clearly defined self-conscious sections, instead of only two or three, contended for victory in the struggle over the commerce power.

The Committee of Detail, which prepared the first draft of a compromise between these various sectional interests, consisted of five members taken from the delegations of

Massachusetts, Connecticut, Pennsylvania, Virginia, and
South Carolina. Thus New England had two votes in the
Committee, the Middle States one, and the Upper and Lower
South one each. The Lower South was so eager for free
trade in slaves that it was willing to desert the Upper South
on the issue of a navigation act. In fact, it was so strongly
opposed to interference by the general government with the
development of a plantation system based on cheap slaves
that it threatened to have no further part in the Convention
unless assured of protection for its peculiar institution. The
commercial interests of New England, on the other hand,
were so eager for the inclusion of all the states in a general
customs and commercial union that they were willing to
deny the federal government power to levy export taxes
and even the unlimited power to adopt navigation acts
rather than lose the advantages of keeping the Lower
South under the authority of the general government. The
Pennsylvania delegates, like those from New England,
would have liked a general government with power to
regulate commerce and adopt a navigation act, but were
not so eager for such measures as to overcome their repugnance to the slave-trade, a business greatly detested in
the Quaker State. Virginia was aligned with Pennsylvania
in opposition to the slave-trade, but could not share the
Pennsylvania attitude toward export duties and a navigation
act. The situation plainly called for some kind of deal between some of the different sections.

This was the situation in which Massachusetts and Connecticut struck their famous bargain with South Carolina.
Virginia and Pennsylvania were voted down in the Committee of Detail, which brought in its report, recommending
that the Congress should have no power to impose taxes on

exports or to prohibit the importation of slaves, but should be authorized to adopt a navigation act by a two-thirds vote. Virginia and Pennsylvania carried their opposition to this so-called compromise to the floor of the Convention, but the two states were unable to work together effectively. When Charles Pinckney of South Carolina, who was unwilling to go along with the majority of his delegation in support of the bargain with the New England delegates, moved to require a two-thirds vote for the adoption of all commercial regulations as well as navigation acts, Virginia gave the motion its warm support. But the majority of the South Carolina delegation remained loyal to its bargain, and Virginia found itself together with the other Southern states in a minority of four against seven. When Pennsylvania moved to strike out the provision of the draft-constitution prohibiting export taxes, only Washington and Madison of the Virginia delegation gave Pennsylvania their support. Massachusetts and Connecticut remained loyal to their bargain with South Carolina, and Pennsylvania found itself together with New Hampshire, New Jersey, and Delaware also in a minority of four. But Pennsylvania was able to eliminate the requirement of a two-thirds vote for the adoption of a navigation act, thus making the final arrangement even more objectionable to Virginia. Virginia's one victory at this stage of the proceedings was the limitation of the prohibition against restricting the importation of slaves to a period of twenty-one years. In this move against the traffic in slaves Virginia and Pennsylvania were able to make a common cause with good results, but in general the bargain between New England and the Lower South was modified on the floor of the Convention more in the interest of Pennsylvania than in that of Virginia. Through the efforts chiefly of the Pennsylvania delegates the finished Constitution was made much more favorable to the free states and to the commercial interests than it would have been under the so-called compromise arranged between New England and South Carolina.

The intersectional struggle between the Northern States, or as they were often termed in 1787 the Eastern States, and the Middle States, the Upper South, and the Lower South did not exhaust the possibilities of sectionalism in the Federal Convention. Another sectional alignment was that of the Atlantic States against the West. This division of interests was discussed several times in the Convention. It came up first in connection with the determination of the basis of representation in the Congress and again in connection with the provision for the admission of new states. But the West was not directly represented in the Convention, and the immediate issue was whether the Atlantic States should take advantage of their existing superiority to limit the power of the states which would eventually develop in the West or should permit the Western people to enjoy a proportionate influence in the government of the Union.

The case against the West was stated most forcefully by Gouverneur Morris. "I look forward," he said, "to that range of new states which will soon be formed in the West. I think the rule of representation ought to be so fixed as to secure to the Atlantic states a prevalence in the national councils. The new states will know less of the public interest than these; they will have an interest in many respects different; in particular they will be little scrupulous in involving the community in wars, the burdens and operations of which will fall chiefly on the maritime states." [This in fact happened in 1812 exactly as he predicted.]

"Provision ought therefore to be made," he continued, "to prevent the maritime states from being hereafter outvoted by them." Later he returned to the subject. "Among other objections," he said, referring to the proposal to give the people of the West representation in Congress on the same basis as those in other sections, "it must be apparent that they will not be able to furnish men equally enlightened to share in the administration of our common interests. The busy haunts of men, not the remote wilderness, is the proper school of political talents. If the Western people get the power into their hands, they will ruin the Atlantic interests. The back members are always most averse to the best measures. . . ." Similar sentiments were expressed by Rutledge of South Carolina and Gerry of Massachusetts. Gerry said he was for admitting Western states on liberal terms, "but not for putting ourselves into their hands. They will, if they acquire power, like all men abuse it. They will oppress commerce, and drain our wealth into the Western country. To guard against these consequences, I think it necessary to limit the number of new states to be admitted into the Union in such a manner that they shall never be able to outnumber the Atlantic states."

In general the opponents of equal treatment for the West were upper-class members of the Convention. The Virginia delegates, however, took the Western side of the argument. Virginians were the largest holders of Western lands and Mason, Randolph, and Madison were leading speakers against Gouverneur Morris' motion to keep the West in a position of permanent inferiority. James Wilson of Pennsylvania, another state with a large interest in Western lands, differed strongly from his colleague, Morris, favoring equal treatment of Westerners, but it was Roger Sherman of Connecticut, conscious doubtless of his state's great Western Reserve in Ohio, who stated most effectively the grounds for the acceptance of liberal views toward the West. "We are providing for our posterity," he argued, "for our children and grandchildren, who would be as likely to be citizens of new Western states as of the old states. On this consideration alone," he concluded, "we ought to make no such discrimination as is proposed. . . ." At the same time the probability that the West would possess special interests of its own, different from those of other sections, was clearly recognized. "The extent and fertility of the Western soil," declared Madison on one occasion, "will for a long time give to agriculture a preference over manufactures." It was not a comforting reflection to the great merchants from the seaboard states, where infant manufacturing industries were already looking to the government for encouragement and aid. Fortunately enough upper-class delegates agreed with the middle-class leaders to secure equal treatment for the West.

The controversy over the admission of new Western states into the Federal Union on equal terms with the old was not the most important intersectional conflict in the Convention from the point of view of its immediate consequences. But the great importance which the West was clearly destined to enjoy in the future made the issue of equal treatment for Western states a major test of Convention statesmanship. The upper-class delegates tended to divide on this issue in accordance with the direction of their interests. It was a lucky accident that the strongest upper-class delegation, that of Virginia, came from a state with a very extensive interest in Western lands. The middle-class delegates seemed generally quicker to recognize

the importance of the question of principle involved in the
controversy. That was the principle of equal rights for
all Americans regardless of section or class. It was the
principle dictated by the spirit of the West. In 1787 the
Western spirit began where tide-water ended. It was predominant in the back-country of the original states all the
way from Maine to Georgia. All the states contained
"Wests" within their own borders, but not all the delegations were capable of representing effectively the Western
spirit. The middle-class delegates tended to be more successful in interpreting that spirit within the Convention,
because the middle-class spirit was also the essential spirit
of the West, the spirit of the average man. The permanent
adjustment of this intersectional controversy upon the
sound basis of equal rights for the people of all sections,
East and West alike, under the leadership of upper-class
Virginians, middle-class Pennsylvanians, and Connecticut
Yankees, was one of the happiest achievements of the
Convention.

It is evident that sectionalism in the Federal Convention
was a complex phenomenon. There were a few questions,
notably that of the representation of slaves in the lower
house of the Congress, which divided the states into two
sections, the North and the South. But on another issue
affecting the institution of slavery, namely, the freedom of
the slave trade, the South itself was divided into two sections. In general the different interests of the states with
respect to slavery were less important causes of sectional
differences in the Convention than differences with respect
to the disposition of public lands, the issue of currency and
the payment of public and private debts, and above all, the
regulation of commerce. With reference to these issues

various combinations of the sections were formed, such as that between New England and South Carolina with reference to the regulation of commerce. If any of these combinations had proved stable enough to carry over into other controversies, there would have been the beginning of a permanent organization of interests in the Convention which might have been recognized as what came later to be called a political party. In fact the sections failed to coalesce into durable parties during the Convention. The conflicts between the sections showed how partisanship might eventually develop under the Constitution but failed to indicate which possible combinations of sectional interests promised sufficient permanence to become true parties.

The absence of organized partisanship on a sectional basis in the Convention contributed greatly to the success of its deliberations. Since no section was strong enough to dominate the proceedings, and no combination of sections was durable enough to determine the result of many different controversies arising out of their conflicting interests, all sections were able to boast some victories and each could find sufficient grounds for satisfaction with the final result. The Virginia delegation suffered the greatest disappointments. At the end Governor Randolph and George Mason refused to sign the finished Constitution, but Washington, seeing that the Convention had built the framework for a strong and serviceable general government, which could be improved in the light of experience by the process of amendment, gave it his invaluable support. The Connecticut delegates were probably best pleased with the Constitution in its final form. The delegations from the Middle States also had fared well in the intersectional contests, having shrewdly exploited the opportunities for exerting a decisive influence afforded by their strategic geographical location. Above all, Pennsylvania's middle-class members, Franklin and Wilson, must have felt great satisfaction in the triumph of their views in the controversies over the tax and commerce powers, the slave trade, and the development of the West. The frame of government was not as democratic as they would have liked, but it was much less undemocratic than the brain-trusters, especially Hamilton, Gouverneur Morris, and Charles Pinckney, had planned, and the upper-class leaders of the Convention, particularly in the Virginia and South Carolina delegations, had desired.

The failure of the Convention to produce durable political parties can not be explained by lack of the materials for the formation of parties. The leading economic interests of the different sections were clearly defined and sharply conflicting. If any particular combination of delegations from different sections had been formed, capable of offering a united front against the other sections on all the leading economic issues, that combination would have constituted a political party which could have written a partisan constitution for the United States. It might even have been able to secure the ratification of such a constitution by the states and to take charge of the government of the resulting partisan Union. Several combinations were formed between the delegations of different sections, such as that between the large states to secure proportionate representation of the states in the Congress, and that between New England and South Carolina to protect the slave trade and secure a navigation act. But none of these combinations was able to hold together on other issues. The principal conflicts of interest between the different sections were adjusted by combinations of delegates specially arranged for each case. Thus, though the Convention contained the elements from which political parties might have been compounded, no organized party actually developed in the course of its deliberations.

There was a clearer alignment of interests in the state ratifying conventions. The various factions which had joined in making the Constitution led the fight for its adoption in the state conventions. Libby's scholarly work on *The Geographical Distribution of the Vote of the Thirteen States on the Federal Constitution* shows where the principal opposition to the Constitution originated. There were dissatisfied members of the leading special interests in all sections of the country who contended that a better bargain might have been made by the representatives of their interest in the Convention. This kind of opposition was particularly strong in Virginia, where some of the leading planters were alienated by the failure of the Virginia delegation to get more consideration for the special interests of aristocratic tobacco-planters. But the strongest opposition in the state conventions came from the representatives of the one major interest which was greatly underrepresented in the Federal Convention. That great division of the landed interest, consisting of the small independent farmers, was suspicious of a constitution in the making of which they had had little apparent influence and no direct part. They distrusted a scheme for the concentration of extensive powers in a central government, which would always be far away and might easily get out of control. These small farmers were influential in every state. They were dominant on the frontier. They constituted the sectional interest which may most conveniently be described as the West, if it be remembered that in 1787 the West began where tide-water ended. The West, as thus defined, was by no means unanimous in its opposition to the Constitution, but by and large it furnished the bulk of the dissenting votes in the state conventions. These Anti-Federalists formed the first organized expression of the political West in American politics. But the Anti-Federalists were not a national party. They were merely a scattered array of state parties.

There has been much discussion of the origin of political parties in the United States. One early writer, the author of a life of Alexander Hamilton, ventured the opinion that the two great parties grew out of the contentions over the appointment of Washington as commander-in-chief of the Continental Army. Another early writer, the author of a life of Aaron Burr, ascribed them to the divisions in the Federal and State Conventions of 1787 and 1788. John Quincy Adams, in an address delivered on the fiftieth anniversary of the Constitution, endorsed the thesis that the major parties originated in the contentions of the partisans of England and of France during the administrations of Washington and John Adams. Martin Van Buren, who knew as much as any early party leader about the practical business of organizing and managing parties, was the author of a posthumous treatise on the subject, entitled an *Inquiry into the Origin and Course of Political Parties in the United States.* In this book he declared that party divisions were founded upon "the great principle first formally avowed by Rousseau, 'that the right to exercise sovereignty belongs inalienably to the people.'" Charles A. Beard's studies of early party history, particularly his book, *Economic Origins of Jeffersonian Democracy*, have demonstrated the inadequacy of the earlier theories. It is now clear that the first national parties in the proper sense of the term did not originate until Washington's administration. It ought to be added, I think, that the two-party system of national politics was not definitely established until much later.

Washington's attitude toward partisan politics is well known. In his Farewell Address he bequeathed to his countrymen a solemn warning against the dangers of parties founded upon geographical distinctions. He also condemned the spirit of partisanship, or as he called it, faction, however founded, if carried to excess. In the conduct of his own administration, however, he was careful to put into positions of political importance only those who were trustworthy friends of the Federal Constitution. It is specially interesting to note how he distributed appointments among the members of the Federal Convention, all of whom were men with whose abilities and characters he was intimately acquainted. Some of them retired from public life at the close of the Convention on account of age. Others preferred to hold office under the state governments. A score of the delegates were elected to the first Congress under the Constitution as senators or representatives. Of the others, Washington appointed to office every friend of the Constitution with only one exception. That single exception was Charles Pinckney, a brilliant but egotistical young man, who seems to have made himself generally disliked by the leaders of the Convention. Washington appointed few of the opposition delegates to office under the Constitution. But Washington did not intend to govern by means of a party. He intended to govern with the aid of members of all the factions which had joined in making the Constitution. He was particularly careful to appoint representatives of all the geographical sections, recognized by him in the Convention, the Northeast, the Middle States, the Upper South, and the Lower South. He wished the Federalists to be as genuine Nationalists as the circumstances of the country and his acquaintance with politicians permitted. If the Washingtonian Federalists were a sectional party, they were a party which combined all the major sectional interests into which the upper classes were divided.

Washington's plans for a non-partisan system of politics, or perhaps it might be more accurately termed a one-party system, were frustrated by the ineptitude of Alexander Hamilton. Hamilton was never Washington's prime minister. He was only one of several political lieutenants to whom Washington entrusted the management of parts of his legislative policy. But the importance of fiscal policy at the beginning of the first administration under the Constitution gave Hamilton's leadership a decisive influence upon the course of national politics. If Hamilton had shown the same solicitude for the interests of the Virginia planters that he showed for those of the New York, Philadelphia, and Boston merchants, he might have held together the combination of interests which Washington had carefully built up in the Convention of 1787. If, for instance, Hamilton had proposed the assumption by the United States of the debts of the Virginia planters to the English merchants as well as the assumption of the debts owed by the various states to domestic, chiefly northern, speculators, he might have kept the Virginians in line with the other supporters of the Washington administration. But Hamilton had poor vision, when his gaze turned in the directon of the debt-ridden tobacco planters of the Upper South. More unfortunately for the future of the Federalist party, he had no vision at all, when his gaze turned in the direction of the small farmers in the back-country and the pioneers in the West.

At the end of the eighteenth century the back-country and the frontier were the most rapidly growing sections of the United States. They were destined to continue to be the most rapidly growing sections of the country through-out the nineteenth century. The unequal rates of growth of the different sections repeatedly upset the calculations of party leaders who failed to understand the trend of the times. Hamilton was the first victim of such miscalcula-tions. He thought the rich merchants and other moneyed interests could dominate enough states to give them control of the national government. For this purpose it would have been sufficient in Washington's time to have held the Northeastern and Middle States. Control of the national government could have been maintained without aid from the South. But by the end of Washington's administration the up-state and back-country population in New York and Pennsylvania had already grown so great that it was difficult for the New York City and Philadelphia mer-chants to maintain their grip upon the state governments. The South and West were already lost to the Federalist party. When the Federalists failed to carry New York in the presidential election of 1800 and also lost most of the electors in Pennsylvania, the doom of the party under Ham-iltonian leadership was sealed.

The Jeffersonian Democracy was founded upon a broader and solider basis. Jefferson's great achievement as a party leader was the assemblage of the bulk of the small inde-pendent farmers and artisans into a single political organization. From New Hampshire and Vermont and up-state New York to the Carolinas and Georgia and the new states beyond the mountains he succeeded in bringing together the bulk of the average Americans, whose distrust of a strong central government survived their defeat in the state ratifying conventions. Strengthened by that part of the upper-class planters who were alienated from the Federalists by Hamilton's fiscal policy, Jefferson's Democratic-Republican party crushed the Hamiltonian party. The Hamiltonians sought to retrieve their political fortunes by selecting their presidential candidate from the South Carolina plantation aristocracy, but the Federalist ticket of Pinckney and King was little more than a revival of the sectional alliance between the upper-class merchants of the Northeast and the planters of the Lower South, who combined at one stage of the proceedings in the Federal Convention to secure a navigation act and save the slave trade, and had been overpowered by the delegations from the Middle States and Upper South. Such a sectional alliance could not possibly win presidential elections against the Jeffersonians. Upon the ruins of the Hamiltonian Federalists Jefferson established a system of one-party government, which succeeded where the Federalist successors of Washington had failed, and maintained its control of the national government for a whole generation.

The one-party system of national politics collapsed in the scrub-race for the presidency of 1824. Federalist opposition to the Jeffersonians had completely disappeared and all presidential condidates were nominally Democratic-Republicans. The combination of John Quincy Adams and Henry Clay brought together enough votes from the Northeast and the West to secure the presidency for Adams and the leadership of the opposition for Jackson. Adams himself clung to his father's political philosophy and sought to govern without the benefit of an organized party. The two Adamses really believed in the principles of the Constitution. They had faith in the possibility of effective nonpartisan government despite the separation of legislative and executive powers. Clay eventually acquired a better understanding of the nature of politics under the Federal Constitution, and contrived to bring together in a single coalition the opposition to the triumphant Jacksonians. With the sophisticated collaboration of Webster and Calhoun, Clay organized their sectional followings into the Whig Party and cemented the foundation of the two-party system in national politics.

The higher strategy of the major-party leaders during the rest of the nineteenth century is revealed in the history of the sectional alignments in presidential elections. Always the effort of the party leaders was to form a combination of sections which could control a majority of the votes in the electoral college. Candidates were brought forward with a view mainly to their sectional appeal. Always the West was growing more rapidly than the other sections of the country, and the balance of power between the sections was shifting in response to the movement of population. Sectional combinations, which once seemed capable of permanent control of the national government, eventually were overpowered by new combinations, and old party leaders were forced to reconstruct their organizations or retire from party leadership. From a study of the population statistics and the reapportionments of congressmen among the different sections after successive censuses, the possible winning combinations of sections can be determined, and the courses of the national parties can be described.

The development of sectionalism in American politics under the Constitution has proceeded along the lines foreshadowed in the Federal Convention of 1787. The four sections which were represented in the Convention, or the five sections, if the West be counted as one, have grown prodigiously, but the important fact throughout the nineteenth century was the disproportionate rate of growth of the West. As the frontier moved west, the boundary between the West and the other sections moved west also. But throughout the century the spirit of the West remained the same, the spirit of the average man. As the West grew in population and in political importance, it tended to disintegrate, and to become more like the Atlantic sections. But as parts of the West became more Eastern in spirit, the East became infected with the Western spirit. Turner's illuminating essay on "The Influence of the Frontier in American History," may have exaggerated that influence, but did not mistake the fundamental fact in the first hundred years of national politics. This fact was the paramount political importance of the average man in the rural areas. The failure to understand it ruined the Hamiltonian party. Its correct understanding made the fortune of the Jeffersonians. Thereafter no major-party leader neglected to reckon with it in planning the strategy of his political campaigns.

The first impressive evidence of the rise of the West in American politics was the shifting of state capitals from the sea-board to inland centers. The removal of the capital of New York to Albany, of the Pennsylvania capital from Philadelphia to Harrisburg, of the Virginia capital from

Williamsburg to Richmond, and of the South Carolina capital from Charleston to Columbia were significant signs of the coming trend. Nevertheless, at the close of Washington's administration the states west of the Appalachian mountains sent only three members to Congress out of a total of 106. A generation later, when Andrew Jackson was first elected, the then Western states sent forty-six members out of a total of 213. After another generation, in the decade ending with the election of Abraham Lincoln, the then West returned one hundred members. Three additional members from the Pacific Coast marked the beginning of the Far West in national politics. The original thirteen states, however, still retained a majority of the total membership of Congress, which had then become 237. By the eighteen-eighties the original states had definitely lost their supremacy, returning only 138 congressmen out of a total of 325. At present the Atlantic states return 165 members out of a total of 435. The West, if it could unite in national elections, would easily control the national government.

The record of elections shows that the West has never been any better united than the East. In the first part of the nineteenth century the cotton-growing states of the old Southwest tended to unite with the original Lower South in national politics. The rest of the old Southwest tended to unite with the original Upper South. The states in the old Northwest between the Ohio River and the Great Lakes tended to occupy a middle position like Pennsylvania, the "Keystone State." The states in the newer Northwest, when they came into the Union, tended to reflect the politics of the rural Northeast, whence came the dominant element among their early settlers. The Far West, in which the tide of settlers from all the older sections of the country finally flowed together, became uniquely western.

The growth of the West not only destroyed the original supremacy of the Atlantic states, but gradually altered the relative importance of the four original sections. In the first half of the last century the Lower South, which had originally lagged behind the Upper South, began to grow more rapidly and eventually gained the leadership of the South in national politics. After the Civil War the bulk of the Upper South joined the Lower South in forming a new sectional combination, which under the name of Solid South has been a major power in national politics down to the present day. The rest of the Upper South, constituting the Border States, has occupied an intermediate position in the intersectional controversies which have continued to dominate the political scene at Washington. In the North throughout the nineteenth century the Northwest was always gaining at the expense of the Northeast. It is only within the last half-century that the industrialization of the Northeast has reversed the relations between these two sections. At the same time the growth of the Far West, especially the Pacific Coast states, has tended to offset the relative decline of the Middle West. This constant shifting of population among the sections has shifted also the location of the balance of power between them, and compelled the national party leaders from time to time to revise their plans for bringing together winning sectional combinations at presidential elections.

At every period in national politics since the final establishment of the two-party system a century ago the plans of the party leaders have rested upon the assumption that there is a standard pattern of sectionalism. In this pattern there have always been three major sections in the United States and a varying number of sub-sections and minor intermediate sections. The major sections have been roughly described as the North, South, and West; the intermediate sections, as Middle or Border States. But the major sections have always had difficulty in maintaining the solidarity which is necessary for the full development of their potential influence in presidential elections, and the intermediate sections have always had difficulty in maintaining the detachment which is necessary for the effective exploitation of the balance of power between the major sections. The South has broken down into Upper and Lower South, or into Solid South and Border States. The North has broken down into Northeast and Northwest. The West has broken down into Middle West and Far West. The original intermediate section consisted of Pennsylvania, the Keystone State, and the other Middle Atlantic states. But Pennsylvania was originally both a Middle state and a Northwestern state and the boundary between the Middle States and the Northwest has always continued to be uncertain and obscure. The resulting complexity of sectional politics has offered abundant opportunities to realistic party leaders for the formation of sectional combinations which might become the basis of victorious and durable parties.

The strategy of the major party leaders since the fall of the Federalists has tended to follow one of two main types. The first type of partisan strategy has been to appeal for political support primarily to the West. This is the exact opposite of the original Hamiltonian party strategy. It is the type which is best illustrated by the Jeffersonian and the Jacksonian leadership. Henry Clay pursued the same type of partisan strategy, though with less wisdom than

Jefferson and less success than Jackson. In the middle of the nineteenth century it offered an attractive prospect of success, because the Western spirit permeated all sections of the country, and Western interests were easily identified with the interests of the country as a whole. Under these favorable circumstances it could build national parties with substantial support in all sections of the country. It is a strategy which may easily be defeated by bad leadership or adverse circumstances. The proof is furnished by the frustrated careers of Stephen A. Douglas and William Jennings Bryan. Nevertheless, this strategy possessed substantial merits which are clearly reflected in the perennial vitality of the Jeffersonian and Jacksonian traditions.

The other type of partisan strategy has been to appeal more particularly to the special interests of two of the three major sections of the country in the hope of effecting a combination between them capable of gaining a majority in the electoral college. The Whig party, as originally designed by Clay, was a coalition between leaders from all three major sections, but Calhoun soon dropped out and eventually led his following in the Lower South into the Democratic party. Webster held the bulk of the big businessmen of the Northeast in line with the remaining big Southern planters and the sundry Westerners from various sections whom Clay was able to bring together under his leadership. This combination could elect to the presidency military heroes who ran on their war records without benefit of platforms, but it could not elect Clay or Webster. It is evident that such success as the Whigs attained was due less to the skillful planning incorporated in Clay's celebrated "American system" of economic policies than to the appeal of Generals Harrison and Taylor to the same kind of voter who had formerly cheered for General Jackson.

The Anti-slavery Republican party was a more successful product of this type of partisan strategy. This party was based upon a combination of the Northeast and Northwest without any regard to the interests of the South. As the northern Democratic leader, Douglas, picturesquely put it, no practical politician would attempt to stand on the Republican platform south of Mason and Dixon's line or the Ohio River. But the Northeast and the Northwest together had grown so strong that those two sections could elect a president without any Southern support. In the campaign of 1856 the Anti-slavery Republicans lost their first battle, because the Democrats shrewdly chose their candidate from the Middle State of Pennsylvania without which the Republicans could not win. But in 1860 the Republicans carried the intermediate section as well as the Northeast and the Northwest, and elected their ticket. Lincoln would have become president, even if the opposition had been united, instead of divided between three sectional candidates.

The trouble with the Republican party, regarded as a combination of sectional interests, was that, while it could elect its candidate for the presidency, it could not so easily control the Congress. It could dominate the electoral college, because the great Northern and Western states cast their electoral votes under the unit rule, whereas it could not control Congress, since the unit rule did not apply to the election of congressmen. For a time the withdrawal of the Southern congressmen and senators gave the Republicans full control at Washington by default, but the return of Southern members after the Civil War in increased numbers (on account of the electoral effects of the Fourteenth Amendment) threatened the Republicans with permanent loss of control in the House of Representatives, unless they could elect some of their candidates in the Southern states. Party strategy reënforced other arguments for negro suffrage and led to the adoption of the Fifteenth Amendment. But it proved impossible to maintain the Republican party in the Solid South except at the point of the bayonet, and public opinion in the North eventually turned against Northern interference with Southern elections. Thereupon the Republican party strategists sought in the Far West compensation for the expected support which they had failed to get in the South. Already in 1864 Nevada had been admitted to statehood in order that there might be enough Republican votes to submit the Thirteenth Amendment to the states before the presidential election. During the Harrison Administration, when for a time the Republicans were again in complete control of the federal government, half a dozen new states were hastily admitted into the Union. A majority of these new states did not contain enough inhabitants to form as much as a single congressional district, but they counted heavily in the Senate and in the electoral college. Again the plans of the Republican strategists were frustrated. The rise of an uncompromising demand in the Far West for the free coinage of silver diverted much of the new voting power to the Populists in 1892 and to the Democrats in 1896. The free-silver issue wrecked the Republican party in the Far West, but gave it by way of compensation what it had never been able to secure through its own strategy, the almost solid support of the business interests in the Northeast and Middle West. Thus at last the Republican combination of sectional interests could hope under normal conditions not only to elect its presidential ticket, but also to command a majority of the votes in both branches of the Congress. This remained the partisan pattern in national politics, with only a temporary interruption caused by the split between the Progressive and Conservative Republicans which brought Woodrow Wilson into the White House, until the advent of the New Deal.

Another product of this type of partisan strategy has been on the whole less successful. This is the combination of sectional interests which was forced on the Democratic party by the development of the Solid South. Basing their campaign upon the assurance of Southern support, the party leaders might seek to combine with the Solid South enough support in either the Northeast or the West to gain a majority in the electoral college. The preference of the Democratic leaders for the former policy seems clear. In eleven campaigns since the Civil War they have taken their candidate for the presidency from New York State. Three times they have taken the candidate from other Northeastern states. The Bryan campaigns are the conspicuous exceptions, where the policy of joining South and West prevailed. Bryan was uniformly unsuccessful, but Wilson in 1916 owed his reelection to his popularity in the West and South, since he failed to carry his own state and was weaker in the Northeast than in any other section. In general this type of partisan strategy, like that of the Whigs under Clay and Webster, has seemed better suited to an opposition party than to a dominant major party.

The type of partisan strategy in national politics, which originally seemed best suited for a dominant major party, has been definitely based upon the ascendancy of the West.

It is not a mere coincidence that the most successful practitioners of this type of leadership, Jefferson and Jackson, though often thought of as Southern politicians, were essentially Westerners. Their appeal was frankly to the Western spirit and to the dominant economic interests of the West. Jefferson's preference for a rural economy of the Western type is well known. "The inhabitants of the commercial cities are as different in sentiment and character from the country people as any two distinct nations," he once declared in a moment of exasperation at the opposition fomented by the Hamiltonian Federalists, "and are clamorous against the order of things established by the agricultural interest. . . ." "Though by command of newspapers they make a great deal of noise," he concluded, "they have little effect on the direction of policy." There can be no question of the predominance of "the agricultural interest" in national politics during the Jeffersonian régime. Jackson was equally candid and explicit in avowing his partiality for the farmers and planters. "The agricultural interest of our country," he declared in his first annual message to Congress, December 8, 1829, "is so essentially connected with every other and so superior to them all that it is scarcely necessary to invite to it your particular attention. It is principally as manufactures and commerce tend to increase the value of agricultural productions and to extend their application to the wants and comforts of society that they deserve the fostering care of Government."

The success of the Jeffersonian and Jacksonian partisan strategy, however, was contingent upon the ascendancy of a rural economy in American life. In the first half of the nineteenth century the agricultural population was definitely predominant in all sections of the United States. The growth of cities and the expanding influence of urban interests in partisan politics gradually shifted the balance of political forces, first in the sections where industry was more advanced and then in the country as a whole, until the simple strategy of the Jeffersonian and Jacksonian party leaders was no longer effective. The early supremacy of the agricultural interests in national politics was further undermined by the division between the Northwest and the Southwest over the slavery question. In the latter part of the nineteenth century it was no longer possible for partisan strategists to ignore urban and industrial interests as completely as in the Jeffersonian and Jacksonian eras. Sectionalism became a more complex phenomenon and national politics became less rustic and more urbane. The nature of the rising interests of the cities and their influence upon the later development of the national parties are topics which will be considered in the next chapter.

At this time I wish merely to call attention to the effect of the Jeffersonian and Jacksonian partisan strategy upon the influence of the different classes in national politics. The essential fact is that agrarianism, as practiced in the Jeffersonian and Jacksonian eras, greatly increased the political importance of the middle class. In fact all the types of partisan strategy which emphasized the political leadership of the West tended to increase the political importance of the middle class. The reason is clear. The typical Westerner throughout the period of predominant Western influence in national politics was a farmer, and the typical Western farmer was a middle-class farmer. This correlation of types was already evident in the time of Jefferson and was clearly defined in the time of Jackson. It was indelibly stamped upon the American character in the time of Lincoln.

The crowning achievement of middle-class agrarianism in national politics was the Homestead Act. Adopted in 1862 in fulfillment of the campaign pledges of the Republican Party, this significant piece of legislation put a heavy premium upon the favorite American qualities of individual initiative and enterprise. At the close of the Civil War more than a million men were mustered out of the Union and Confederate armies. The Homestead Act offered a matchless opportunity for the average veteran to make a new start in life. The cultivation of the standard allotment of a quarter section of land ensured the development of a standardized kind of citizen. The successful homesteader on his one-hundred-sixty-acre freehold could not be less than a middle-class man. As long as he lived on his limited holding he could not easily be more than a middle-class man. For at least a full generation after the Civil War the homesteaders formed the most important single element in Western politics. Under the circumstances of the time they were necessarily also the most important single element in American politics. It is this achievement of the Anti-slavery Republicans — made doubly important by the exclusion of slavery from the Far Western territories — which clears the title of Abraham Lincoln to a place with Franklin and Jefferson and Jackson among the greatest leaders of the middle class in American politics.

The typical homesteader in the latter part of the nineteenth century was the veritable symbol of true Americanism. The great task of the American people up to that time had been the subjugation of the wilderness. The great task of the federal government had been to bring the West under a reign of law. The chief instrument of both tasks was the independent enterprising pioneer who settled the successive frontiers. This pioneer, regarded as an individual, was the average man. Regarded as the unit of a class, he stood for the supremacy of the middle class. He made the rural middle class what it was in this period of American politics, the senior partner in the business of government under the Federal Constitution.

3. The Influence of the Urban Middle Class under the Constitution

In the previous chapters I have tried to show, first, that there was a middle class in American politics at the beginning of our national existence, which exerted a greater influence upon the framing of the Federal Constitution than has been generally recognized, and, secondly, that after the adoption of the Constitution the influence of the rural middle class, resulting from the rapid settlement of the West, became greater than that of any other single class of Americans. But middle-class agrarianism always had to fight for its high place in national politics, and that place became increasingly precarious with the expansion of capitalistic industry and the growth of the cities in which such industry has flourished. These developments brought new divisions among the people, particularly among the urban population, and, as I believe, have produced an urban middle class, which is destined to exert in the twentieth century a political influence not inferior to that of the rural middle class in the nineteenth. What are the grounds for this belief is the subject of the present chapter. But, before discussing the political influence of the urban middle class, it is necessary to establish the existence of such a class, to trace its origin and development, to estimate its present strength, and to appraise its general character.

The urban middle class certainly could have exerted little direct influence in national politics at the time of the Federal Convention of 1787. Sam Adams and men like him in the larger commercial centers of New England and the Middle States doubtless were typical urban middle-class leaders. They made an important place for the urban middle class in local politics and even in state politics in Massachusetts, New York, and Pennsylvania. But they lacked the means of playing the political game at the national capital in competition with the great merchants. The middle-class members of the Federal Convention were more influential than has been generally supposed, but they were mainly lawyers from the smaller towns, dependent for their political importance largely upon the support of the rural population.

The urban population was well represented in the Federal Convention, but its representatives were chiefly members of the upper class. The social connections of the delegates to the Convention have already been analyzed. Nearly all the merchants and lawyers from the leading centers of commerce belonged to the upper class. Benjamin Franklin's middle-class urbanity was a conspicuous exception to the predominantly aristocratic tone of the businessmen in the Convention. Among the lawyers from the larger commercial centers only James Wilson showed much understanding of or sympathy for the democratic ideas characteristic of middle-class thinking at that time. The Boston merchant, Gorham, when a land-holding qualification for the suffrage was under consideration, might enter a plea on behalf of the little businessmen, the independent artisans and craftsmen, who were indispensable in a flourishing seaport, but his argument makes it clear that he was governed more by expediency than by principle in championing the cause of the middle class. His colleague, Gerry, was outspoken in condemnation of such middle-class notions as residential suffrage and frequent popular elections.

The urban upper class indeed possessed a much greater

representation at the Philadelphia Convention than it would
have been entitled to on the basis of the urban population
alone. At that time less than four per cent of the people of
the United States lived in places of as many as eight thousand inhabitants. But the urban upper-class delegates, who
mostly represented the commercial interests of the leading
seaports, accounted for more than one quarter of the total
number of delegates. All eight of the Pennsylvania delegates in the Convention resided in Philadelphia, and the
control of the delegation was clearly in the hands of its
upper-class members. New York City was also much better
represented than it appeared to be on the face of the election
returns. The only member of the New York State delegation who resided in the city was Hamilton, and he was
out-voted by his up-state colleagues. But Gouverneur
Morris of the Pennsylvania delegation belonged to the New
York Morris family, Governor Livingston of the New Jersey delegation belonged to the New York Livingstons,
Rufus King of the Massachusetts delegation had recently
married into a leading New York mercantile family and
thereafter made New York his home, and Dr. Johnson of
the Connecticut delegation, having recently become president of Columbia College, was also a capable spokesman
for the New York point of view. Two of the upper-class
Massachusetts delegates were closely associated with the
commercial interests of Boston, and both the upper-class
New Hampshire delegates represented the similar interests
of Portsmouth. Baltimore, the leading commercial center
of the Upper South, was also represented by upper-class
delegates who were well qualified to speak in the Convention for the commercial interests. These upper-class merchants and their lawyers controlled outright three of the

twelve state delegations and exerted a disproportionate influence in at least three other delegations.

The urban upper class was not able to hold the position of leadership in national politics which its members shared with the great tobacco and rice planters at the Federal Convention. While Washington remained at the head of "the new and more perfect Union," his policy of combining the sectional interests, which had joined in making the Constitution, in support of his administration, ensured to the leading merchants in the commercial centers an influential voice in public affairs. But Washington could not always hold the helm. Hamilton's partisan strategy was designed to perpetuate the leadership of the upper classes, particularly the urban upper class, but Hamilton's party was a failure. His successors at the head of the commercial interests in national politics were more adroit, but the circumstances of the age were against them. At the close of Washington's administration more than a hundred of the 106 congressmen came from districts which were dominated by rural voters, and agrarian politics of some kind necessarily prevailed at the national capital. As late as Jackson's time there were only four cities in the entire country large enough to be entitled to more than a single congressman, and only three or four others whose voters could easily have dominated the congressional districts in which they lived. There were ten or a dozen smaller cities in districts where urban interests may have exerted a disproportionate influence, but more than two hundred of the 240 congressmen came from districts in which rural interests must have been predominant. By that time manhood suffrage, at least for white men, was generally established throughout the United States, and the practice of voting at national elections had become genuinely popular. The leading Boston, New York, and Philadelphia merchants could no longer play the part in national politics which had seemed so natural and right in 1787.

The growth of cities during the nineteenth century gradually transformed the basis of national politics. A century ago modern capitalism was in its infancy in the United States. The industrial revolution had begun not much more than a generation earlier, but already it was proceeding at an ever quickening pace. Transportation and communication facilities were on the verge of rapid improvement through the development of railways and the introduction of the telegraph. The business corporation, uniting the control of extensive capital with limited liability on the part of the management, was no less important an instrument of modern capitalism than steam and electricity. By 1840 it was becoming a favorite instrument of commercial and industrial enterprise. Large accumulations of capital under integrated management were drawing labor to the most convenient power sites, and the great migration to the cities was definitely under way. At the last census ten years ago there were 960 cities in the United States with more than ten thousand inhabitants. Ninety-three of these cities had more than one hundred thousand inhabitants. Forty of them were large enough to send at least one congressman of their own to Washington. These cities of more than ten thousand inhabitants accounted altogether for 47 per cent of the total population of the United States. By the census of 1940, they may account for a clear majority of the total population.

The Census Bureau draws the line between urban and rural population at incorporated places of 2500 inhabitants.

According to this classification the majority of the American people ceased to be rural and became urban at about the time of the World War. By the census of 1910 the portion of the people classified as rural was 54.2 per cent. Ten years later the rural portion had fallen to 48.6 per cent of the total. By the census of 1930 it was estimated at under 44 per cent. By the census of 1940 the portion of the population classified as rural seems likely to be lower than in 1930. Another measure of the growth of cities in the United States is afforded by the development of what the Census Bureau calls metropolitan districts, of which there were ninety-five in 1930. At that time the metropolitan districts, each of which includes a city of at least fifty thousand inhabitants and adjacent suburban territory populous enough to bring the total for the district up to at least one hundred thousand, already contained a total population equal to the total rural population of the United States. The smaller cities held the balance of power between the metropolitan districts and the rural areas. The current census may show that the smaller cities no longer hold the balance and that the metropolitan districts actually contain a clear majority of the American people.

This great shift of population from country to city can not have taken place without profoundly altering the distribution of political power between the urban and rural portions of the people. It is not necessary to argue that it has greatly increased the importance of urban interests in national politics. But how has it affected the distribution of influence between the various classes of the urban population? Has the urban upper class been able to regain the high place in national politics which it held in 1787? Or has the urban middle class been able to secure a share in the preponderance of power won by the rural middle class under the leadership of Jefferson and Jackson and Lincoln? What indeed is the urban middle class in the year 1940? Or is it a mistake to suppose that class divisions of this kind possess any importance in contemporary national politics?

Statistics showing the distribution of wealth and income among the American people are abundant. There are some interesting statistics of this kind in a recent report of the National Resources Committee, entitled *The Structure of the American Economy*. For example, there is a table showing the distribution of what the report calls aggregate consumer income among the individuals and families composing the consumer units in the American economy. These individuals and families are divided into ten groups, containing equal numbers of consumer units in each group. The top group, containing the richest tenth, receives approximately 36 per cent of the aggregate consumer income of all the American people. The bottom group, containing the poorest tenth, receives approximately 2 per cent of the aggregate income of the American people. In order to make up the full number of the top tenth, it is necessary to include consumer units, that is, independent individuals and families, with as little as $2,600 a year. The bottom group is composed of independent individuals and families, none of whom receives as much as $340 a year. But what is the middle class? Does it comprise the eight groups which stand between the top and the bottom, that is, all those receiving more than $340 a year but less than $2,600? These groups include 80 per cent of the consumers and receive 62 per cent of the aggregate income. Or does it include the two groups which stand in the middle of the array, including 20 per cent of the consumers and receiving 13 per cent of the income? The income range of these two groups runs from $880 to $1,275 a year. Is that the American middle class? Or is it some other combination of the intermediate groups? In short, how is the middle class to be defined in terms of income, or can it be so defined?

One easy answer to this question is to deny the existence of such a class. This is the answer of the Marxists. They say that there are only two basic classes in modern industrial society, the capitalists and the proletariat. It is obvious that this can not be true, if the farmers are taken into account, since the independent small farmer is neither a capitalist nor a worker in the Marxist sense of the term, or rather he is both a capitalist and a worker. There are also other important classes which do not fit logically into the Marxist system of classification. There is an intermediate class of professional men and public employees, who are neither capitalists nor proletarians but rather are the servants of all classes. There is a transitional class of independent artisans and craftsmen, who represent the vestigial remains of an earlier economic order of society. There is a mixed class of tenant farmers, who control small properties without owning them, and wage-earners, who possess some of the securities of great corporations or bank deposits or life-insurance policies and share to some extent the point of view of capitalists as well as that of the proletariat. Finally, there are the unemployed, the vagrants, and the criminals, who fall outside the system of classification. In an abstract form of society, such as the Marxists sometimes seem to be talking about, these classes may be ignored, but in reality they have to be accounted for and are accounted for by practical politicians.

If these various classes are taken into account as precisely as statistics permit, it is possible to make a rough calculation of the proportions of capitalists and proletarians in modern industrial America, according to the Marxist formula. It shows that a majority of the American people belong to the proletariat. As nearly as I can conveniently reckon, the proportion of the population in the proletariat, estimated according to the Marxist formula, would be 51.7 per cent for the whole United States and much higher for industrial states like Massachusetts and New York. According to Lewis Corey, the only Marxist who has attempted to make such an estimate, as far as I am aware, the proportion of proletarians in the whole population of the United States is 59.3 per cent. His estimate, published in his book, *The Crisis of the Middle Class*, is an approximation for the year 1935; mine is based on figures taken from the census of 1930, which I have not attempted to bring down to date. We agree that the proletariat, as defined by Marxists, contains a majority of the American people. But that does not dispose of the question whether there is in fact a middle class. It merely raises another question, namely, have the Marxists adopted a realistic system of classification?

Lewis Corey has made the most noteworthy attempt to vindicate the validity of the Marxist classification. In his book previously referred to, published five years ago, he concedes that there is in fact an important middle class in the United States, consisting of the elements noted above. He argues however that this middle class can not hope to pursue an independent political policy of its own, but must cast in its lot with the proletariat. This, he asserts, is inevitable, because the middle class can no longer find the opportunities for profitable enterprise which formerly abounded in this country, and will therefore prefer security to the risks of unprofitable enterprise. Security, he claims, can be achieved only through such a program of collectivization on a proletarian basis as is advocated by the Marxist theorists. Hence the middle class will find that its interest requires it to accept the dictatorship of the proletariat. By this process of reasoning Corey contrives to reach the conclusion that only the two basic classes, which are recognized by the Marxists, need be reckoned with by political analysts and far-sighted politicians.

The fatal defect in this Marxist reasoning is its failure to recognize the essential nature of political classes. Classes may be defined by economists in terms of property, income, or position in the economic order. Such objective classifications possess indubitable utility in economic analysis. But politicians need classifications which are subjective as well as objective, for they wish to know not only how voters stand in the economic order, but also how they think and feel and are likely to act. The Marxists have recognized the importance of thought and feeling in their emphasis on class-consciousness, but have been slow in learning that group-consciousness of various kinds can be produced by education and by propaganda as well as by material interests. In the United States the middle class has long been great, not only because the farmers, professional men, government and corporate officials, technicians, small businessmen, independent craftsmen, and property-owning wage-earners have always been numerous, but also because most Americans, regardless of their position in the economic order of society, have long been accustomed to think of themselves as something fundamentally different from members of a proletariat as defined by Marxists.

This fatal defect of the Marxist system of political thought is convincingly illustrated by the results of a recent poll published by *Fortune* magazine. The February, 1940, issue of *Fortune* was devoted to a sociological description of the United States. Among a number of articles, which treated of the various classes of American economic society, was a survey of opinion, designed to show what the American people think of themselves in terms of their relative position in the economic order. The result of the poll, which was conducted by time-tested and reliable methods of sampling the opinion of all kinds of people, must be discouraging to Marxists as well as to Fascists and agitators of all sorts who think that the American people are or should be in a revolutionary state of mind.

The first question which was put to a fair sample of the American people was this: What word would you use to name the class in America you belong to? There was an amazing variety of words offered in reply, and no less than 27.5 per cent confessed at first that they didn't know what word to use in describing the class, if any, to which they belonged. Two per cent described themselves as members of the business, executive, or white collar class, and miscellaneous answers which defy classification amount to another 5.7 per cent. Only 1.6 per cent definitely called themselves members of the upper class. Enough others called themselves upper-class by other names to bring the total, who admitted or claimed a place in the top class, up to 2.9 per cent. Only 14.9 per cent called themselves members of the lower class, or used other terms of equivalent meaning. Of these 1.2 per cent actually used the term, lower class; 10.8 per cent put themselves in the working or laboring class; 2.8 per cent employed similar expressions;

and 0.3 per cent admitted that they should be classified as unemployed, idle, or unfortunate. Between these two groups were 47.0 per cent of the total who put themselves into the middle class, either under that name or its equivalent or similar expressions. Of these, 2.5 per cent further described themselves as upper middle class or the equivalent, and 0.4 per cent as lower middle class. The remaining 44.1 per cent thought of themselves as plain middle class, or the equivalent. When these answers had been obtained by the investigators who conducted the poll, those who had not actually used the words, upper class, middle class, or lower class were requested to indicate which of these three expressions they would choose, if they had to describe the class to which they belonged by one of them. More than two-thirds of these persons answered that they would call themselves middle class. By combining these answers with the others, the *Fortune* survey reached the final conclusion that 7.6 per cent of the American people regard themselves as upper class, 79.2 per cent as middle class, and 7.9 per cent as lower class, and that 5.3 per cent can not or will not tell to what class they belong. Approximately four-fifths of all Americans apparently regard themselves as members of the middle class. Not one in a dozen thinks of himself as a proletarian.

The results of this subjective classification of the American people are not astonishing to practical politicians. They have long known that Americans have a strong aversion to thinking of themselves as markedly different from the average man. In this poll many upper-class persons, judged by objective standards, insisted that they really belonged to the middle class. Only a quarter of the factory workers, and an even smaller proportion of farm and miscellaneous labor, called themselves members of the working or labor class. The majority in every occupation and social position, including farm-laborers and the unemployed, decisively considered itself middle class. Even that minority of the factory workers, who originally put themselves in the working class, when pressed to choose between upper, middle, and lower class, mainly swung into the middle class. The major party politicians, who have long tended to personify the American people as the average man, have shown a far better understanding of the realities of American politics than the Marxists with their talk about a self-conscious proletariat which scarcely exists outside the minds of the Marxists themselves.

The American middle class, as constituted by the people themselves, is very different from the same class, as estimated objectively by statistical methods. This is also convincingly illustrated by the editors of *Fortune* magazine. In all their surveys of opinion in the United States *Fortune*'s editors have divided the people into four classes for the purpose of disclosing the distribution of attitudes at the principal different levels of society. These four classes are an upper class, consisting of the relatively prosperous, an upper middle class, consisting of persons ranging from successful farmers and foremen in factories to those on the way to becoming major executives, a lower middle class, consisting of independent self-sustaining workers and those regularly employed at wages, and a lower class, consisting of those who are poor, working when they have an opportunity. Negroes have been polled separately. The proportions in these classes have presumably varied at different times. At present they are stated to be as follows: the prosperous, 6 per cent; the upper middle class, 23 per cent; the lower middle class, 41 per cent; and the poor (including the negroes), 30 per cent. Thus the middle class, as objectively determined by *Fortune*'s editors, is divided against itself. Though its two divisions together account for 64 per cent of the white population, it lacks the solidarity of the middle class as subjectively determined by its own members.

In *Fortune*'s recent survey of class-attitudes the middle class appeared to be much more self-conscious than the statisticians had supposed. Less than 3 per cent of the total poll described itself explicitly as either upper middle class or lower middle class, the leading categories of *Fortune*'s own objective classification. Nearly two-fifths of the poll thought of themselves definitely as plain middle class people without any suggestion from the poll-takers, and approximately four-fifths accepted that classification when suggested to them. A large majority of the persons in each of the four objective classes, recognized by *Fortune*'s editors for their statistical purposes, claimed membership in the middle class, including three-fourths of the prosperous and seven-tenths of the poor. Even among the negroes, who seem to have adopted separate standards of classification for their own race, a greater number put themselves in the middle class than in either of the other classes. So widespread is the existence of middle-class consciousness that it is no great exaggeration to pronounce this kind of class-consciousness the characteristic American state of mind. The United States, according to the findings reported by *Fortune*'s survey, is middle class.

The dominant middle-class consciousness of the American people is confirmed by the attitudes which the *Fortune* survey reported with reference to issues testing further its state of mind. For example, the majority of the people wish to go into business for themselves, a thoroughly middle-class attitude. A majority desire success more than security, as revealed by their preference for a better position with an equal chance of advancement and of failure over an inferior position with little risk of dismissal. A majority favor private business over the government as an employer. A majority believe that the employer and worker go hand in hand together. This attitude is shared by all groups, including even factory workers. A majority believe that the future is still bright for themselves personally, and that opportunity for the advancement of one's children is greater than ever before. A majority have sent their children to college, or intend to do so, and a majority feel a sense of obligation to pass on something to the next generation. These are all middle-class attitudes, and could not exist unless the bulk of the people really were what they profess to be, members in spirit of the middle class.

In the light of these findings it is necessary to revise the estimates of the size of the proletariat, made in accordance with the Marxist formula. In a country where such habits of thought exist, the boundary between middle class and proletariat must be drawn in another way than in countries where the so-called lower classes have been taught to know their place and to keep it. American white-collar workers almost universally refuse to admit that they are proletarians, and, by refusing, elevate themselves into the middle class. Many of the other workers also, including not a few of the unskilled, make the same leap from the inferior class, to which the Marxist philosophy consigns them, into a higher class more compatible with the traditions of the country and their own natural state of mind. If only half of the white-collar workers be transferred from the proletariat, where the Marxist dialectic puts them, into the middle class, and only a fourth of the other skilled workers be similarly transferred, the middle class would surpass the proletariat in the American population as a whole. If two-thirds of the white-collar workers and one-third of the other skilled workers be transferred from the proletariat, as estimated by Marxist methods, to the middle class, the proletariat would lose its superiority of numbers, even in the non-agricultural part of the population. If most of the white-collar workers and a majority of the other skilled and semi-skilled workers be so transferred, as they should be in view of their actual state of mind, the proletariat would fall far behind the middle class, even in highly industrialized states like Massachusetts and New York. Since a political class is mainly a state of mind, it may be large or small, as thinking makes it so. In the United States public opinion has made the middle class large, the urban middle class as well as the rural middle class.

The overwhelming predominance of middle-class senti-ment among the urban as well as the rural sectors of the American people simplifies the task of political analysis in the present state of national politics. As long as the public mind remains in its present state, urban middle-class senti-ment will inevitably dominate the political scene in most of the congressional districts within the great metropolitan areas. New York City, for instance, sends twenty-four congressmen to Washington under the present apportion-ment and districting laws, and in the entire metropolitan area of which it is the center, including parts of three states, there are no less than thirty-six congressional districts. The majority of these districts can hardly fail to reflect a predominantly middle-class attitude in national politics. Middle-class districts are numerous also in the other leading metropolitan areas, Chicago, Philadelphia, Los Angeles, Boston, Detroit, and Pittsburgh. They would be more numerous, if some of these states, particularly New York and Illinois, would adopt fair districting laws.

The influence of urban middle-class sentiment in the national House of Representatives is limited, however, by the nature of the system of representation. Most congressional districts contain a mixture of urban and rural population, and class sentiment of any kind must be correspondingly mixed. Under the present apportionment and districting laws there are 115 districts in which more than 80 per cent of the inhabitants are what the census calls urban. Urban middle-class sentiment is likely to predominate in most of these districts. There are seventy-one other districts in which between 60 and 80 per cent of the population are urban. Urban middle-class sentiment presumably predominates also in many of these districts. Altogether 186 districts are predominantly urban and offer an opportunity for the direct representation of urban middle-class sentiment at Washington. But there are 177 districts in which the rural population exceeds 60 per cent of the total, and rural middle-class sentiment must be more influential than urban. The other seventy-two districts are closely divided between urban and rural voters, and neither type of sentiment can be dominant. If fair reapportionment and redistricting laws follow the present census, the ascendancy of the urban over the rural voters in the national House of Representatives should be definitely established, and the urban point of view should preponderate in the expression of middle-class sentiment at Washington. Heretofore, however, the House

of Representatives has not been the most important organ
for the development of urban middle-class influence in national politics.

The Senate is less important than the lower house as an
agency of urban middle-class interests and feeling. This
results from the capital fact that a large majority of the
urban population resides in a minority of the states. At the
census of 1930 a majority of the population was urban in
only twenty-one of the forty-eight states, and in several of
these the urban population exceeded the rural by only a
slender margin. Hence a majority of the senators are dependent for their offices upon bodies of voters which are
still predominantly rural. By the census of 1940 the ascendancy of the rural states is not likely to be changed. Not
more than one or two states at most can swing over from the
rural to the urban category, and the majority of the senators
must remain dependent for at least another decade upon the
support of bodies of voters in which the rural vote will
exceed the urban. Rural middle-class sentiment will continue to be a factor of the first importance in the United
States Senate.

It is in the electoral college that the urban population
exerts its greatest political influence. Under the apportion-
ment which followed the 1930 census, the twenty-one urban
states received 310 electoral votes. This is a clear majority
of the total electoral vote, which is 531. Since the electoral
vote of each state is cast under the unit rule, the urban
voters might choose all the electors from an urban state, if
they should combine together for the purpose. If the urban
states should combine together for the purpose of controlling presidential elections, they could dominate the presidency. The paramount influence of the urban states in

presidential elections is enhanced by the accidental circumstance that the largest states are almost all urban states, and under the established system of electing presidents the largest states occupy a strongly preferred position. So important has this preferred position of the large states in presidential elections become, that the influence in national politics of the urban population in general and of the urban middle class in particular can not be understood without examining the nature and operation of the presidential election system.

It is a truism to say that the most radical changes which have taken place in our system of constitutional government have been brought about by the unplanned growth of new political practices, gradually acquiring the force of popular customs and sanctioned by the development of a sort of unwritten constitution. Outstanding in the unwritten constitution of the United States is the system of partisan politics, the product of the organization and operation of national political parties. If sectionalism and class-consciousness are important in national politics, they possess importance because they find expression in the major parties and largely determine the course of party government.

Of political parties the written Constitution has nothing to say. It is evident from the debates in the Federal Convention that the spirit of party was viewed with grave suspicion. The animosities between public men and the collisions between the agencies of government, which partisanship tends to produce, were evils which the framers of the Constitution deplored and sought to avoid as far as possible. They sought to devise a system of government which could be operated without permanent standing parties. A two-party system of politics, such as has actually developed in this country and imparted to the unwritten constitution its peculiar and distinctive character, if the Founding Fathers could have imagined such a development, would have been condemned by them as unnecessary, improper, and dangerous to the perpetuity of free institutions.

The capital defect of the written Constitution, regarded as a plan for a system of government to be operated without the aid of permanent organized parties, is the method of electing the president. No part of the original frame of government gave the framers more trouble than the arrangements for the election of the chief executive. Whether there should be one chief executive or several, whether he should be aided and also kept in his place by a council, or allowed to act alone, whether he should serve for only a short term of years, or for a longer term, or even for life, if his behavior should be good, whether he should be eligible for reëlection at the end of his term or required to retire, at least for a time, from the presidential office, whether he should be elected by the Congress, or by the people, or by some novel device such as that of special electors in the several states: these were the questions to which the Federal Convention found it extraordinarily difficult to give satisfactory answers. One of the first decisions reached by the Convention was that the chief executive should be a single person. One of its last decisions, reached more than three months later after many debates and several changes of opinion, was that he should be elected by independent presidential electors, chosen expressly for the purpose, subject to a final decision by the House of Representatives if the electors should fail to cast a majority of their votes for any one person.

This method of election deserves to be examined more

carefully, since it has operated very differently from what the framers hoped and has thereby profoundly altered the whole system of constitutional government. The electors, who were to be equal in number for each state to the sum of the senators and representatives in Congress from that state, were to be elected in each state by the state legislatures, or in a manner to be determined by the state legislatures, and were to vote for two persons for president, who should not be residents of the same state. But if none of the persons voted for by the electors should receive a clear majority of all the votes cast, the lower house of Congress should choose between the five [1] persons receiving the most electoral votes, and in making its choice the members of the lower house should vote by states. In this final election the representatives of each state should cast a single vote, regardless of their number, so that all the states, though unequally represented at the primary election in the electoral college, would have an equal voice. The framers of the Constitution believed that there would rarely be a sufficient concert of opinion in the electoral college to produce a clear majority of the electoral votes for any one person. General Washington, it was conceded, would surely be chosen as the first president at the primary election in the electoral college, but it seemed to most members of the Federal Convention likely that thereafter the House of Representatives would generally be called upon to make the final choice. One delegate, George Mason, declared that in his opinion this would happen nineteen times out of twenty. Though another delegate, Abraham Baldwin, suggested that the growth of better acquaintance between the different sections of the country would eventually

---

[1] Changed by the Twelfth Amendment to three.

secure national reputations for the leading men in the different sections, the prevailing opinion was that the final election of the presidents would normally be made in the House of Representatives.

This method of election would have been extraordinarily undemocratic. While the electoral college represents the states roughly in proportion to their respective populations, giving only a slightly disproportionate number of votes to the smaller states, the equal vote of the states in the House of Representatives makes the smallest state as influential as the largest in the final election. In Washington's time it would have been possible for states possessing less than one-quarter of the total population of the United States to elect the president of the United States in the House of Representatives against the combined opposition of the states possessing the other three-quarters of the population. At the present time it would be possible, if the election of the president were thrown into the House of Representatives, for the representatives of states possessing less than one-fifth of the total population to elect their candidate against the combined opposition of states possessing four-fifths of the population of the United States. The right of the majority to elect the person they desire for president is so firmly established today in the opinion of the public that an election by the representatives of so small a minority of the people might seem to be intolerable.

In the early years of the Federal Union, when the principle of majority rule was less firmly established than now, elections by the House of Representatives proved highly unsatisfactory. In 1801 there was a tie vote in the electoral college and the House of Representatives was forced to choose between Jefferson and Burr. Attempts by political intrigue to throw the election from Jefferson, the acknowledged leader of the Democratic-Republican party, who was clearly the popular choice, to Burr, whom many of the Federalists preferred for partisan reasons, caused bitter feeling. Happily this ill-conceived intrigue failed to accomplish its purpose. In 1825 the election of John Quincy Adams by the House of Representatives, when Jackson had received a large plurality of the electoral votes, though not a clear majority, also caused bitterness. The irreconcilable opposition of the followers of the defeated candidate ruined the credit of the Adams administration and frustrated its best efforts to serve the country. In 1877 the constitutional arrangements for the election of the president broke down completely. The result of the balloting by the presidential electors was in dispute between the followers of Hayes and of Tilden, and no decision could be reached by the Congress. An appeal to arms was happily averted by a compromise between the parties and the establishment of a special electoral commission.

Presidential elections by the House of Representatives are likely to be as objectionable in the future as in the past. The twenty-five smallest states, which now possess less than one-fifth of the population of the United States, would no doubt find it practically impossible to unite in the House of Representatives in support of any candidate for president who could qualify as one of the three highest in the electoral college, but victorious combinations of states possessing much less than a majority of the total population are readily imaginable. There are, for example, several leading issues, springing out of the conflicting interests of agriculture and industry in the United States, which sharply divide the representatives of the rural and urban states. The struggles

over farm relief and wages and hours bills in recent con-
gresses afford abundant illustrations of the ease with which
such issues may arise. A combination of twenty-five rural
states from the South and West is not hard to imagine.
Such a combination could elect its candidates in the House
of Representatives, though these states possess considerably
less than a majority of the total population, provided that
the electoral votes could be split among three or more
candidates in such a way that no one of them obtained a
clear majority. On the other hand, fifteen of the leading
urban states possess a clear majority of the electoral votes,
and could elect the president of the United States by uniting
in support of a single candidate. Yet they would be in a
hopeless minority in the House of Representatives and
would be doomed to defeat, if there were no convenient arrangement for nominating a candidate and the election were
finally determined in accordance with the constitutional
rule. These mathematical possibilities may afford fascinat-
ing opportunities for electoral combinations by practical
politicians, but offer little comfort to believers in democracy. It is unpleasant to contemplate the state of feeling
which would be caused at the present time, if the leading
candidates for the presidency were defeated in the electoral
college through a division of votes among several different
candidates and in the House of Representatives through a
combination of small states in support of a less popular
candidate. It is at least clear that the constitutional arrangements for a final election in the House of Representatives
introduce an element of chance into the electoral process,
which constitutes a serious menace to the principle of
majority rule in presidential elections, and that only a
system of party government under which the people can

chose between the candidates of two major parties offers any security against a highly objectionable form of minority rule.

The principal obstacle, indeed almost the only obstacle, to unpopular presidential elections under the Constitution, as it was originally written and as it stands today, is the system of bipartisan politics. The prime constitutional function of national party leaders is to form such combinations of states as will afford a fair prospect of winning a majority of the electoral votes and thereby preventing an appeal to the House of Representatives for a final decision. In forming such combinations the party leaders seek to bring together the representatives of interests which are strong enough to gain the support of a majority of the voters in states which collectively possess a majority of the presidential electors. They begin with states in which the dominant interests are already committed or will readily respond to a particular type of leadership in national politics. They build up winning combinations by adding states in which control is more evenly contested between those interests which favor that type of leadership and those which incline towards a different type. The doubtful states become the main objects of contention between the major party leaders. Candidates who can carry most of the doubtful states are certain to carry enough of the so-called safe states to ensure their election. Among the doubtful states the biggest are the most important, because all presidential electors are elected at large on a general ticket. The inducement is very great to select candidates and plan campaigns in such a way as to obtain at least a good fighting chance of victory in such states.

This means that those voters who hold the balance of

power in the big doubtful states exert a greatly disproportionate influence upon the calculations of the party leaders.
If such voters belong to a well-defined class, that class,
whatever it may be, becomes a major and perhaps decisive
factor in national politics. My thesis is, that for a large
part of our national existence that class was the rural middle
class and that increasingly in our own time it tends to
become the urban middle class. For many years under the
leadership of Jeffersonian, Jacksonian, and Lincolnian politicians, the rural middle class was the decisive factor in
national politics. At present the system of presidential elections tends more and more to shift the balance of power to
the urban middle class.

The first step in the proof of this thesis is to identify the
big doubtful states. They are not necessarily the same as
the close states in any particular election. In 1936, for example, the closest state was New Hampshire, which the
Democrats took away from the Republicans by a narrow
plurality of the popular vote. But New Hampshire was not
a doubtful state in the technical sense of the term, as understood by the major-party leaders. New Hampshire was a
strongly Republican state. There were only two states in
the whole country, Maine and Vermont, where the Republicans were stronger than in New Hampshire. The Republicans can not hope to win a presidential election
without carrying states in which the Democrats were much
stronger in 1936 than in these northern New England
states. The doubtful states, from the standpoint of the
major-party strategists, are those in which the division of
the voters in a particular election is about the same as the
average for the country as a whole. In 1936 the Democratic
candidate polled a little over sixty per cent of the total

popular vote throughout the United States and the Republican candidate polled less than forty per cent. States in which there was a similar distribution of the popular vote between the candidates of the two major parties were the doubtful states in the technical sense of the term. They were the states which a major-party candidate needed to carry in order to win the election. If successful in these states, he was sure to be elected. If unsuccessful in these states, he could not hope to defeat his opponent by holding merely those states in which he started the campaign with more favorable prospects. The true battle-ground in presidential campaigns consists of the states with an average distribution of voters between the major parties. Among the doubtful states, in this sense of the term, the biggest are necessarily the scenes of the hottest fighting, because in the biggest doubtful states the greatest number of electoral votes are at stake.

The doubtful states, in the technical sense of the term, are easily identified by the fact that in these states the popular votes were divided between the two major parties in approximately the same proportions as in the country as a whole. In the campaign of 1936 there were fourteen such states in various sections of the United States. Two were in the Northeast, namely, New York and New Jersey. Two were in the old Northwest, namely, Ohio and Illinois. Five were on the border between North and South or South and West. They were Maryland, West Virginia, Kentucky, Missouri, and New Mexico. Five others, Minnesota, North Dakota, Colorado, Wyoming, and Idaho, were in the new Northwest or in the Far West. In these states approximately three voters out of each five voted for President Roosevelt, which was the ratio in the country as a whole. These are the states which must be won back by the Republicans, if they are to win back the presidency, unless there is a radical change in the existing alignment of parties.

Most of these states were also doubtful states at the presidential election of 1932. In the Northeast, New York was the principal doubtful state at that election, and Rhode Island took the place of New Jersey. In the old Northwest, Illinois was a doubtful state, but Indiana and Michigan took the place of Ohio. Along the border between North and South and South and West, Maryland, West Virginia, and Kentucky were in the doubtful class, but not Missouri and New Mexico. In the new Northwest and in the Far West, Minnesota, Colorado, Wyoming, and Idaho were in the doubtful class, but North Dakota was replaced by Montana and Utah. In 1932 also the three Pacific Coast states fell into the doubtful class. If the doubtful states at presidential elections during the entire period since the close of the World War are determined in this manner, a fairly stable pattern of partisanship emerges. In this pattern each state finds a more or less definitely fixed place in relation to the other states. The doubtful states find their place between the definitely Democratic and Republic states, and among them the biggest are New York, Ohio, and Illinois. These are the states, therefore, in which presidential elections must be won or lost.

The strategic position of the big doubtful states in presidential elections consolidates the influence of the urban middle class in national politics. These are the states in which the character and interests of the doubtful voters are matters of primary importance in the calculations of the major-party leaders. It happens that all three of them are states in which the urban population constitutes a large majority of the total population. In fact, the predominance of the urban population is more decisive than appears from the ordinary statistics of urban and rural population. In all three the inhabitants of the great metropolitan areas alone constitute a majority of the total population. The most influential political element in these states must be the urban middle class. The kind of leadership which will be most likely to win these states in national elections will be leadership responsive to the interests and feelings of the urban middle class. Such leadership will respond in some measure also to the interests and feelings of the urban middle class in other states. Thus the urban middle class attains a decisive position in presidential elections. Well-informed and sagacious politicians will be heedful of its state of mind, and will secure for it in the conduct of national affairs an influence suited to its circumstances.

The relations between the urban and rural portions of the middle class in the three big doubtful states must be explored in order to understand the electoral strategy of the major-party leaders. In New York State the rural middle class lives mainly in the Dairy Belt, and, like the same class in Vermont and elsewhere in the rural Northeast, is strongly Republican. The balance of power, therefore, in state-wide elections in New York lies definitely with some part of the urban population. The part which is excluded by its position from a share in the balance of power is that which is devoted to Tammany Hall. This is a situation which gives a disproportionate influence to the independent urban voters, who, the election returns suggest, are chiefly to be found among the middle class. In Ohio and Illinois the rural middle class lives mainly in the Corn

Belt. The Corn Belt farmers have been traditionally inclined to favor the Republicans more than the Democrats, at least since the Civil War, but they have not been so constant in their preference for the Republican party as the dairymen in up-state New York. On the other hand, the Republican party organizations in Chicago and in the larger Ohio cities have been more vigorous rivals of the local Democratic organizations than in New York City. The balance of power in Ohio and Illinois, therefore, is divided between urban and rural voters and can not be so definitely located as in New York. The major-party leaders in presidential campaigns must never forget to consider the interests and cater to the prejudices of urban middle-class voters in all three states, but in Ohio and Illinois they must also pay special heed to the interests and prejudices of the corn-growers.

These preoccupations of the national party politicians, who have been responsible for the conduct of presidential campaigns, are plainly reflected in the choice of candidates. The Democratic candidate has been taken from New York in eleven of the nineteen campaigns since the reorganization of the party during the Civil War. The Republicans have taken two-thirds of their candidates from the Corn Belt, chiefly from Ohio and Illinois, and have often balanced their ticket by taking the vice-presidential candidate from New York. Only in the three Bryan campaigns was the urban point of view openly flouted by the Democrats. It has never been entirely neglected by the Republicans. It is evident that since the Civil War the Democrats have generally directed their appeal in presidential campaigns primarily at the urban middle class. The Republicans have divided their principal attentions in presidential campaigns between the urban middle class and the middle-class farmers in the Corn Belt. In recent years the trend on the Republican side has been unmistakably to shift the emphasis more and more from the rural to the urban middle class. The presidential election returns in the big doubtful states strongly support the thesis that the urban middle class is tending to become the most powerful single factor in national politics.

This is a tendency which must be very discouraging to Communists. Advocates of a dictatorship of the proletariat, if they face the facts of American politics, can not console themselves with the thought that the middle class has entered upon a decline. The influence of the rural middle class in national politics is doubtless declining. But the middle class as a whole is finding full compensation for the decline of the rural middle class in the rise of the urban middle class. As long as the more or less skilled industrial workers in the large cities remain in their present state of mind, there is no room for a class-conscious proletariat strong enough to support a Communist dictatorship. The urban middle class may reasonably look forward to greater rather than less influence in national politics in the future. Under the circumstances there is no ground for the belief that they can be persuaded by Communist propaganda to think of themselves otherwise than as average Americans of the time-honored kind.

The poor prospects for Marxist Communism in national politics mean equally poor prospects for Fascism. Fascists, unlike Communists, do not underestimate the importance of psychological forces in politics. They have built their power abroad partly upon the antagonism of capitalists to the economic program of the Marxists, but chiefly upon the reaction of the middle class against the threat of Communist dictatorship in the state. They have exploited the weakness of middle classes which were unsure of themselves and felt forced to choose between competing forms of dictatorship. Between dictatorship pretending to operate in the name of the proletariat and dictatorship pretending to operate in the name of the nation the middle class naturally chose the latter. But the necessity for such a choice can not exist, nor be made to appear to exist, in a country where the middle class is strong and self-confident. It can not be made to appear to exist in the United States under the existing conditions or under any conditions that seem likely to exist in a predictable future. The prospects for an American Fascism, therefore, are no better than for an American Communism.

The ascendancy of the middle class under the American Constitution, I conclude, seems likely to be maintained, and to endure through a period of time of which no end is in sight. Middle-class consciousness, it must be added, furnishes a solid foundation for a reign of law sustained by the consent of the governed. The foundation is solid, because middle-class consciousness is not primarily class self-consciousness, but rather consciousness of equal participation in a rational organization of the state for the common good. It produces an attitude toward the state which gives to political ideals an intrinsic force of their own, independent of economic interests and psychological complexes. It tends to give reality to the vision of the state as a true commonwealth, in which power rests ultimately, not on physical force and organized official violence, but on the good will of the people.

III

The Future of Democracy in America

THE miscellaneous reflections on topics not elsewhere specified, with which Bryce filled the last part of *The American Commonwealth*, have gained added interest from the passage of time. For Bryce was the happy possessor of a temperament which we now recognize as no less typically American in its easy-going tolerance of Democracy's deficiencies and errors and in its stubborn optimism in the face of Democracy's unsolved problems than it was typically Victorian in its complacent assurance of effortless superiority on the part of the nineteenth-century Englishman. He was also profoundly convinced that he lived in the midst of a period of great changes and that the future therefore was destined to be radically different from the past. "Changes move faster in our age," he wrote, "than they ever moved before, and America is the land of change." [1] This is what Americans are still repeating to themselves, and if they are also viewing the future with a somewhat greater degree of alarm than was thought decent for Americans in the nineteenth century, they merely resemble by so much more the Victorian Englishmen for whom the half-Americanized Bryce was consciously writing.

How valiant a prophet of change Bryce was in the eighteen-eighties deserves to be recalled. "Even in England," he wrote, his pen wandering for a moment from his Amer-

---

[1] Bryce, *The American Commonwealth*, Vol. 3, Ch. 115, p. 648.

ican theme, "it is impossible to feel confident that any one of the existing institutions of the country will be standing fifty years hence." [2] Though to Victorian Conservatives this lack of confidence in the stability of English institutions must have been a shocking revelation, to his fellow Liberals in the tight little island Bryce's subversive vision of the future at home could only have confirmed his reputation for invincible optimism. But Bryce's optimism was also prudent. He looked forward with hope, but he guarded himself against the perils of precise prediction. "All we can ever say of the future," he observed in concluding this chain of thought, "is that it will be unlike the present." And he turned again to his reflections upon the future in America.

Now after fifty years it is clear how right Bryce was in emphasizing the prospect of change. The population of the United States is more than twice what it was when Bryce was writing his book. Its character also has changed along with the change in size. The French-Canadians and Germans and Irish, whose influx he noted without sharing the alarm of some of the earlier English stock, have continued to come, and have been joined by immense numbers of immigrants from southern and eastern Europe, whose coming had barely begun when he was first in America. French and Germans and Irish, he observed with manifest approval, tend to produce a racial mixture not radically different from that produced in England by the blending of the Anglo-Saxons and Normans with the original Britons. Hence the American people of the future, he reflected with natural satisfaction, might well become a kind of rejuvenated English, capable of reproducing on a grander scale in the New

[2] Bryce, *op. cit.*, Vol. 3, Ch. 96, p. 338.

World their characteristic achievements in the old. But this prospect is evidently altered by the influx of the Latin races, the Slavic peoples, and the Semites.

The growth of cities has brought even greater changes than the growth of the country as a whole. They have grown faster than the rest of the country. They have received more than their share of the newer immigrants. They have gained population also at the expense of the rural districts by the movement of young people from the country into the urban areas. In the cities the birth rate has declined more rapidly than elsewhere and the inevitable distinctions between town and country have thereby been accentuated. Bryce viewed the growth of cities in the light of the experience of the preceding fifty years with greater apprehensions than were aroused by his contemplation of any other feature of the American scene. Now after another half-century a majority of the American people dwell in cities and the American scene is more radically transformed than even Bryce ventured to anticipate.

The growth of cities has been accompanied by an unparalleled development of mechanical industry and commerce. Along with increased size goes diversification of function and accelerated technological change. The electric dynamo and the internal combustion engine, little known and less exploited in the middle 'eighties, give contemporary mankind a phenomenal command of physical power, making the age of steam, so dazzling in the eyes of Bryce's contemporaries, seem now almost as primitive as the earlier age of wind and water. The improvement in the means of transportation and of communication surpasses even the advance of manufacturing, if an anachronistic name may still be applied to the basic processes of production. The motion picture and the radio revolutionize both a nation's means of amusement and the fundamental processes of politics. Bryce possessed a rare fertility of political and social imagination. But even Bryce could not foresee the transformation of society and politics which has been produced in America by the ingenuity, persistence, and resourcefulness of our Edisons, Wrights, and Fords.

The consequences of technological change have been matched by the advance in the art of business organization itself. The modern business corporation is a phenomenon so familiar in the contemporary business world that it already is accepted by businessmen as an integral part of the order of nature itself. The impatient reformer who would curb its abuses and render the new device in the field of business organization more serviceable to mankind tends to be regarded with the same suspicion as one who would tamper with the Bill of Rights or otherwise profane the handiwork of the Founding Fathers. Bryce offers some suggestive thoughts for such defenders of the orthodox economic faith. "No invention of modern times," he wrote with disarming innocence, "has so changed the face of commerce and delighted lawyers with a variety of new and intricate problems as the creation of incorporated joint-stock companies." [3] It has indeed delighted lawyers. It has also revolutionized the practical administration of the business system.

These changes bring us to the heart of modern capitalism. Bryce did not fail to include in his book a chapter on Wall Street. But he wholly failed to perceive its future significance. He discussed organized speculation in securities and commodities from the standpoint of its effect upon the

[3] Bryce, *op. cit.*, Vol. 3, Ch. 101, p. 415.

manners and the nervous systems of Americans. The habit of speculation, he thought, might tend to increase the nervous tension of that already tense and nervous people. But "so far as politics are concerned," he added, "I do not know that Wall Street does any harm." [4] Perhaps no change during the last half-century in America strikes the contemporary observer as more significant than the change in the relations between Wall Street, Main Street, and Pennsylvania Avenue. It is more than a change of attitude. It is a change in the essential character of the American Commonwealth.

Bryce's anticipations concerning the future influence of businessmen in general went as far astray as those concerning the political influence of Wall Street. The Coolidge era was definitely beyond his horizon. He could not believe that businessmen as a class would continue to play so important a part in American life as they were playing in the eighteen-eighties. Victorian Englishmen felt an inherited deference for the administrator of public affairs which they could not feel towards the ordinary private businessman. Bryce as a University graduate possessed perhaps more than his share of this traditional attitude. The general tone of American business, particularly that part of it dominated by the great capitalists and exploiters of natural resources, seemed to him definitely below the level of the best elements in American life. He was sanguine enough to predict that the supremacy of the businessman in America would not last. "As the pressure of effort towards material success is relaxed," he wrote, "as the number of men devoted to science, art and learning increases, so will the dominance of what may be called the business mind decline." [5] Time may

---

[4] Bryce, *op. cit.*, Vol. 3, Ch. 101, p. 421.
[5] Bryce, *op. cit.*, Vol. 3, Ch. 113, p. 633.

yet prove Bryce right in this opinion, but meanwhile the extent to which the "business mind" succeeded in dominating the American scene attests the limitations of the most intelligent foresight.

The American Bar also failed to receive the appreciation that might have been expected from a man of Bryce's high legal scholarship. The Bar, he opined, counted for less than formerly in practical politics. The evidence in support of this opinion does not now seem as convincing as it did to Bryce. In the Federalist era lawyers had certainly held a prominent place. Though neither Washington nor Franklin received any legal training, the actual framing of the Constitution of 1787 was largely the work of the lawyers in the Federal Convention. Subsequently the Supreme Court under John Marshall's vigorous leadership gave the legal fraternity a paramount influence in the development of American institutions which was as surprising a performance to contemporary politicians as it is impressive in the eyes of posterity. But in Bryce's time also lawyers held a place in the practical working of the institutions of the country which only seems less impressive today because public affairs were then less spectacular than in the time of the Founding Fathers. Leading planters and merchants were in fact no less prominent in American politics in the Federalist era than the captains of industry and other millionaires a century later who made such an unfavorable impression upon Bryce.

It was the influence upon the Bar of the great business corporations that most disturbed Bryce in the eighteen-eighties. The "decadence in the Bar of the greater cities," he wrote, was due to "the growth of enormously rich and powerful corporations, willing to pay vast sums for questionable services." [6] The businessmen connected with the great corporations seemed to him to form a class apart from ordinary businessmen. They personified a new phenomenon in the business world, to Bryce a strange and ominous phenomenon, the peculiarly American system of corporate enterprise. This system at once fascinated and disturbed him.

The development of corporate enterprise a half-century ago reached its peak in what Bryce described with evident admiration as "that prodigy of labor, wealth, and skill — the American railway system." He was deeply impressed by the "splendid boldness with which financial operations are conducted," by the "autocratic character" of railroad management, and by the great power of the railroads as revealed in their "inevitable conflicts with State governments." "War," he believed, "was the natural state of an American railway towards all other authorities." [7] No talents of the practical order, he thought, could be too high for such a position as that of a railroad president, and he dwelt with obvious relish upon the concentration of power in their hands and upon their "almost uncontrolled" discretion. "These railway kings," he declared in a final burst of enthusiasm, "are among the greatest men, perhaps I may say,

---

[6] Bryce, op. cit., Vol. 3, Ch. 98, p. 382. Seventeen years after the publication of The American Commonwealth the author renewed his criticism of American lawyers, as follows: "Lawyers are now to a greater extent than formerly business men, a part of the great organized system of industrial and financial enterprise. They are less than formerly the students of a particular kind of learning, the practitioners of a particular art. And they do not seem to be quite so much of a distinct professional class. . . . They still comprise a large part of the finest intellect of the Nation. But one is told they do not take so keen an interest in purely legal and constitutional questions as they did in the days of Story and Webster, or even in those of William M. Evarts and Charles O'Conor. Business is king." The Outlook, Vol. 79, p. 734 (March 25, 1905).

[7] Bryce, op. cit., Vol. 3, Ch. 100, p. 400.

are the greatest men in America." [8] And he goes on to marvel at their wealth, their fame, and their power. They travel in "palace" cars; their journeys are like "royal" progresses. They yield in grandeur only to the very greatest authorities in the land, the President of the United States and the Speaker of the House of Representatives.

Such great power, Bryce clearly recognized, brought with it great problems. "It may therefore be conjectured," he concluded, "that the railroad will stand forth as a great and perplexing force in the economico-political life of the United States. It cannot be left to itself — the most extreme advocate of *laissez faire* would not contend for that, for to leave it to itself would be to make it a tyrant. It cannot be absorbed and worked by the National government — only the most sanguine state socialist would propose to impose so terrible a strain on the virtue of American politicians, and so seriously to disturb the constitutional balance between the States and the Federal authority. Many experiments may be needed before the true mean course between these extremes is discovered. Meanwhile, the railroads illustrate two tendencies specially conspicuous in America — the power of the principle of association, which makes commercial corporations, skillfully handled, formidable to individual men; and the way in which the principle of monarchy, banished from the field of government, creeps back again and asserts its strength in the scarcely less momentous contests of industry and finance." [9]

How right Bryce was in estimating the power and the menace of the great railroad corporations and of their dictatorial executives the history of subsequent years abun-

[8] Bryce, *op. cit.*, Vol. 3, Ch. 100, p. 412.
[9] Bryce, *op. cit.*, Vol. 3, Ch. 100, p. 414.

dantly demonstrated. The struggle to assert the superiority of public over private interests in the management of the American railway system was hard fought and long doubtful. Years passed after Bryce first published his warning before Theodore Roosevelt was able to force the Hepburn Act through Congress and definitively establish the supremacy of the public interest. Now after half a century the desperate plight of the American railway system has nearly obliterated the memory of its former grandeur and the pride of the once-mighty railroad president has yielded to a new and almost incredible humility. It is scarcely possible to believe that a perspicacious observer as sanguine as Bryce was once so pessimistic as to have written: "I doubt whether any congressional legislation will greatly reduce the commanding positions which these potentates hold as the masters of enterprises whose wealth, geographical extension, and influence upon the growth of the country and the fortunes of individuals, find no parallel in the Old World."

If Bryce could not foresee the adoption and consequences of effective measures for the regulation of railroads, still less could he foresee the influence of the World War and the Great Depression upon the power of accumulated wealth and specially of the great corporations. The World War transformed the United States from a debtor into a creditor country and at the same time transformed the American Government from a minor factor in the world of business and finance into the greatest both of debtors and of creditors. Finance-capital reached the zenith of its power in the decade culminating in the Wall Street crash of October, 1929. In 1929 the head of one of New York's greatest banks could flout the warnings of the Federal Reserve Board and defy the wishes of the United States Treasury itself. But the pride of the Mitchells and the Wiggins went before a very great fall, and the power which had been theirs slipped from the less resolute hands of their chastened successors in Wall Street and drifted away into the clutches of the New Dealers on Pennsylvania Avenue. More appropriate than ever were Bryce's prophetic words about the speed of change in our age. America is indeed a land of change.

What, it is now in order to inquire, were the grounds for Bryce's stubborn, though not unqualified, optimism concerning the results of the process of change, and what further are the grounds for believing that the Americans of today are entitled to cherish the same optimism as the Bryce of a half-century ago? Already in 1888 he was convinced that the economic changes which he noted would provoke legislative attacks upon accumulated wealth, directed in the first instance against the great business corporations. He foresaw the growth of special taxes upon corporations and of stricter regulation of public franchises. But the prospect of drastic anti-trust laws and of vigorous action against the railroads and other public utilities did not disturb the equanimity with which he habitually viewed the future of the American Commonwealth. What then were the reasons for his serene confidence in the success of reform, and how valid are they today?

Bryce offered three reasons for his conviction that the tendency of the times was towards the improvement of democracy in America and that the public life of the country would eventually be brought nearer to the ideal which he believed democracy was bound to set before itself. The first of these reasons was the absence of class distinctions and of class hatred. In Europe hatred of the privileged classes rested upon ancient and persistent distinctions between them and their inferiors and was an accepted feature of the political scene. In America, he observed, class distinctions were comparatively obscure and lightly regarded. The traditions of the country worked strongly against the growth of class-consciousness among the white population, and seemed capable of sustaining the official creed summarized in the phrase, equality of opportunity.[10]

The second reason for Bryce's optimism was the diffusion of wealth among an immense number of small proprietors all of whom were interested in the defense of property. In Europe peasant proprietorship was widely extended in the French Republic and in other countries which had been deeply touched by the French Revolution, but even in these countries the average size of the holdings was small, and jealousy, if not hatred, of the privileged classes was rampant. Generally in Europe the great landlords continued to retain many of their hereditary privileges as well as most of their estates, and the attitude of the peasantry was as definitely conditioned by their circumstances as was that of the industrial wage-earners dependent upon mass-employment by capitalistic enterprise. In America the independent farmers were owners as well as workers, and were accustomed to look upon the government as something designed primarily for their service. They might hate particular politicians whom they suspected of undue subservience to special interests. They might even hate the great corporations in an abstracted kind of way. But they could not hate the capitalists as a class. "I do not think," Bryce wrote, "that the ruling magnates are themselves generally disliked. On the contrary, they receive that tribute

[10] Bryce, *op. cit.*, Vol. 3, Ch. 115, p. 660.

of admiration which the American gladly pays to whoever has done best what everyone desires to do."

The third reason was the exemption of the American people from chronic pauperism and what Bryce called "economical distress." The poor, of course, the Americans, like other peoples, had always with them. But poverty in America was a personal accident rather than a social maladjustment. For the able-bodied and industrious man without property there was always the possibility of a farm of his own from the public lands at the cost of the labor of reducing it to cultivation. In 1888 neither the public lands in the West nor the older soils in the East were exhausted. For those whose misfortunes denied them access to these opportunities there was always charity. Under such circumstances the acceptance of charity involved no stigma and, in fact, charity was cheerful and abundant.

This sanguine view of the future in America, Bryce conceded, omitted certain considerations. First, it assumed that the country would be left to itself. Yet it was certain that the country could not be left altogether to itself. There was the rising tide of alien immigration, a tide destined to sweep into the United States vast numbers of foreigners ignorant of American traditions and steeped in hostile traditions of their own. At this point in the argument Bryce's stubborn optimism comes to the aid of his logic. "The intellectual and moral atmosphere into which the settlers from Europe come has more power to assimilate them than their race qualities have power to change it; . . . the future of America will be less affected by this influx of new blood than any one who has not studied the American democracy of today can realize." [11]

[11] Bryce, *op. cit.*, Vol. 3, Ch. 116, p. 674.

The second consideration which, according to Bryce, should not be omitted was that the chronic evils and problems of old societies and crowded countries would reappear on American soil with the further growth of population and of its congestion in great cities. He cited "high economic authorities" for the opinion that the exhaustion of good land in the public domain was imminent and that pressure on the resources of the country would be felt within a measurable period of years. Diminishing returns to the industry of the farmer could not fail to react upon the conditions of life in the cities. Increasing recourse to the cities by the surplus population from the country districts as well as from abroad could not fail to sharpen the struggle for existence. The traditional equality of opportunity in America would have less meaning for those upon whom the burden of the struggle would rest most heavily, and permanent discontent, as in Europe, would tend to prevail among the underprivileged.

In response to such doleful anticipations Bryce had not much to offer beyond evidently wishful thinking. There were elements of strength in America, he opined, lacking in Europe: notably (1) the unlikelihood, as he saw it, of class hatred growing out of the struggles between capital and labor, as carried on in America; (2) the likelihood of a continuance of the equable distribution of land; (3) the likelihood that the habit of moderation in thought and action would stand unimpaired; and (4) "the restraining and conciliating influence of religion." In view of these possibilities he stoutly adhered to his conclusion that "we may look forward to the future, not indeed without anxiety, when we mark the clouds that hang on the horizon, yet with a hope that is stronger than anxiety." [12]

[12] Bryce, *op. cit.*, Vol. 3, Ch. 115, p. 664.

Now after fifty years — and that was the period of time Bryce had in mind as he wrote with his thoughts on the future — it is clear that he was correct in admitting the necessity of allowing for these two considerations. Was he also correct in minimizing their practical importance? Do they seriously affect the soundness of the conclusions which he drew from his three manifestly good reasons for believing that the prospects for the successful reform of the then-existing evils were favorable?

In the first place, it is impossible to deny that Bryce was over-sanguine concerning the tendency of the struggles between capital and labor in America. Both capital and labor are much better organized now than they were fifty years ago. The C.I.O. has succeeded to the position then held by the Knights of Labor as the leading rival of the A.F. of L., and the unification of the labor movement seems as remote as ever. Nevertheless, labor is definitely more self-conscious than it was, and capital, which was very self-conscious then, seems no less so now. The self-consciousness of labor and capital, respectively, is certainly not identical with class-consciousness in the European style, but the influence of European attitudes has spread to America and class-consciousness of a sort has evidently sprung up to an extent not anticipated by Bryce. Class-hatred is far from constituting a social evil of the same order as in Europe, but there is enough of it to lower perceptibly the barriers against the reappearance on American soil of what Bryce called the chronic evils and problems of old societies and crowded countries.

Secondly, the equable distribution of land has proved an institution of less vitality than Bryce anticipated. Speculative operations in farm lands, the increasing burden of debt upon farmers working their own holdings, and the ominous growth of farm tenancy and absentee ownership, have rudely disturbed the predominant uniformity of the American system of free and equal proprietorship in agriculture. In all sections of the country divergent class interests have emerged in rural areas, and in the South the special problem of the sharecroppers has further complicated the general situation. Agricultural laborers everywhere seem further removed from land-ownership than a half-century ago, and capitalists whose investments have been secured by farm lands likewise seem further removed from the working farmer. The calamitous loss in recent years of European markets for the surplus products of American farms and the prodigal intervention of the Federal Government in the processes of raising and marketing farm products has profoundly altered the nature of the agricultural interest in American politics. The most sympathetic reader of *The American Commonwealth* after fifty years must concede that the author's optimism under this head has not been sustained by the course of events.

Thirdly, there is to be considered Bryce's confidence in the habitual moderation of American thought and action. On this point, there is much to be said in favor of the view that no grave impairment of this invaluable habit on the part of a self-governing people has been suffered in the course of the last half-century. If it be assumed that Bryce was correct in imputing to the Americans of the eighteen-eighties, as compared with their European contemporaries, the quality of political moderation, it seems justifiable to conclude that on the whole that excellent quality has been remarkably well preserved. The two-party system in national politics — the most decisive evidence of the moderation of political behavior under a representative govern-

ment — continues to flourish despite the attacks of radicals
and reactionaries. Repeated attempts on the part of ambitious politicians to effect the formation of influential third
parties have come to nothing. It has not been possible even
to bring about a drastic realignment of the existing major
parties, though exceptionally spirited campaigns, notably
the Bryan campaign of 1896 and the New Deal campaign
of 1932, seem to have brought about some permanent
changes in the distribution of partisans. The history of
partisan politics up to now seems to justify Bryce's confidence in the American habit of moderation.

To the contemporary observer criticism of the administration in power almost always seems extraordinarily violent and reckless. To one who takes a long view of the
political scene contemporary partisan controversy seems
extraordinarily restrained and temperate by comparison
with the tone of similar controversy abroad or at various
earlier periods in American politics. To a New Dealer,
smarting under the criticisms of a publicity agent for an
economic royalist, the traditional habit of political moderation may seem ruined beyond hope of redemption. To the
dispassionate historian the manners, if not the actual temper, of partisan controversy form a striking contrast with
the customary intemperate strictures upon the conduct of
public affairs in the times of Lincoln, Jackson, Jefferson,
and Washington. As long as the two great parties continue
to be dominated by middle-class attitudes and sentiments,
the habit of political moderation, which Bryce rightly regarded as one of the important grounds for optimism
about the future of the American Commonwealth, seems
likely to continue unimpaired.

Finally, what shall be recorded after fifty years about

the restraining and conciliating influence of religion? Concerning religion in general Bryce's published observations were tantalizingly inadequate. "Few mistakes are more common," he noted in a chapter on the influence of democracy on thought, "than that of exaggerating the influence of forms of government." Presently he added the further reflection: "The presence of evangelical Protestantism has been quite as important a factor in the intellectual life of the nation as its form of government." [13] Holding such opinions as these, the reader of his comprehensive treatise on democracy in America would expect to find him devoting a large space to the discussion of the influence of religion. In fact there are only two short chapters on that subject in all his great work. He notes that free government has prospered best among religious peoples and adds that America seems unlikely to drift from her religious moorings. For the rest, religious ideas and religious institutions alike are studiously ignored.

Whatever importance Bryce may have attached in his own mind to the influence of evangelical Protestantism upon the development of American democracy, it is beyond contradiction that that particular form of the Protestant religion can not contribute as much to the stability of the political institutions of today as it contributed to the stability of the institutions of fifty years ago. The varieties of religious practice in contemporary America are much greater than in Bryce's time and the relative importance of different varieties is changed. It is questionable whether religion on the whole exerts as great an influence in America as formerly, though certain religious bodies have grown greatly in political importance. Yet the impress of colonial

[13] Bryce, *op. cit.*, Vol. 3, Ch. 107, p. 554.

Protestantism remains deeply marked upon the fundamental processes of political thought. The eighteenth-century notion that there is a higher law than that embodied in written constitutions by the hand of man remains a force to be reckoned with by the advocates of that favorite creed of dictators, the modern doctrine of national sovereignty. The revolutionary practice of appealing to the conscience of the common man against the arbitrary pretensions of tyrannical rulers can still be cited in support of resistance to the harbingers of returning despotism. Religion is undoubtedly a latent force of great potentiality in American politics, but whether it be a force likely to exert a restraining and conciliating influence remains to be seen.

This brief survey of "the elements of strength" upon which Bryce relied for justification of his hopeful attitude in looking forward to the future of the American Commonwealth will perhaps suffice to show how precarious were his grounds for believing that the future in America would be greatly different from that in Europe. To be sure, even Bryce's sanguine disposition failed to foresee some of the circumstances which would add new elements of strength in America. Most important among these seem to have been the restriction of immigration, the reduction of the size of families, technological improvements in the production of wealth, and above all the astonishing flow of new and valuable ideas for the gratification of human wants. Cheap electricity, new sources of power, the automobile, the motion picture, the radio, the whole amazing variety of unforeseen and useful products of inventive genius and organized research have overruled the law of diminishing returns. Yet the cold facts remain that the exclusion of European immigrants can not prevent the importation of European ideas from threatening the predominance of the domestic traditions, and that family limitation can not prevent the growth of human wants from outstripping the means of gratifying them. Technological improvements make unemployment as well as work, and the abundance of new and valuable ideas in the field of material production may reveal all the more disastrously the dearth of new and valuable ideas in the field of human relations. Certainly the condition of the American Commonwealth after fifty years is greatly changed, as Bryce anticipated, but what has been most clearly vindicated by the process of change is his too-candid avowal that all he could surely say of the future was that it would be unlike the present.

What then is to be said, in the light of the actual experience of the last half-century, concerning the tendency towards the improvement of democracy in America, which Bryce thought he discerned, and the grounds of his hope that the public life of the country would eventually be brought nearer to the democratic ideal? We are constrained by the course of events to admit that poverty seems more likely to become chronic than Bryce anticipated, the diffusion of wealth more likely to be less equable, and class-consciousness more intense. Are we then to conclude that Bryce was over-sanguine and that the future of the American Commonwealth can not be as bright as anticipated? Must we radically revise the horoscope which he cast so hopefully and which two generations of Americans have found so comforting? For answers to these questions we may turn from theoretical speculations, as Bryce himself would doubtless have done, and examine the actual record of events for signs of their intrinsic meaning.

The most adequate test of the trend of the times in

America, as far at least as concerns the future of the American Commonwealth, is the influence of events upon the particular institutions which Bryce himself considered most significant in this connection. These institutions are: (1) federalism; (2) the separation of powers and their distribution among the three branches of the constitutional government; and (3) the party system. Bryce analyzed with care the processes of change as he saw them operating in each of these institutions. He noted the effects of the changes which had already occurred upon the stability of the political system as a whole. In the light of these effects he proceeded to forecast future trends with more confidence than one would have expected from his general observations on the hazards of prediction. These forecasts of the future in the concluding chapters of his great work made a deep impression on the minds of contemporary readers. In order to appraise the present value of Bryce's work the same task needs to be performed again in the light of the evidence afforded by the subsequent half-century.

On the future of federalism Bryce wrote with prudent circumspection. Secession, a vivid recollection in the minds of Bryce's contemporaries, was an experiment the repetition of which he pronounced improbable. The extinction of the states by absorption into the central government was also in his opinion improbable. It had been generally believed in Europe, he reminded his readers, when the Unionists triumphed over the Confederates in 1865, that the federal system was virtually at an end. But this had not happened. Nevertheless, it was impossible, Bryce believed, to ignore the growing strength of the centripetal and unifying forces. The importance of the states, he concluded, would decline as the majesty and authority of the national government increased.

This pleasantly vague prediction has been abundantly confirmed by the course of events. The authority of the national government, whatever may be thought of its majesty, has certainly increased, and the states have become relatively much less important in the American political system. Traditional phrases about the rights of the states continue to be repeated by opposition statesmen in need of rhetorical weapons against the measures of the statesmen in power. But the phrases reveal lack of imagination as well as lack of votes and are rarely remembered by those who use them when they become in their turn responsible for the conduct of public affairs. It is clear that the centripetal forces have proved stronger than Bryce anticipated and the decline of the states has gone further than he ventured to predict. It is still too soon, doubtless, to speak of the extinction of the states, but the virtual end of the federal system in its original form is already in sight. The states have lost beyond the possibility of recovery every claim to the substance of sovereign statehood and have definitely sunk to the status of mere organs of local government.

Many factors have contributed to the transformation of the federal system, but most important among those not foreseen by Bryce are the increased demands which the people of modern commonwealths have learned to make upon their governments. The preamble to the Constitution of the United States says nothing about economic security, though broad phrases like domestic tranquillity and the general welfare, which its framers with happy prescience incorporated in it, may easily be construed by sympathetic interpretation to authorize such expansion of the functions of government as the changing spirit of the times may deem necessary and proper. Farmers and industrial workers feel the need of better protection against the hazards of the business cycle and clamor for more generous assistance in their efforts to acquire the goods which they can not produce for themselves in exchange for the products of their own labor. Unorthodox but persuasive economists assure them that their lives might be much more comfortable and secure, if governments would do what they might to bring law and order into industry. Businessmen grieve at political encroachments upon their once-profitable functions, but the need for a longer view in planning for the satisfaction of common wants than is compatible with the requirements of annual balance-sheets continues to clear the way for the extension of collective enterprise.

The need for greater foresight and comprehensiveness in planning and for greater efficiency in the execution of the plans puts new stresses and strains on the machinery of government. It is necessary that the machinery of government be more powerful, as well as more intelligently directed, if the services of the modern commonwealth shall be adequate under the conditions of modern times. Not only must larger numbers of civil servants be employed, but also more technical and professional competence must become available, to the end that the officers in charge of the public business may hold their own with the capitalists and the labor-leaders, the politicians and the lobbyists, with whom they have to deal. Public business management must gain and retain the confidence of the public. The organization and operation of public business must be improved and made more efficient without sacrificing the rights of the individual.

In meeting the new requirements of our time the governments of the states have been notoriously inadequate. It is by no means universally true that the tendency of modern government is to move the functions of government to successively larger units, but it is perfectly clear that the smaller states are far less competent than the larger states to perform many of the most important functions of the states in the American federal system. The largest state in the Union contains more than one hundred times as many inhabitants as the smallest, and sends more congressmen to Washington than the eighteen smallest states combined. While the largest states maintain governments in which the organization of public business can take full advantage of the progress of the science of public administration, if their politicians are willing, for the average state this is scarcely possible. One-third of the forty-eight states possess less than half the population of the average state, and in these states the small scale upon which the public business is conducted does not admit of such a division of labor in public administration as is requisite for true economy and efficiency. Whatever may be thought of the states as instruments for the protection of individual rights, it is incontestable that the greater number of them are too small to be equal to the exacting requirements for the successful management of the kind of public business a state is expected to carry on in the modern world.

The incompetence of the states resulting from the small size of many of them is magnified by the consequences of their unequal financial resources. It has been estimated that the yield of a standardized tax plan for defraying the cost of government in the states will vary from less than twenty dollars per capita in several of the Southern states to more than one hundred dollars per capita in New York and Delaware. Several of the larger Northeastern states can probably raise by taxation four or five times as much per capita as most of the Southern states can raise with the same effort and sacrifice on the part of their inhabitants. These financial inequalities are reflected in the expenditures for important public services. Ten of the states, for instance, spend more than ninety dollars a year per pupil in the public schools. Eleven spend less than half of that amount. The states in which the public schools are most generously supported spend more than four times as much per pupil as those in which the least is spent. To bring these states with inferior educational opportunities merely up to the present average for the country as a whole would require hundreds of millions of dollars annually in addition to the sums now raised for the public schools in those states. It is evident that under these conditions the states can not be equally acceptable instruments of government and that many of them can not be expected to maintain even a tolerable standard of public service.

Lack of population and of tax power tend to undermine the governing capacity of many states. "The small unit of government," as another English critic of American government, Harold J. Laski, has observed recently in discussing what he calls "the obsolescence of federalism," is "impotent against the big unit of giant capitalism." The obvious exaggeration in this statement does not destroy its probative usefulness. The scale of industrial operations in the United States has grown enormously in the last half-century, while the boundaries of the states remain as before. The practical incapacity of the states to deal effectively with the great combinations of capital is no more clearly revealed by the history of the anti-trust laws than is the inadequacy of state efforts to repress ordinary crime emphasized by the enactment of the Lindbergh laws. Only a few of the greater states can command the reserves of professional skill and technical talent necessary to enable them to vie with the national government in the utilization of the most modern methods of government and administration. For the great number of the states there seems nothing ahead but a vista of growing inadequacy and declining public confidence.

Universal recognition of the impaired efficiency of the federal system was long delayed by the reluctance of the Supreme Court of the United States to give to the commerce clause of the Constitution the broad interpretation demanded by the march of time. The effect of the stubborn adherence by a majority of the Court to a narrow view of the constitutional provisions which distribute power between the national and state governments will be considered presently in another connection. In this connection it should suffice to call attention to the recent decisions which have sustained congressional legislation concerning matters formerly deemed to be within the exclusive province of the state governments. Since the validation of the Wagner Act and of the Agricultural Adjustment Act of 1938, to say nothing of the abdication of state authority under the stimulus of federal subsidies and subventions, it is apparent that the traditional federal system can not survive. To think of the members of the Federal Union as free and sovereign states, as many Americans once did and some professed to do again in the years of the Eighteenth Amendment, is a meaningless anachronism.

To think of the extinction of the states, however, is

manifestly unjustifiable. The stronger states serve as convenient instrumentalities of regional opinion and local self-government. They facilitate the expression of various points of view concerning the functions and practice of government; they help to maintain the rights of the people against threatened encroachments from reckless leaders and subversive movements; they constitute one of the principal securities against the denial of due process of law. Doubtless the governments of the states could serve these purposes more effectively, if at least half of them could be abolished and their inhabitants redistributed among the remaining states or among new and more perfect states created for the purpose. But it is impossible to suppose that those in charge of the smaller state governments would consent to this, especially as long as the smallest among them can find demoralizingly profitable ways of exploiting their privileges as equals of the greatest under the fundamental law of the Federal Union.

The unforeseen extent of the decline of the states and the practical impossibility of reorganizing the weaker among them have created for the national government the problem of finding new safeguards against the excessive centralization of power. This becomes all the more necessary, since the weaker states, regarded as agencies of the national government, have proved little less unsatisfactory than as independent instrumentalities of local self-government. A striking phenomenon of recent years has been the attempted utilization of the state governments for the administration of national policies under the supervision of the national government. But the results have been disappointing. Experience under the Social Security Act has confirmed the fears of those who argued that in general the national government should rely for the execution of its laws upon agencies under its direct control. The advantages of such a course are obvious. But the continued expansion of the activities of the national government increases the importance of proper measures of decentralization in the actual conduct of public business. It is not prudent to permit all the authority of the modern service state to be gathered together at a single point.

The first step in the decentralization of federal power is the organization of suitable administrative districts for the activities under the direct control of the national government. Even more striking than the expansion of federal influence in recent years through the grant of financial aid to the state governments has been the multiplication of regional and district offices of federal administrative agencies. In 1935 more than seventy such agencies maintained a total of over a hundred separate systems of administrative districts. To bring the administrative branch of the national government into closer touch with local opinion it is necessary to establish better order in the tangled skein of district administration. Effective decentralization requires the selection of convenient regional centers, where the multifarious activities of district officers may be coördinated under the watchful eye of local interests in each region. Already New York, Chicago, and San Francisco have become outstanding centers of federal administration. The emergence of perhaps half a dozen other regional centers of federal administration would provide the framework for the gradual development of an effective system of collaboration on the part of regional interests in the work of the federal agencies.

It is not necessary to look forward to the creation of

any single standard system of administrative areas to make federal decentralization an acceptable substitute for obsolescent federalism. Federal Reserve districts, army corps areas, the geographical jurisdictions of the Circuit Courts of Appeal, and many other regional schemes may continue to serve their various needs. It is not uniform boundaries between administrative districts but a stable arrangement of regional centers, that forms the requisite basis of effective federal decentralization. But of such problems there is no discussion in Bryce's *American Commonwealth*. The rise of federal administrative centers in regions instead of states lay beyond his horizon.

Bryce's concluding reflections concerning the separation of powers and their distribution among the three branches of the constitutional government, like those on federalism, were for the time bold and perspicacious. He noted the great vicissitudes which had marked the relations between the Congress, the President, and the Supreme Court. That no permanent disturbance of the balance between them had resulted "shows how well the balance had been adjusted at starting." Bryce was convinced that "at this moment there is nothing to show that any one department is gaining on any other." [14] The national government might be gaining authority at the expense of the states, but the relations between its several parts, Bryce was convinced, tended to remain as before.

Congress, Bryce observed, was the branch of the government with the largest facilities for usurping the powers of the other branches. It had constantly tried to encroach on the authority of the Chief Executive. The struggles between them gratified his fondness for political drama. He

[14] Bryce, *op. cit.*, Vol. 3, Ch. 115, p. 654.

dwelt at length and with obvious zest upon the conflict between "King Andrew" Jackson and the great Whig leaders in the Senate. The conflict between the Radical Republicans and Andrew Johnson furnished another dramatic illustration of his theme. The balance between President and Congress seemed to have swung far from the point of equilibrium. But hitherto it had not failed to swing back.

With persuasive logic Bryce reached the negative conclusion that "Congress has not become any more distinctly than in earlier days the dominant power in the state." In fact, its power, as compared with that of public opinion, seemed to him rather to have declined. The Senate, he believed, had "lost as much in the intellectual authority of its members as it [had] gained in their wealth." The House "suffers from the want of internal organization, and seems unable to keep pace with the increasing demands made on it for constructive legislation." [15] Congress would retain its established position, he thought, because of the inability of the people to provide a better servant. Bryce's poor opinion of the House may be recalled by the present generation with little surprise. His unflattering description of the Senate gives a greater shock to present-day Americans, especially those who have believed that the Senate was not improved by the substitution of direct popular elections for the original practice of election by the state legislatures.

Few contemporary Americans will contest Bryce's dictum that the inability of the people to provide a better servant affords the best assurance we possess that the Congress will retain its established position. The Congress labors

[15] Bryce, *op. cit.*, Vol. 3, Ch. 115, p. 655.

under many disadvantages in the struggle for popular favor. It gets no praise for doing what the public wants it to do, since this is what is expected of it. If it does the unpopular thing, it may serve the public interest well, but it naturally can not expect to gain popularity thereby. Always it must do its thinking out loud, and make up its mind in what appears to be an agony of indecision. It must strive ever to protect the public interest against selfish private and local interests, but it is nobody's business to thank it for so doing. If it works harmoniously with the President, it is accused of being a rubber-stamp, and if it resolutely opposes the presidential wishes, it is denounced as obstructive.

The rise of well-organized special interests and the growth of pressure politics has deprived the Congress of much of the initiative in legislative policy which it formerly possessed. The increase in its size has reduced the importance of the individual Congressman and Senator. Better organization and more businesslike rules of procedure have doubtless improved the efficiency of the House, but the resulting enhanced prestige has benefited a handful of leaders and reduced still further the importance of the ordinary member. The Senate on the whole has probably gained from the practice of direct election, which gives its members a clearer mandate to speak for public opinion in their respective states, but the costs of election remain excessively high, and the introduction of the radio has favored a few of the more conspicuous leaders, as better organization has done in the House, at the expense of the ordinary Senators. There seems no ground for challenging the conclusion that Congress has not become more distinctly the dominant power than in Bryce's time.

The weakness of the Congress, according to Bryce, is

the strength of the President.. What Bryce called the un-
developed possibilities of greatness in the presidency seem
to be implicit in the office. The changes of the last half-
century have manifestly tended to emphasize these possibilities. Yet Bryce's caution in dealing with them is as
clearly called for now as in his time. The realization of
these possibilities, he affirmed, depends "on the wholly un-
predictable element of personal capacity in the men who
may fill the office." [16]

The appraisal of presidential capacity must be conducted
in accordance with the appropriate point of view. From
the view-point of their relations with the Congress, presidents may be roughly classified under three types. First,
there are those masterful presidents who have been able to
establish their supremacy in national politics on the firm
basis of executive independence combined with the leadership of a great national party. Secondly, there are those
rugged and indomitable individuals who have maintained
the independence of their office, though unable to gain or
keep the leadership of a dominant party. Finally, there are
the ordinary politicians and military heroes who have attained the presidency without developing the capacity
either to lead a major party or to secure themselves against
dependence on partisan or congressional leaders.

The record of the relations between the Congress and
the presidency since Bryce's time seems at first sight to confirm his conclusions. The balance between the two has
oscillated to and fro, but no permanent disturbance of the
equilibrium seems to have followed. Woodrow Wilson
and the two Roosevelts have been denounced as dictators,
but the first Roosevelt and Wilson were followed by presi-

[16] Bryce, op. cit., Vol. 3, Ch. 115, p. 656.

dents whom no one would accuse of dictatorship and of the second Roosevelt's successor it is obviously too soon for prudent political analysts to speak. The Congress has dominated the political scene at Washington with little regard to the wishes of the occupant of the White House during more than one administration in the last half-century, as it had done more than once when Bryce was studying American politics. Yet there are clearer signs than in Bryce's time that the future may not be altogether like the past.

The first sign of possibly impending change in the relative positions of the presidency and of the Congress is the apparent decline in the frequency of administrations under which there is a well-adjusted balance between the two institutions. More often in the last half-century than formerly one or the other of the two has been definitely in the ascendant. In the first century of American politics under the Constitution of 1787 there were four presidents who fell clearly within the first of the three categories described above. They were Washington, Jefferson, Jackson, and Lincoln. There were seven in the second category: the two Adamses, John Tyler, Zachary Taylor, Andrew Johnson, Rutherford B. Hayes, and Grover Cleveland. Cleveland is the only president clearly of this type in the period since 1888, while there have been three outstanding examples of the first type. It seems to be more necessary than before that a president be the leader of his party in order to be an independent and influential chief executive. Or perhaps the proper inference is, that a president who is strong enough to maintain the independence of his office will also under modern conditions be able to dominate his party as well. In short, it may not be clear whether the presidency or the Congress tends to gain authority at the expense of the other, but it seems increasingly difficult to maintain the nice balance between them which the framers of the Constitution originally had in view.

Another cause of disturbance to the constitutional balance of powers is the immense growth of the business of government. The resulting demand for the services of capable public business administrators tends to bring into the service of the national government a large class of men of superior energy and talent. These men throw the weight of their influence on the side of the executive. Congressmen may deplore the presence and activities of the brain-trusters, but the need for more brains in government is so great that by one means or another it is bound to be filled. It may be suspected that an important, if unavowed, reason for opposition in Congress to the Reorganization Bill of 1938 was the blow to the patronage implicit in the planned extension of the merit system. Lame-duck Congressmen, it may be conceded, often bring a needed human touch into the business of government, and political experience such as theirs is an indispensable ingredient in a thoroughly competent administrative system. But for the multifarious special skills which are increasingly in demand in federal administration it will be necessary to look more and more outside of politics.

Bryce's typically English and Victorian blindness to the importance of technical *expertise* in the administration of public affairs caused him to miss much of the significance of the fight for civil service reform which raged hotly at Washington in his time. The merit system is needed not only to weaken the power of professional politicians. It is needed also to strengthen the executive in order that it may cope effectively with the heavier demands upon government in a more highly organized age. This aspect of the merit system appears most clearly in its application to what has always been, and bids fair to continue to be, the most important field of public administration, namely the administration of justice. The spoils system has clung tenaciously to the appointment of government lawyers, and especially federal judges, and the effort to take the judges out of politics and to effect a redistribution of power between the judiciary and the more definitely political branches of the national government is perhaps the most significant development of recent times.

Bryce was clearly wrong in his estimate of the future of the judicial branch of the government. "The judiciary," he wrote, "if indeed the judges can be called a political department, would seem to have less discretionary power than seventy years ago, for by their own decisions they have narrowed the scope of their discretion." [17] He was thinking of the Dred Scott and legal tender decisions and of the heavy blow dealt by them to the prestige of the Supreme Court. A few years later the ill-considered attempt on the part of the Court to reassert its influence in national politics by the income tax decision seemed to confirm Bryce's opinion that the Court could claim political authority for itself only at the cost of popular confidence and prestige. Yet it is now clear that the courts generally were on the eve of a rapid advance in political power and public importance.

The unprecedented growth of the power of judicial review, particularly under the due process clauses in the Fifth and Fourteenth Amendments, gave the judiciary a practical capacity to nullify controversial measures of the Con-

[17] Bryce, *op. cit.*, Vol. 3, Ch. 115, p. 654.

gress and state legislatures unforeseen by Bryce. The disposition to interpose the judicial veto was not restrained by differences of opinion among the judges. During the terms of Chief Justices Fuller, White, and Taft political enactments to which a majority of the Supreme Court were opposed were vetoed with growing frequency and with little regard for the objections of the minority. William Jennings Bryan displayed remarkable prescience in his reference to this practice in his famous "cross of gold" speech at the Democratic National Convention of 1896. "Our opponents criticize us," he shouted, "because, they say, we criticize the Court. But we do not criticize the Court. We only call attention to what you already know. If you seek criticism, read the opinions of the dissenting judges."

The political activity of the Supreme Court reached a climax under Chief Justice Hughes. Despite the able and conciliatory leadership of the Chief Justice leading measures of the New Deal were vetoed, some of them by narrow majorities, over the strong protests of dissenting judges. "A tortured construction of the Constitution," to quote from the dissenting opinion of Justice Stone in the case which ended in the destruction of the first Agricultural Adjustment Act, could not be justified by such reasoning as was employed by the majority of the judges, and he reminded his heedless colleagues that "Courts are not the only agency of government that must be assumed to have capacity to govern." Forced to choose between an attack upon the Court and acquiescence in a course of construction which threatened to destroy the usefulness of the Constitution in times of crisis, the Roosevelt Administration led the attack. Fresh appointments to the Court have brought about a more tolerant attitude toward controversial legislation, and redressed the balance between the judiciary and the political branches of the government.

Banished from the center of the stage as a censor of political policy, the Supreme Court returns to the scene as a guardian of due process of law in the execution of public policies. This is a development which promises not only to conserve the influence of the judiciary but also greatly to strengthen the executive branch of the national government. It should lead to a sound division of labor between the judges and the other groups of technical experts in the public service. It should improve the work of public business administrators by the exercise of a kind of judicial review for which trained lawyers are well fitted. If the judges can resist the temptation to enforce their personal views concerning administrative policy under the guise of maintaining lawful processes of administration, thereby repeating the error into which they were drawn in the exercise of the power of judicial review in the field of legislative policy, they seem destined, like other groups of technical experts in the coming years, to play a bigger role in the conduct of public affairs than Bryce anticipated.

A redistribution of authority in the national government between the strictly political branches and those more particularly concerned with administration, so as to increase the influence and prestige of the latter, seems inevitable. This is a turn in the evolution of the doctrine of the separation of powers which Bryce did not foresee. The modern distinction between politics and administration originated in Great Britain and was already recognized in his time as sound. The delicate adjustment of the relations between the Cabinet Minister and the Permanent Undersecretary is one of the valuable British contributions to the art of constitutional government. Its adoption in the United States, partly as an addition to and partly as a substitute for the traditional separation into three kinds of power, though it has complicated the practice of government at Washington, promises for the future a more competent, and hence more powerful, administrative system than could be easily imagined in the days of the almost unrestrained operations of the spoilsmen. During the hot debate over Franklin D. Roosevelt's Reorganization Bill the cry of dictatorship was successfully raised to delay the advance of the new and higher-powered system of administration. The alarm was false, and the temporary success of the politicians can not be expected permanently to check the shifting of power from the political branches of the government, the presidency being by no means excluded, to those which are more strictly administrative in character.

The future of the party system was the third of the principal subjects of political speculation by which the value of Bryce's predictions may conveniently be appraised after fifty years. In discussing the political parties Bryce was more influenced by contemporary conditions than in dealing with federalism and the separation of powers. Both of these features of the American political system had been fixed in the written constitution, and the processes of change were preconditioned by the letter as well as the spirit of the fundamental law. The party system, on the contrary, was alien to the thought of the Founding Fathers, and received no sanction from the original principles bequeathed by them to their successors. Any system of political parties was a dreaded accident in a country where no system had been wanted.

The particular bi-partisan system, which eventually developed, was one to which the leaders of American opinion only slowly became reconciled. Washington plainly envisaged a one-party system, in which all friends of the new and more perfect Union would rally to the leadership of "the wise and the good." Nothing during his presidency distressed him more than the persistence of what seemed to be merely factious opposition. Jefferson in his celebrated first inaugural claimed that all Americans were at heart both Federalists and Democratic-Republicans, like himself. In fact under his prudent leadership, sustained by the moderation of his successors, organized opposition to the governing party eventually collapsed. The true origin of the American bi-partisan system dates from the party struggles of the Jackson era. The Whig coalition, deliberately formed by the anti-Jackson leaders in all sections of the country, was the first genuine opposition party in the modern sense of the term.

Bryce formed an unfavorable opinion of the system of bi-partisan politics practiced in America. In Great Britain the struggles of Liberals and Conservatives seemed to him to turn upon questions of principle, as the names suggest. He conceded that partisan controversies in America also in the days of Jackson and of Lincoln appeared to have been inspired by questions of principle. But in his own time all traces of principle had been lost, he thought, and the battles of the parties were waged solely for the spoils of victory. War cries, slogans, and symbols the parties possessed, but rational causes of controversy seemed totally lacking.

Bryce was deeply interested in the psychology of politics. The motives of politicians, the technique of campaigning, the temper of the voters, these engrossed his attention.

On the whole, he did not like what he saw. "Nothing in recent history suggests," he wrote, "that the statesmen who claim to be party leaders, or the politicians who act as party managers, are disposed either to loosen the grip with which their organization has clasped the country, or to improve the methods it employs." [18] Even his inveterate optimism almost deserted him. "Changes in party methods there will of course be in the future, as there have been in the past; but the professionals are not the men to make the changes for the better." His hopes for real betterment rested with the civil service reformers and the Mugwumps.

It is evident that political psychology is not enough to produce an adequate interpretation of partisan politics. The Mugwumps and many other independent political movements have come and gone in the last half-century, while the professional politicians seem as busy and influential as ever. The official ballot, the merit system, and many another reform in the processes of government have been introduced, and have accomplished genuine improvement. Still the system of bi-partisan politics flourishes as before. There have been great vicissitudes in the fortunes of the two great parties, but neither success nor failure has greatly altered the character of a major party or the practical operation of the bi-partisan system.

It is difficult to avoid the conclusion that Bryce's analysis of the American party system was superficial. The truth seems to be that a more complete answer to the riddle of the parties must be sought by analysis of the interests which become involved in the partisan struggles. America had always been a predominantly agricultural country and partisan politics was still dominated by agricultural interests

[18] Bryce, *op. cit.*, Vol. 3, Ch. 115, p. 656.

when Bryce was writing *The American Commonwealth*. The most powerful single interest was that of the grain-growers, and the most important factors in national politics grew out of the conflicts of interest between them and the sugar, cotton, and tobacco planters, who bounded the grain-growers on the south, and the mixed farmers and dairy-men who bounded them on the north. The commercial and industrial interests necessarily played a minor role on the political scene in a period when the inhabitants of cities were a minority, and for a long time a small minority, of the American people.

In the last half-century the economic basis of American politics has been profoundly transformed. The growth of cities has destroyed the earlier ascendency of rural interests in the major political parties. Urban industry, commerce, and finance have replaced agriculture in the center of the stage, and new combinations of interests have had to be effected in order to maintain the authority of the party leaders. Industrial capitalists and organized labor have insisted on receiving greater consideration from the party leaders than formerly, and the characters of the major parties have reflected the changes in the circumstances of their membership. Politicians operate under the influence of the same motives as before, but the bi-partisan system serves radically different ends than when Bryce was making his observations.

The most significant change in the American party system is the rise of the urban middle class to a more influential position in national politics. Like the grain-growers a half-century ago, the urban middle class need not be identified exclusively with either one of the major parties. It may merely divide its members between them in such a manner that the possibility of shifting a portion of them from one to the other gives the class as a whole a disproportionate influence in the inner councils of the leaders of both parties. Thus it gains a share in the balance of power among the contending interests involved in national politics, and strongly affects the whole course of political controversy. This seizure of a share in the balance of power, formerly an almost exclusive possession of the grain-growers, by the urban middle class marks a revolution in the party system which Bryce's method of political analysis prevented him from foreseeing.

The same defective methodology prevented Bryce also from properly appreciating the real merits of the American system of bi-partisan politics. Political principles are doubtless subordinated too much to mere partisan expediency, as Bryce insisted, but partisan expediency serves an important public purpose. It serves to mitigate the violence of political controversy by compelling such compromises between conflicting interests within the party as will enable the party to agree upon candidates and enter upon campaigns with a fair prospect of commanding the confidence of a majority of the voters. The wide extent and diverse interests of the major parties afford the best guarantee which the people of the United States can hope to possess that the power to govern will be used with moderation. Since the practical business of government consists largely in the adjustment of the conflicts of interest arising among the people, it follows that politicians, who understand the nature of the people's interests and are responsible for their use of power to either of the major parties, may well be the most serviceable rulers that the people may reasonably expect to obtain.

It may indeed be argued that two major parties, differently constituted from those which divided the bulk of the voters between them in Bryce's time, or in our own, would be more serviceable instruments of government. It is clear that both the Democratic and the Republican parties had serious defects then and have them now. They were founded, and still rest, largely upon geographical differences, and yet fail to represent the different sections in due proportion to their real importance. But it would be difficult to shuffle the leading interests in national politics about and rearrange them in more logical combinations without sacrificing one of the principal advantages of the existing bi-partisan system, namely, the ascendency of moderate elements and the maintenance of the balance of power in the middle classes. It is easy to grow impatient with the uninspiring leadership which often dominates the American political scene, but it will not be easy to find a safer and more useful party system than the traditional bi-partisanship. The composition and character of the two great parties will continue to change as the circumstances of the people change. The organizations themselves, if all goes well, may yet last a long time.

Bryce enjoyed the good fortune of surviving for many years the publication of his forecasts concerning the future of the American Commonwealth and of seeing many of his hopeful anticipations vindicated by the course of events. Writing for *The Outlook* seventeen years after the first appearance of his book he expressed the opinion that the major trends described therein were still dominant.[19] One great change, which however nobody had predicted, he admitted — namely the emergence of the United States as

[19] *The Outlook*, Vol. 79, pp. 733, 846 (March 25, April 1, 1905).

a colonial power following the war with Spain. To this momentous development he devoted several paragraphs which reveal his wide knowledge and ripe wisdom. Even in old age Bryce retained his interest in the study of government and in the fate of democracy, incorporating his latest observations and impressions in a final work, *Modern Democracies*, published after the World War and devoted to a discussion of the outlook for democracy throughout the world. A third of a century had passed since the appearance of the first edition of his study of democracy in America. It was an extraordinary opportunity to reconsider his earlier opinions. It was also an extraordinarily changed world to which he had to readjust them.

Bryce was profoundly disturbed by the consequences of the World War. The rise of Communism depressed him more than the triumph of democracy elated him. Democracy, where it triumphed, seemed to be desired not for what it was, but for what it might be used to win for the masses. It was valued merely as a means, and not as end in itself, precious because of the embodiment of liberty. He thought that there had probably been no moment in history since the fall of the Roman Empire, which had struck mankind with such terror and dismay as "the world-wide disasters which began in 1914 and have not yet passed away." That many millions of men should perish in the strife which brought disasters to the victors only less than those it brought to the vanquished seemed to him an event without parallel in the annals of modern civilization. "The question, whether men will rise towards the higher standard which the prophets of democracy deemed possible," he wrote, "has been exercising every thoughtful mind since August, 1914, and it will be answered less hopefully now than it would have been at any time in the hundred years preceding."

Bryce nevertheless clung in his old age to the hopeful attitude which had characterized the work of his prime. But hope seemed to be at the end more an effort of the will than a product of the study. The assumption that democracy is the final form of government he dismissed as unwarranted, "for whatever else history teaches, it gives no ground for expecting finality in any human institution." He returned to his earlier philosophy of change. "All material things are in a perpetual flux." What then shall he finally say about democracy? Only this: "Hope, often disappointed but always renewed, is the anchor by which the ship that carries democracy and its fortunes will have to ride out this latest storm as it has ridden out many storms before. . . . Democracy will never perish till after Hope has expired." But would Hope soon expire? He did not venture to say.[20]

The disappointing character of Bryce's final reflections upon the future of democracy in America is clearly foreshadowed in his earlier comments on the future of the American Commonwealth. "In Europe," he remarked near the close of the earlier work, "whose thinkers have seldom been in a less cheerful mood than they are today [that is, in 1888], there are many who seem to have lost the old faith in progress." [21] Yet there were others, he noted, who remained convinced that, though the ascent of man is slow, it is also sure. This less somber type of thought, he added, was more common in the United States than in Europe.

[20] Bryce, *Modern Democracies*, Vol. 2, Ch. 80, pp. 606–609. Whether Bryce's hopefulness would have survived the renewal of war in 1939 is an interesting but perhaps futile topic of speculation.
[21] Bryce, *The American Commonwealth*, Vol. 3, Ch. 116, p. 685.

Was it justified and could it endure? To this implicit question Bryce offered no better than an equivocal reply. "America has still a long period of years stretching before her," he wrote, "in which she will enjoy conditions far more auspicious than England can count upon. . . ." [22]

Since Bryce finished writing *The American Commonwealth* a long period of years, measured by the life of a man, has elapsed. The conditions now existing in the United States are not as much more auspicious than those in England as they were formerly. It is difficult to escape the conclusion that Bryce, were he alive today, would be little, if any, more hopeful about the prospects of democracy in America than he once was about the future of British institutions. He himself had written that it was impossible to feel confident that any of those institutions would remain standing after fifty years. In fact they still stand, though their future certainly seems even less bright than a half-century ago. Would Bryce give American institutions another fifty years? The somber conclusion seems irresistible that Bryce's methods of reasoning about politics would lead him to a negative answer.

Hope in the field of politics needs to rest upon a firmer foundation than was afforded by Bryce's system of political science. Hope, it must be admitted, is not a scientific attitude. Scientists can discuss the chances of a future political event, if the available observations on the data of politics are sufficiently precise. The theory of probability possesses scientific standing. But hope is an emotional or sentimental attitude. It has no place in science. If hope is to be durable, it must be closely associated with faith. But of a political faith Bryce has little to say. For the building of a political

---

[22] Bryce, *op. cit.*, Vol. 3, Ch. 116, p. 686.

faith, science is not enough. Political philosophy must be summoned to political science's aid.

Many of Bryce's contemporaries believed in the theory of organic evolution. They believed that all the capacities implanted in a creature by nature are destined to unfold themselves, completely and conformably to their end, in the course of time. Science seemed to them equal to the task of demonstrating that proposition. Some of them went further and believed also that all the capacities implanted in organized society were destined to unfold themselves, completely and conformably to its end, in the course of time. Political science was not capable of demonstrating that proposition. Those who believed it were forced to accept it on faith, fortifying their faith as best they could by an appropriate political philosophy. But the philosophy of evolutionary politics, as distinguished from the science of comparative politics, appeared not to interest Bryce.

The most appropriate philosophy then available for the support of an intelligent faith in political progress was that of Kant. A century before the first publication of Bryce's *American Commonwealth* Kant had written a short essay, unfortunately little known in English-speaking countries, entitled, *The Natural Principle of the Political Order*. The eighth proposition in this essay stated the evolutionists' political faith in the most suitable scientific context. Never has there been a more resolute or more convincing declaration of faith in the political progress of mankind. Bryce possessed no such political faith as this, but without it his high hopes for democracy, even in America, seem to rest upon a foundation of sand.

The Political Interpretation of History

EVER since the inquisitive age in which Voltaire wrote his *Philosophic Dictionary*, reflection upon the course of human events has caused scholars to persist in the search for a rational interpretation of history. They have not been discouraged by the skepticism of historians who, like Froude, have argued that the address of history must be less to the understanding than to the emotions. "A science of history," according to this historian, "implies that the relation between cause and effect holds in human things as completely as in all others; that the origin of human actions is not to be looked for in mysterious properties of the mind, but in influences which are palpable and ponderable." Froude believed that "natural causes are liable to be set aside and neutralized by what is called volition," and that in consequence "the word Science is out of place" in connection with the study of history. If, as Froude intimated, the origin of human actions can be found only in mysterious properties of the mind, the outlook for a rational interpretation of history may well be poor.

Despite the skeptics, political scientists, I think, will prefer to believe with Kant that "whatever metaphysical theory may be formed regarding the freedom of the will, it holds equally true that the manifestations of the will in human actions are determined, like all other external events, by universal natural laws." Hence, as Kant persuasively argues in his epoch-making essay, *The Natural Principle of the Political Order*, it may be hoped that, when the play of the human will is examined on the great scale of universal history, a regular march will be discovered in its movements. Thus, as Kant himself pointed out, marriages, births, and deaths appear to be incapable of being reduced to any rule by which their numbers may be calculated beforehand, on account of the great influence which the free will of man exercises upon them; and yet the vital statistics of all countries prove that these events take place according to constant natural laws. He compared them with the very inconstant changes of the weather, which can not be determined beforehand in detail, but which maintain the flow of rivers, the growth of plants, and the existence of the animal world. Men, viewed as a whole, are not guided in their efforts merely by instinct, like the lower animals; nor do they proceed in their actions, like the citizens of a purely rational world, according to a preconcerted plan. Nevertheless, Kant concluded, it may be possible to discover a universal purpose of nature in this paradoxical behavior of human beings. We may not choose to speak of a science of history, but we may hope to collect with the aid of the historians the materials by means of which the history of creatures who act without a conscious plan of their own can be rationally interpreted according to a determinate plan of nature.

Kant did not believe that he himself knew enough about the history of mankind to explain the laws of human development, but he did venture to offer a clue to such an explanation. This clue is embodied in the famous eighth proposition of his essay on *The Natural Principle of the Political Order*. "The history of the human race," he declared, "viewed as a whole, may be regarded as the realization of a hidden plan of nature, to bring about a perfect political constitution as the only state in which all the capacities implanted by her in mankind can be fully developed." This is the great hypothesis which gives Kant his transcendent position among those who have sought a rational interpretation of history. It calls for an interpretation of history in terms of a constitutional history of mankind. Since the essence of every kind of constitution is the system of education which gives the constitutional forms their vital force and practical significance, a constitutional history of mankind becomes a history of the growth of the political ideas and ideals which animate the constitutions. Kant's formula for a rational interpretation of history, therefore, calls for the systematic and purposeful study of political ideas as reflected in political structures and processes. Such an interpretation may be termed for convenience a political interpretation of history.

Of all the political interpretations of history which have been inspired by the Kantian hypothesis, the most important is that of Hegel. The Hegelian conception of the history of mankind as a record of the gradual broadening and deepening of the idea of liberty is the grandest in the history of political philosophy. But Hegel's idea of liberty was conditioned by the circumstances and the temper of his time. With one eye doubtless on the fundamental verities, but with the other on the king of Prussia, he reached a conclusion which was better suited to gratify the pride of patriotic Germans than to satisfy the needs of dispassionate political thinkers. The resulting discredit of the Hegelian interpretation of history tended to depress the value of the Kantian hypothesis itself.

We Americans, without devoting much attention to philosophical interpretations of history, have always cherished our faith in the independent power of political ideas and ideals. The democratic-republican creed, if I may so describe the traditional principles of American politics, emphasizes the importance of securing the blessings of liberty. But we reject the Hegelian idea of liberty as too narrow and too negative. We doubt if there can be any satisfactory definition of liberty except in terms of some more positive concept. The idea of liberty seems to us to be closely associated with that of justice. We prefer to define it as the absence of political restraints upon personal behavior except those imposed by just laws. We identify justice with the interest of the whole body of people. We believe that a reasoned and settled determination to establish justice, and thereby also to secure the blessings of liberty, has been one of the active forces in building the American Commonwealth. For democratic-republican Americans, therefore, it is not difficult to believe further that a philosophical attempt to work out the universal history of the world with the aid of the clue furnished by Kant may eventually succeed in giving it a rational meaning in terms of a gradual broadening and deepening of mankind's natural sense of justice.

Abroad, however, doubt on the part of professional students of politics that an acceptable interpretation of history could be achieved by the method of Hegel helped to clear the way for the favorite theory of a large part of the contemporary world, the economic interpretation of history. The most recent statement of the economic interpretation of history comes from the skillful pen of the leading political theorist of the British Labor party, Harold J. Laski.

No advocate of the Marxist political philosophy can be expected to make out a better case than Professor Laski in his two volumes, *The State in Theory and Practice*, and *The Rise of European Liberalism*. Laski is not unmindful of criticism which has been directed against the Marxist philosophy of history. He is much too intelligent to argue that the selfish desire for personal gain on the part of members of governments affords an adequate clue to public policy, or even that the use of power is always governed by the private advantage of the economic class which dominates the state. He admits that statesmen may be sincere in their belief that they employ the authority of the state for the highest ends they know. He contends merely that what the rulers of the state can know and desire is conditioned by the economic relationships which the state, he thinks, exists in order to maintain; that these relationships give birth to an appropriate body of ideals; and that these ideals possess political validity because of their supposed power, as Laski puts it, "to maximize the possibilities of production." History, he concedes, is meaningless when read as nothing but a struggle between conflicting selfish interests. So to regard it, he insists, "is to defame the quality of human nature." History, he believes, is rather the record of the competition of ideals for survival, the character of which is determined by their power to exploit productive possibilities in the existing economic order. In other words, the latest and most refined version of the economic interpretation of history clothes the naked facts of the class struggle in the splendid raiment of triumphant ideals. These ideals remain, nevertheless, nothing more than rationalizations of economic interests.

A preliminary answer to such an interpretation of history

is to match it against another which offers a conflicting interpretation of the same phenomena. For this purpose, Pareto's psychological interpretation of history comes conveniently to hand. Instead of rationalizations, Pareto offers us residues and derivations. The terms are not inconvenient, though hardly self-explanatory. Derivations, according to Pareto, are the ideas and ideals which may be advanced by those concerned to explain and justify their behavior. Political ideas and ideals, he concedes, may spring from attempts to justify rational interests in the economic order. They are more likely, he argues, to spring from attempts to justify the persistent feelings and sentiments which, when manifested as political behavior, he pedantically calls residues. Upon these residues and derivations Pareto relies as heavily in developing his philosophy of history as Laski upon his rationalizations. The Liberalism of the eighteenth and nineteenth centuries, for example, began, according to Laski, as a method of emancipating the rising capitalist class, and changed after 1789 into a method of disciplining the modern industrial proletariat. According to Pareto, this same Liberalism may have been merely an ingenious device for aiding the natural leaders of a changing world to win the new struggle for power and then to hold their gains. From this point of view, Laski's capitalists and proletarians are but the specific modern forms of the elite and the masses, into which, according to Pareto, mankind is universally divided.

It is not necessary for the advocate of a political interpretation of history to argue that both Laski and Pareto are wrong. Indeed it may be conceded that each has grasped a portion of the truth concerning the interpretation of history. But if each is partly right, neither is likely to be wholly right. Whether rationalizations or derivations are the more important factors in modern politics is a matter concerning which much can be said. The Fascist triumphs and Communist humiliations in recent years suggest that the derivations have been more potent than the rationalizations. Even the greatest of the Communist triumphs, the successful establishment of the Soviet Union, a devotee of Pareto's interpretation of history would probably say, was a vindication rather of the Paretian than of the Marxist technique. Be that as it may, it is clear that Communist as well as Fascist leaders can exploit the residues of the mob. They too can qualify for places among the elite in lands where the masses seem to be far from ready for a genuine dictatorship of the proletariat. Pareto's *Mind and Society* is not only a practical working manual for demagogues; it is an effective rejoinder to the more extravagant claims of the historical materialists.

All that is contended for the political interpretation of history is that political ideas and ideals may be something more than either rationalizations or derivations. They may be natural inspirations, exerting an independent influence upon the course of events. It is, of course, obvious, that many political ideas depend upon the special interests of those who come to believe them or serve the private ends of those who exploit their belief by others. But it has never been shown that all political ideas belong wholly to these two categories. It probably can not be shown that all so belong. This probability is enough for the advocate of the political interpretation of history. He will never rest content with the view that political ideas and ideals are nothing but rationalizations and derivations.

The advocate of the political interpretation of history

knows that a satisfactory interpretation of history can not be based upon any simple formula. Teggart has exposed the speciousness of some of the most plausible of the simple formulae of the past. Toynbee and Alfred Weber have made clear the enormous complexity of historical processes. Amidst the variety of interpretations which possess some measure of validity, there is abundant room for a political interpretation. Scholars who still persist in the search for a rational interpretation of history need not hesitate to go back to Kant, and to conclude with him that a philosophical attempt to work out the universal history of the world according to the plan of nature in its aim at a perfect civil state must be regarded as possible, and as even capable of helping forward the purpose of nature.

Belief in the political interpretation of history does not require the unqualified rejection of economic and psychological interpretations. It is possible to agree with Charles A. Beard that there is an economic basis of politics. It is possible also to agree with Charles E. Merriam that there is a psychological basis of politics. It is essential to believe merely that there is a political basis of politics as well, and that the existence of a political basis of politics involves the possibility of a political interpretation of history. In other words, political ideas, like the economic relationships by which Laski sets such great store and the persistent sentiments which give rise to what Pareto calls residues, may possess intrinsic powers of their own, enabling them by themselves alone to influence, if not altogether to determine, the policies of governments and the development of states.

The claims of the various interpretations of history may be further tested by trial in the court of universal history itself. The classical Roman Empire was organized by politicians and defended by soldiers, but it was administered mainly by lawyers. In the Holy Roman Empire, however, at least during its greatest centuries, lawyers were relegated to a minor role, and the leading parts in the administration of imperial affairs were taken by priests. Modern Marxists, aided by the solid advantages of hind-sight as well as by the Marxist dialectic, can offer a plausible explanation of the preference for a legal education in the training of civil servants in ancient Rome and for more attention to theology in training for the public service in the Middle Ages. But can Marxists offer any convincing explanation in terms of their peculiar dialectic for the fact that the Chinese Empire was administered mainly by students of political ethics rather than by either lawyers or theologians? Confucianism, whatever may have been its merits as a religion, was certainly one of the most effective systems of training civil servants that any great empire has ever possessed. Whether the Confucian scholars were better prepared for the public service than the lawyers and priests of the Western world, it would be unprofitable to debate. That they were on the whole, until very recent times, well prepared for the duties they were called upon to perform, the long, if checkered, history of the Chinese Empire affords abundant evidence.

But what was there in the economic condition of the Far East under the Chow Dynasty from which some unknown precursor of the modern Marxists could have predicted that the Confucianists, and not the lawyers of whom there were then a plenty, would eventually gain the favor of the occupants of the Dragon Throne and administer the affairs of the Celestial Empire? The modes of producing wealth were doubtless not precisely the same in ancient China as in ancient Rome or in the medieval West; nor were they the same in China throughout the course of her imperial history. Yet did not the Chinese Empire continue through many vicissitudes to be administered predominantly by Confucian scholars? It is impossible to escape the conclusion that the political and ethical ideas taught by the Confucianists constituted one of the bases of politics, independent of economic relationships and sentimental residues, and that the general acceptance of the Confucian political ethics in China explains in no inconsiderable measure the development of the Chinese Empire. By the same process of reasoning, we may conclude also that legal and religious ideas have played a more independent part in the development of Western institutions than Marxists and Paretians are willing to admit.

The objection may be raised to the political interpretation of history that it does not enable us to know in advance the course of human events. Laski, for instance, in his plea for the economic interpretation of history, makes a great deal of this objection. Referring to some of the rival philosophies of history, he declares that "the trouble with all such theories is a simple one. They do not enable us to predict the probable future of events. They leave us blindfold before our fate." The Marxist theory, as understood by Laski, presumably avoids this trouble. The head of the Marx-Engels-Lenin Institute at Moscow, Comrade Adoratsky, is of the same opinion. In a recent exposition of the theoretical foundation of Marxism-Leninism, he quotes with warm approval the observation of Engels that "Marxism is not a dogma, but a guide to action." As a guide to action, the course of events since 1848 enables us to take its measure. Before condemning the political interpretation of history, therefore, for its alleged defective powers of prediction, it may be well to inquire how accurately the Marxists have been able to predict. In fact, the record of their miscalculations is well known. One illustration of their incapacity to predict will suffice — an illustration taken from the experience of Marx himself in attempting to grasp the meaning of one of the most sensational events of his own time.

During the years when Marx was earning a precarious living by writing European correspondence for the New York *Tribune*, the center of the political stage in the Far East was held by the sanguinary Taiping rebellion. On June 14, 1853, shortly after the Taiping rebels reached the peak of their power by the conquest of Nanking, the *Tribune* published an article in which Marx read the lesson of the rebellion for the people of the West. "Now England," he wrote, "having brought about the revolution in China" (that is, as he believed, by forcing opium on the Chinese), "the question is, how the revolution will in time react on England, and through England on Europe." His answer to his own question was as follows: "It may safely be augured that the Chinese revolution will throw the spark into the overloaded mine of the present industrial system and cause the explosion of the long prepared general crisis, which spreading abroad will be closely followed by political revolutions on the Continent." That fatuous prediction was written over eighty-three years ago. Again, only ten years ago, Marx's spiritual heir, Trotsky, was equally confident that another Chinese revolution, then in progress, would cause the long overdue explosion in the "overloaded mine" of the capitalist system. But the revolution of the Kuomintang, like the Taiping rebellion, has run a very different course from what was predicted by the Marxists. As a guide to action, the orthodox dialectical materialism has been thoroughly tried and found wanting.

If it were true that the political interpretation of history affords only an uncertain guide to the future, it would not on that ground be more objectionable than other interpretations. But the question may fairly be raised, Is it desirable that men should be urged to believe that they can predict the course of future events? Consider, for example, the present plight of the Communists, who have been taught to have faith in their powers of prediction. They have persuaded themselves that a dictatorship of the proletariat is inevitable. The Fascists, on the other hand, while repudiating the notion that the basis of politics is exclusively or even mainly economic, appear eager to spread the opinion that the peoples of modern states must choose between the dictatorship of the poor under the leadership of the Communists and that of the strong under their own natural leaders. Holding, as the Fascists do, that there is a psychological as well as an economic interpretation of history, they willfully believe that strong men can be the masters of their fate. This belief is one of the important causes of the momentary success of Fascism in its struggle with Communism for power. The Fascist is confident that men can choose between Communism and Fascism, and consequently strives to bring about what he thinks is the proper choice. The genuine Marxist, on the contrary, assumes that in the long run the circumstances make the choice for the man, and, finding himself apparently on the losing side, concludes that he has been mistaken in his analysis of the situation. Thus, fatalism under adverse circumstances becomes defeatism, and power passes to the more vigorous leadership of the Fascists.

It is not only Fascists, however, who can profit by the faith in man's practical capacity to make a real choice. Democratic-republicans also, armed with a political philosophy which holds that accredited ideas, as well as vested interests and persistent sentiments, may be mighty for good or for evil, may believe both in human capacity to choose and in a wider range of choice than either Communists or Fascists. It is not the power of prediction, but the power to inspire faith in one's self and one's associates, that makes a political philosophy a vital factor in the course of events. A political philosophy which emphasizes the independent force of political ideas and ideals possesses that power. It puts formidable obstacles in the path of those who would discourage the taking of thought for the improvement of human relations by urging the inevitable failure of all but one of the possible courses of political action.

Democratic-republicans are not blind to the signs of the times. They can see that modern methods of producing wealth are changing the structure of economic society and tend to bring about corresponding changes in the dominant ideas of sound public policy. They can understand how the profound modifications of the competitive system now visibly taking place compel the abandonment of the time-honored principle of *laissez faire* as the cardinal maxim of enlightened statesmanship. They may even concede that, since there is an economic basis of politics, there must be some alterations in the processes of government and in the structure of the state itself. It is clear that in the years ahead the sharper differentiation of economic classes and disturbances in their relative strength, like the unequal growth of different sections of the country in the nine-teenth century, must have important effects on the course of American politics.

But it is very far from clear that democratic-republican-ism must inevitably succumb in the coming struggle for power. The division of the peoples of modern states into two economic or political classes does not exhaust the pos-sibilities of classification in modern society. There are mid-dle classes as well as upper and lower classes. The middle classes can believe in the possibility of rejecting both the policy of proletarian dictatorship and that of a dictatorship of the elite. They can believe further in the possibility of rejecting the economic individualism of the age that is passing away, without sacrificing also their democratic-republican principles of politics. The fates of American constitutional government and of *laissez faire* economics are not inextricably bound up together. Collectivism in its various forms presents possibilities for economic and political programs from which democratic-republicans as well as Communists and Fascists can choose. Those who believe that political ideas constitute one of the independent bases of politics may well believe also in the practicability of such a choice and in the mission of the middle classes to maintain freedom to choose.

These considerations lead to the condemnation of all theories of politics which divide mankind into two sharply differentiated classes, whether superciliously termed the elite and the masses or harshly called exploiters and ex-ploited. There seems to be a tacit conspiracy between those who believe in an unqualified economic interpretation of history and those who intend to profit by that belief on the part of others without accepting it for themselves, to force the rest of mankind to choose between their two types of leadership. Professional students of politics will not be stampeded by any such conspiracy. They do not believe in the necessity for any such choice. There is no such simple dichotomy of the body politic. The classes into which the peoples of modern states may be divided are more numerous, less clearly defined, and more interdependent. The various theories of class struggle, whether advanced by Communists or by Fascists, make too little allowance for the observable facts of social and political classification. Above all, they make too little allowance for the existence and the power of the middle classes.

It is one of the great merits of a belief in the intrinsic power of political ideas and ideals — under the existing conditions, perhaps its greatest merit — that the classes which are most likely to gain strength through their faith in suitable political ideas and ideals are the middle classes. These are the classes which give character to modern states. By their nature and situation, they are clearly destined to be the guardians of rational ideals of justice and liberty. They are the classes which naturally find the greatest harmony between their own special interests and the general interests of the community to which they belong. Their political ideas and ideals are most likely to be what may fairly be called the democratic-republican ideas and ideals. The political philosophy which most promotes the strength of the middle classes constitutes, therefore, one of the best guarantees that democratic-republicanism will continue to flourish. The proper basis of such a political philosophy is a political interpretation of history.

NOTES ON BOOKS

Notes on Books

PART I

UNREFLECTING faith in the good and supposedly manifest destiny of the United States, characteristic of the first century of the Federal Union, has gradually yielded in recent years, in the face of a growing volume of adverse criticism of the traditional American way of life, to a broadening search for firmer foundations of a new and better reasoned faith. Generally the criticism and the search have been combined in the same hands, though the proportions of criticism and ideological reconstruction may be very different. The range of criticism has been wide, including the Communist and Fascist critics, who would abandon the foundations of the traditional American way, but the bulk of it has rested on the assumption that the new order will develop without violent interruption from the old. An interesting specimen of the more moderate type of critical and ideological literature is *The American Way* by David Cushman Coyle, together with three additional discussions by Carl Dreher, Carl Landauer, and Gerald W. Johnson (Harper and Brothers, 1938), a selection of essays submitted in a prize contest conducted by the publishers in the previous year. A suggestive selection of titles from this recent literature will be found in *Tomorrow in the Making*, edited by John N. Andrews and Carl A. Marsden (McGraw-Hill Book Co., 1939), which contains a comprehensive summary of different points of view by representative authors.

The essentials of the American way have presumably stood fast from the beginning. What they were, however, has been the subject of interminable controversy. As good a point of departure as any for the exploration of this controversy is afforded by James Truslow Adams' *Jeffersonian Principles and Hamiltonian Principles* (Little Brown, 1932). An excellent survey of the course of the controversy, which brings it to the point reached at the commencement of the New Deal, is Charles A. Beard, *The Idea of National Interest* (Macmillan, 1933). See also V. L. Parrington, *Main Currents in American Thought* (3 vols., Harcourt Brace, 1927), and R. H. Gabriel, *The Course of American Democratic Thought* (Ronald Press, 1940).

Liberalism, which has often been regarded as the essence of the American way, is a creed which was not definitely formulated until long after the Founding Fathers had passed from the stage. Some of the important antecedents of Liberalism, though not the fully developed body of principles and policies which came to bear that name in the latter part of the nineteenth century, are interestingly discussed in Harold J. Laski's *The Rise of Liberalism, the Philosophy of a Business Civilization* (Harper and Brothers, 1936). The attitude which became associated with the liberal movement in American politics at the time of its greatest influence is best reflected in Herbert Hoover's *American Individualism* (Doubleday Page, 1922) and *The Challenge to Liberty* (Charles Scribner's Sons, 1934). The best recent attempt at a reasoned vindication of this attitude is Walter Lippmann's *An Inquiry into the Principles of the Good Society* (Macmillan, 1937). The same writer's *The Method of Freedom* (Harvard University Press, 1935) marks an earlier stage in the development of his thought, revealing a stronger disposition to reconsider the Liberalism of the nineteenth century with a view to its adaptation to the changed circumstances of the twentieth.

The advent of the New Deal brought a reconsideration of the traditional Liberalism from various points of view. Some of the noteworthy contributions to the discussion of American Liberalism by the revisionists are the following: John Dewey, *Liberalism and Social Action* (G. P. Putnam's Sons, 1935); Charles A. Beard, *The Open Door at Home* (Macmillan, 1934); Stuart Chase, *A New Deal* (Macmillan, 1932), and *The Economy of Abundance* (Macmillan, 1934); David Cushman Coyle, *Roads to a New America* (Little Brown, 1938); Max Lerner, *It Is Later Than You Think* (Viking Press, 1938); Herbert Agar, *The Land of the Free* (Houghton Mifflin, 1935); and John A. Ryan, *A Better Economic Order* (Harper and Brothers, 1936). The views of these writers, all self-styled "Liberals," cover a wide range of opinion, extending from Coyle's qualified individualism to Lerner's "democratic collectivism." Agar urges a return to the agrarian Liberalism of the nineteenth century and Ryan advocates an advance towards an industrial democracy in harmony with the Papal encyclicals. John Chamberlain's *The American Stakes* (Carrick and Evans, 1940) registers the effect of time and experience upon youthful radicalism as expressed in the same writer's *Farewell to Reform* (Liveright, 1932).

Systematic and comprehensive formulations of American political philosophy have not yet been produced. Much of the best political thinking has been done by those charged with the responsibility for the interpretation of the written constitutions of the United States. Instead of authentic treatises on the foundations of American

political beliefs there are the judicial opinions of the great
Supreme Court justices. The spirit of American politics
must be distilled from the occasional writings of those
statesmen who have been most successful in voicing the
unspoken thoughts of the people. Foremost among the
modern sources from which this spirit may be caught are
Theodore Roosevelt's *Autobiography* (Macmillan, 1913),
and Woodrow Wilson's *The New Freedom* (Doubleday
Page, 1913), to say nothing of the writings of statesmen
now living.

PART II

I

The relations between economics and politics have been
the subject of frequent and extensive discussion in recent
years. Whatever metaphysical theory may be held regarding the freedom of the will, it is a convenient hypothesis
for the scientific study of political phenomena that the
manifestations of the will in human actions are explicable
in accordance with natural laws of universal validity. It
follows that the economic basis of politics may be usefully
studied with a view to explaining the course of political
events, even though the existence of other bases of politics
be recognized. The arguments in favor of making a greater
use of economic data than formerly in the study of politics
are effectively stated in Charles A. Beard's weighty little
essay, *The Economic Basis of Politics* (A. A. Knopf, 1922).
Their limitations are clearly pointed out in the same writer's
"Memorandum on Social Philosophy" in *The Journal of
Social Philosophy*, V, 7–15 (October, 1939).

The pioneer among modern scholars, seeking to give a scientific explanation of American politics, was Frederick J. Turner, whose *Influence of the Frontier in American History* (Publications of the American Historical Association, 1893), employed economic data in a striking manner to explain the development of political ideas. This method of approaching the study of American politics has been carried further by Turner in later studies, published in his *Significance of Sections in American History* (Holt, 1932). For a valuable discussion of the limitations of Turner's method, see B. F. Wright, "American Democracy and the Frontier," in *The Yale Review*, XX, 349–365 (December, 1930). Charles A. Beard's application of the method is best illustrated by his work, written in collaboration with Mary R. Beard, *The Rise of American Civilization* (2 vols., Macmillan, 1927). See also their *America in Midpassage* (Macmillan, 1939). An analysis of the economic interests, rural and urban, which are represented in the Congress of the United States, and factual material designed to show their relative importance in national politics, will be found in my two books, *The Political Parties of Today* (Harper and Brothers, 1924; 2nd ed., 1925), and *The New Party Politics* (Norton, 1933). See also my article, "American Politics at the Crossroads," in *Facts and Factors in Economic History*, *Articles by Former Students of Edwin Francis Gay* (Harvard University Press, 1932), pp. 535–556.

There is no satisfactory official compilation of national election statistics in the United States. Unofficial congressional election returns for recent years have been published in the *Congressional Directory* (Government Printing Office, Washington, D. C.), and for earlier years may be found in the *World Almanac*, *Tribune Almanac*, and *Whig Almanac*, published annually in New York during various periods for more than a century. Presidential election returns may be found in the same newspaper publications. A carefully edited compilation of presidential election returns for the period 1896 to 1932, inclusive, is Edgar E. Robinson's *The Presidential Vote, 1896–1932* (Stanford University Press, 1934). Official returns for other federal elections must be sought in the various yearbooks and manuals published by the state governments, or in manuscript records at the state capitals or county seats throughout the country. A comprehensive account of the sources of presidential election statistics will be found in Robinson's work, noted above, "General Note on Sources" (pp. 379–399). An instructive set of maps, showing the distribution of electoral votes by states at all presidential elections down to 1928, will be found in Charles O. Paullin and John K. Wright, *Atlas of the Historical Geography of the United States* (published jointly by the Carnegie Institution of Washington and the American Geographical Society of New York, 1932).

II

The most valuable work for the study of the proceedings in the Constitutional Convention of 1787 is Max Farrand, *The Records of the Federal Convention of 1787* (Yale University Press, 3 vols., 1911, and a fourth volume, 1937). Another careful edition is Gaillard Hunt and James Brown Scott, *The Debates in the Federal Convention of 1787, which framed the Constitution of the United States of America, reported by James Madison, a Delegate from Virginia* (Oxford University Press, New York, 1920). See also the Library of Congress, *Documents Illustrative of the Formation of the Union of the American States* (selected, arranged, and indexed by Charles C. Tansill, Government Printing Office, 1927). This valuable publication of 1115 pages emphasizes the evolution of the Constitution in the Convention of 1787, and may be found in any complete set of Congressional documents (69th Congress, 1st sess., House Doc. no. 398). The standard edition of the debates in the State ratification conventions is Jonathan Elliot, *The Debates in the several State Conventions, on the Adoption of the Federal Constitution, as recommended by the General Convention at Philadelphia in 1787*, 5 vols. (2nd edition, Philadelphia, 1836). This work contains also the Journal of the Federal Convention and much more material relating to the adoption and interpretation of the Federal Constitution.

The most complete and instructive account of the proceedings in the Federal Convention is Charles Warren, *The Making of the Constitution* (Little Brown, 1928; 2nd ed., 1937). This very useful work contains copious summaries of the debates, conveniently arranged to show the actual development of the Constitution, and much other relevant material. Other valuable accounts are: George Bancroft, *History of the Formation of the Constitution of the United States of America*, 2 vols. (Appleton, 1882); Max Farrand, *The Framing of the Constitution of the United States* (Yale University Press, 1913); Charles A. Beard, *An Economic Interpretation of the Constitution of the United States* (Macmillan, 1913); Robert L. Schuyler, *The Constitution of the United States, An Historical Survey of its Formation* (Macmillan, 1923); and Hastings Lyon, *The Constitution and the Men Who Made It*

(Houghton Mifflin, 1936). Of these last writers, Lyon emphasizes the personal factors in the making of the Constitution; Schuyler, the points of agreement among the framers; Beard, the differences among them, especially those growing out of their economic interests; and Bancroft, the politics of the Convention. A work of special value is O. G. Libby, *The Geographical Distribution of the Vote of the Thirteen States on the Federal Constitution, 1787–8* (University of Wisconsin, 1894).

The influence of the agrarian middle class in American politics has been obscured by the phenomena of sectionalism. This is evident upon examination of any of the standard party histories, such as Frank R. Kent, *The Democratic Party, A History* (Century Co., 1928), and William Starr Myers, *The Republican Party, A History* (Century Co., rev. ed., 1931). More penetrating is the analysis of party history in Herbert Agar's *The Pursuit of Happiness, the Story of American Democracy* (Houghton Mifflin, 1938), which stresses the role of the independent farmer in national politics. With this should be compared another recent political analysis from the Southern point of view, Walter Prescott Webb's *Divided We Stand, the Crisis of a Frontierless Democracy* (Farrar and Rinehart, 1937). Broader points of view are emphasized in Arthur M. Schlesinger, *New Viewpoints in American History* (Macmillan, 1922). See also T. V. Smith, *The Promise of American Politics* (University of Chicago Press, 1936).

Emphasis upon the class-basis of American politics has been the special concern of the Communists and Fascists. Much of the Communist and Fascist literature, published in the United States, is of obvious European inspiration and shows little understanding of the American way of

life. Most noteworthy, among radical writings of the
Communist type, are Harold J. Laski, *Democracy in Crisis*
(University of North Carolina Press, 1935), and Lewis
Corey, *The Decline of American Capitalism* (Covici Friede,
1934); and among those of a Fascist type, Lawrence Dennis,
The Coming American Fascism (Harper and Brothers,
1935). Recognition of the important role of the middle
classes has been slow, and on the part of radical writers
reluctant, as Lewis Corey's *The Crisis of the Middle Class*
(Covici Friede, 1935) bears witness. Among more moderate and realistic writers, John Corbin, author of *The
Return of the Middle Class* (Charles Scribner's Sons, 1922),
made the sound point that, under the changing conditions
of the present age, the middle class must not only play a
leading part in creating rational public opinion, but also
assume a special responsibility for the administration of
"bureaucratic" institutions in the public interest. Alfred M.
Bingham's *Insurgent America, the Revolt of the Middle
Classes* (Harper and Brothers, 1935) and *Man's Estate, Ad-
ventures in Economic Discovery* (Norton, 1939), develop
in an interesting and persuasive way the implications of a
political philosophy which accepts the middle classes rather
than the proletariat or the elite as the leading element of
the modern state. F. C. Palm's *The Middle Classes, Then
and Now* (Macmillan, 1936) contains a valuable survey of
the origin and spread of middle-class attitudes in history
and literature.

III

Anticipation of future changes must rest upon past tendencies and present conditions. Convenient compendiums
of significant facts and fruitful analysis of economic and

social factors underlying contemporary political forces
are: (1) Report of the President's Research Committee on
Social Trends, *Recent Social Trends in the United States*,
2 vols. (McGraw-Hill, 1933); (2) National Resources
Committee, *Report on Our Cities* (Government Printing
Office, 1937); and (3) the same committee, *The Structure
of the American Economy, Part I, Basic Characteristics*
(Government Printing Office, 1939). R. S. and H. Lynd,
authors of *Middletown in Transition* (Harcourt Brace,
1937), furnish an illuminating test of the main conclusions
of the statistical investigators by their careful observations
in a typical urban community of the Middle West. Wise
comment on the inferences of social and political analysts
is contained in Charles E. Merriam's *The Rôle of Politics in
Social Change* (New York University Press, 1937). Those
who would venture to forecast the future should study not
only James Bryce's *The American Commonwealth*, 2 vols.
(1st ed., Macmillan, 1888), but also Alexis deTocqueville's
Democracy in America, 2 vols. (1st ed., Paris, 1835–40;
Bowen's 1st American ed., 1862).

IV

There is an abundance of reading for those with a taste
for the philosophy of history. Arnold J. Toynbee's mam-
moth work, *A Study of History*, 6 vols. (Oxford University Press, 1934–39), although unfinished, states the issues
clearly and indicates the vast scope of the subject and the
enormous mass of materials. Other particularly noteworthy
recent works are: Vilfredo Pareto's *The Mind and Society*,
4 vols. (English translation, Harcourt Brace, 1935); Oswald
Spengler's *The Decline of the West*, 2 vols. (English translation, A. A. Knopf, 1927–29); and Pitirim A. Sorokin's

Social and Cultural Dynamics, 3 vols. (American Book Co., 1937). The temper of these three works is utterly alien and hostile to that of Kant and Hegel, the fathers of the philosophy of history. See especially Immanuel Kant, *The Natural Principle of the Political Order, considered in connection with the Idea of a Universal Cosmo-Political History* (republished in *Eternal Peace and Other International Essays*, World Peace Foundation, Boston, 1914).

INDEX

Adams, John 6, 7, 8, 9, 10, 11, 28, 29, 30, 42, 43, 45, 162, 257
Adams, J. Q., 176, 180, 181, 216, 257
Adams, Sam, 194
Administration, 258–259
Adoratsky, 281
Agrarianism, 95–96, 100, 106–110, 115, 191–193, 240
Anti-Federalists, 12, 153, 176
Aristocracy, 5, 6, 8, 9, 11, 149, 150, 154
Aristotle, 10, 40, 43, 49
Authority, 21, 22

Baldwin, 136, 147, 214
Bar, 231
Beard, 85, 176, 279
Blaine, 92
Bluntschli, 52
Border, 81, 82, 83, 88
Bourgeoisie, 45, 46
Brougham, 45
Bryan, 82, 86, 93, 94, 186, 189, 260
Bryce, 59, 98, 226ff.
Burr, 215
Business corporation, 229
Businessman, 230, 232
Butler, 140, 162

Calhoun, 85, 112, 181, 186
Cannon, 51, 52, 53
Capitalists, 236
Class, classes, 5, 9, 27, 28, 42, 127, 235, 285
Class consciousness, 56, 57, 155–157, 236, 239
Class system, 28, 127, 129, 156, 286. *See also* Lower class, Middle class, *Mittelstand*, and Upper class

Clay, 85, 112, 180, 181, 185, 186
Cleveland, 257
Climate, political, 89, 94
Clinton, 4, 145
Communism, 24, 50, 126–127
Communists, 50, 59, 60, 125, 155, 156, 224, 278, 283
Confederationists, 142, 146, 148
Congress, 253–255
Coolidge, 92
Corey, 46, 202
Cox, 70

Davis, 70
Decentralization, 251–253
Democracy, 40, 41, 59, 138–142, 235–238, 244, 268–271
Democratic republicanism, 124–125, 150, 180, 213, 275, 284, 285–286
Democrats, 65, 66, 68, 69, 71, 78, 92–94, 104–106, 118–122, 189–191, 219–224, 267
Dickinson, 140
Douglas, 83, 186, 187

Elite, 50, 60, 126
Ellsworth, 134, 135, 137, 139, 141, 147
Equality, 40
Evolution, 13, 271

Fascism, 24, 50, 126–127
Fascists, 50, 59, 60, 125, 155, 156, 224, 278, 283
Federalism, 245–253
Federalists, 75, 85, 142, 147–151, 178, 263
Few, 136
Fortune Magazine, 204